EBONY PICTORIAL HISTORY OF BLACK AMERICA

EBONY PICTORIAL HISTORY OF BLACK AMERICA

By the Editors of Ebony

Introduction by
Lerone Bennett Jr.

Volume I

AFRICAN PAST TO THE CIVIL WAR

THE SOUTHWESTERN COMPANY, Nashville, Tennessee
By arrangement with Johnson Publishing Company, Inc., 1971

Library of Congress Catalog Card No. 71-151797

Series ISBN No. 0-87485-049-5
Volume ISBN No. 0-87485-050-9

First Printing

Johnson Publishing Company, Inc.
Chicago, Illinois

Printed in the United States of America

Norman L. Hunter
Design and Layout

PICTURE CREDITS

Photographs and other illustrations are identified by page number and, where necessary, by letters, a, b, c, etc. in sequence on the page. Credits are listed separately for each chapter.

1

L. Bandoni, 27
Ebony collection, 8, 12, 17, 19, 25, 26, 29, 30, 35, 39, 41, 47, 48
Cecil L. Ferguson, 37
G. A. Hoskins, 20, 22, 23
Norman L. Hunter, 32
Metropolitan Museum of Art, Rogers Fund, 13
Segy Gallery, 45
University of Chicago Library, 10, 14
University Museum, Philadelphia, 42

2

Ebony collection, 50, 54
Historical Pictures Service, Chicago, 52, 57, 58

3

Ebony collection, 60
Historical Pictures Service, Chicago, 61, 64
Schoenfeld Collection, Three Lions, 63, 66

4

Ebony collection, 68, 73, 74, 77, 78, 80, 82, 89, 91, 92, 93, 95
Historical Pictures Service, Chicago, 96
United Press International, NYC, 85, 86, 70

5

Ebony collection, 102a,b, 103, 104, 105a, 106b
Historical Pictures Service, Chicago, 101, 105b, 106a

6

Charleston Museum, 148a,b
Jack Delano, 158
Ebony collection, 113, 121, 125, 129, 131, 157
Cecil L. Ferguson, 155
Harpers Weekly, 108, 126, 133, 136, 139, 141, 143, 145, 146, 147b, 150, 153, 156a
Historical Pictures Service, Chicago, 111, 117, 118, 135, 137, 147a, 149, 154, 156b
Library of Congress, 114, 123
Three Lions, Inc., 152

7

Chicago Historical Society, 190
Ebony collection, 161, 162, 163, 166, 167, 169, 171, 172, 173, 174, 117, 178a, 178b, 179a, 179b, 181, 182, 185
Hughie Lee-Smith painting, 176
New York Public Library, 187, 188

8

J. N. Black, 234
Ebony collection, 195, 198, 204, 205, 206, 207, 208, 209a,b, 213, 214, 220, 224a,b, 227, 228, 236a,b, 237, 239, 240, 242
Historical Pictures Service, Chicago, 198, 201, 202, 203, 217, 218, 219, 230, 231
Bertrand Miles, 196
Missouri Historical Society, 233
Thomas Noble, 223
Schoenfeld, Three Lions, 192, 199, 200, 210, 212, 229

9

Chicago Historical Society, 266, 269, 274, 276, 277, 278, 279, 282, 285, 291, 292, 295, 296
Ebony collection, 244, 247, 249, 250, 251, 258, 259, 264a,b, 265a,b, 272, 280a,b, 281, 286, 288, 303, 305, 308, 309, 311
Historical Pictures Service, Chicago, 252, 267, 270, 271, 298, 300, 307
Library of Congress, 260, 262
National Archives, 256
Wide World, 255

Contents

Introduction

by Lerone Bennett Jr.

THIS IS AN EXTENDED ESSAY on the odyssey of a people. Spread over three volumes, and matriced in the latest advances of modern scholarship, this essay uses photography, typography, and prose to give a new dimension to one of the great adventures of the human spirit.

This adventure, as recounted by the editors of *Ebony*, spans centuries and continents. The story begins at the dawn of recorded history on the banks of the Nile and the Niger and it ends, after a journey through the empires and cultures of ancient Africa, the holds of slave ships and the horrors of slavery, with renaissance and rebellion on the banks of the Hudson and the Mississippi. As the story unfolds, with emphasis on the human element and the agency of black people, the lost years echo and re-echo with the sounds and struggles of forgotten men and women. And it should be said at once —though we will return to this point later in greater detail—that no American can understand himself or his country without a confrontation with the multifaceted images of the experience presented here.

For twenty-five years, the editors of *Ebony* have been involved in the struggle to make this experience intelligible and illustrious. Like all black media, *Ebony* came into being to project and to protect the images of the black experience. As publisher John H. Johnson said in a speech on the twentieth anniversary of the magazine, *Ebony* was started as "a vehicle for building and projecting the image of the Negro in America—an image that had long been shattered and distorted in media oriented primarily to whites." He added: "We felt then—and we feel now—that a man must be at home somewhere before he can make a home anywhere."

From the very beginning, *Ebony* and its sister magazine, *Negro Digest* (now *Black World*), published in-depth articles on the black experience by men like W. E. B. Du Bois, Arna Bontemps, Richard Wright, and others. In the early sixties, the magazine pioneered in extended popular series on African-American history. A Book Division was later organized to meet the demand for facts and interpretation of the black experience. In the course of these activities, *Ebony* magazine accumulated a great deal of material and the world's largest collection of pictures on African-Americans. *The Ebony Pictorial History of Black America* grew out of an awareness that this huge repository of material should be made available to a larger public.

The volumes were produced by a team of editors, artists, and photographic specialists who consulted hundreds of books and documents and reviewed thousands of pictures before preparing the final material.

The complete volumes are significant because of their scale, structure, and content.

This is the most extensive attempt to date to present a total visual image of the black experience. The 960 pages of these three volumes include more than one thousand pictures. The first volume carries the story from the Golden Age of Africa to the Civil War. The second volume focuses on the formative experiences and events from the Reconstruction to the Supreme Court Decision of 1954. The third volume deals with the most vibrant story of our times, the Civil Rights movement and the Black Revolution. There are also sections on Religion, Sports, and the New (Cultural) Renaissance. There is a summary index in Volume III.

The story is developed in an interesting manner. There is, in each section, a complete photographic essay supplemented by a prose summary. The two separate but complementary stories provide a unique bifocal view of the germinal events in African-American history.

The emphasis throughout is on history as revelation, on history as a way of understanding and transformation. The volumes are based on the premise that you have to understand the past in order to make the future. The editors of *Ebony* believe Santayana was right when he said, "People who cannot remember the past are condemned to repeat it."

We were struck—and we think you will be struck—by the variety of the material, the variety of places, of faces, of strategies, of dreams. There is variety, tumultuous variety, but there is also an underlying sameness—the sameness of the obstacles, the sameness of man's inhumanity to man, and the sameness of the black man's tenacity and hope.

This material also reveals and makes comprehensible the depth of the black man's involvement in American life, and the prodigality of his gifts. Here are the forgotten founding fathers, the black pioneers of East and West, the creators of cities and rhymes, the builders of railroads, the makers of America's only original song and dance, the unsung inventors, theorists, and activists. Here are the men and women who made Mount Vernon and Monticello and Charleston and New Orleans possible. Here also are the victims, the long thick black line of victims, the casualties of wars for freedom which did not pay off in their own lives, the casualties of mobs and repressive legislation, the casualties of a sociopolitical process which condemns to death twice as many black babies as white babies and permits white men to live seven years longer than black men. The victims are here, and so are the dreamers: the men and women, black and white, the Nat Turners and the John Browns and the Frederick Douglasses and the Harriet Tubmans, the Marshalls, the Kings, and the Malcolms, all the men and women who repeatedly forced Americans to the high ground of principles enunciated but not lived. They are all here, the victims and the dreamers, the activists and the builders. And no one, I think, can read their story without gaining a new sense of the meaning and destiny of America.

What emerges from these volumes is the image of a people with deep and inextricable roots in the soil of America. And that image tells us that the destiny of this land is tied up with the destiny of this people. More than one hundred years ago, Fredrika Bremer, a European visitor, told white Americans, "The romance of your history is the fate of the Negro." Her words, as these volumes indicate, are still true.

For one hundred years now, we have evaded the implications of that truth, to the detriment of both blacks and whites. We tend to identify the American heritage with the Euro-American heritage, forgetting that America is an African as well as a European invention. There is a tendency in all media to identify the American experience with the Euro-American experience and to call the history of Euro-Americans the history of America. Even today, most history textbooks project a white national image of a multinational reality. The history of African-Americans is a standing refutation of that presumption. African-American history tells us that there is another history, another reality, *another America.* It tells us further that it is impossible to create "American" history without recognizing the false universality of the white history our media propagate.

Within recent years, largely as a result of the work of black historians and the direct action of black demonstrators, there has been a new appreciation of the centrality of African-American history. But despite the gains, many people still regard African-American history as an intellectual ghetto. Even worse, some people regard it as a minor-league pastime involving the recitation of dates and the names of black greats. But African-American history, read right, is a much more fateful encounter than that. Read right, within the context of social forces struggling for dominance, African-American history raises total questions about the meaning of the historical process and the orientation of our lives. In its essence, as I have said elsewhere, African-American history is a radical reappraisal of a society from the standpoint of the men on the bottom. And this means that black people have experienced violation and exclusion as the truth of the American experience. Because of what they have been through, because of the irrefutable evidence of their scars, they are the creative negation of all the placid myths about American history. And if truth, as Jean-Paul Sartre noted, is the perspective of the truly disinherited, then the history of the black man is the truth or close to the truth of our reality.

Do not take lightly the evidence presented here. This is the story of a history which is inside you, working; it is the story of a history which is engraved on your skin and in your viscera, the story of a history which made you and which you are now making, perhaps without even knowing it.

A final and perhaps even more important reason for the importance of African-American history is that it mirrors in microcosm the history of the overwhelming majority of the peoples of the earth. One could even say that the history of the African-American is the history of man taken to the nth degree. The story of the African-American, which is also the story of man, is a story of slavery, segregation, blood, cotton, roaches, rats. But it is also a story of human faith, human strength, and human weakness, which is to say that it is a story relevant to the lives of all men. Ralph Ellison put it very well, saying: "Any people who could endure all that brutalization and keep together, who could undergo such dismemberment and resuscitate itself, and endure until it could take the initiative in achieving its own freedom is obviously more than the sum of its brutalization. Seen in this perspective, theirs has been one of the great human experiences and one of the great triumphs of the human spirit in modern times, in fact, in the history of the world."

1

Golden Age of Africa

CONTRARY TO WIDESPREAD misinformation, the history of black Americans does not begin with their arrival in the New World on slave ships. It has its true beginning in remotest antiquity on their ancestral continent, Africa. Recent archaeological findings identify Africa not only as the source of much of Western culture but as the cradle of mankind.

Among the major discoveries which have forced historians and anthropologists to discard their condescending picture of Africa as a continent without historical importance are Dr. L. S. B. Leakey's find at Lake Victoria in Tanzania of Proconsul, man's immediate predecessor, who is estimated to have lived some thirty million years ago; and his discovery in 1959 at Olduvai Gorge—also in Tanzania—of what are believed to be the fossil remains of the first man (estimated age 600,000 years). Similar discoveries of stone tools and fossil bones throughout Africa indicate that the first men roamed across the continent in pursuit of food. On the basis of this evidence, it is generally accepted today that during this crucial period, the Paleolithic or Old Stone Age, Africa led the rest of the world in man's early development.

Other important finds of the subsequent Neolithic or New Stone Age were made at Shaheinab in the Sudan on the banks of the Rivers Nakuru and Njoro where archeologists unearthed, among various stone tools and pottery, a great number of querns or handmills which indicate that their users had a knowledge of growing grain crops and consequently the baking of some type of bread. Rock drawings discovered in caves in various parts of the African continent indicate that Africans were creative and skilled artists as long ago as three thousand years before the birth of Christ.

Although the gathering of archeological evidence for the reconstruction of Africa's past is far from complete, enough is available today to convince serious scholars that long before civilization had spread to Europe, it was an accomplished state in many parts of Africa. In the face of incontrovertible evidence, a growing number of scientists are beginning to conclude—however reluctantly—that while Caucasoid man was living a relatively primitive existence, his dark-skinned counterpart in Africa was already solving mathematical problems, drawing and writing messages, building temples and homes of brick, growing crops, raising cattle, mining metals and fashioning them into useful objects such as weapons, utensils, tools, ornaments, and objects of art. Moreover, Africa's excavated ruins of palaces, fortresses, and temples tell us that during this early period, Africans organized social communities, then cities, states and, finally, empires with complex political structures, laws, and religious institutions.

THE FIRST ascertainable African state to attain prominence and power was the ancient empire of Ethiopia (as distinguished from modern Ethiopia). It derived its name from the Greek word *Aithiops*, meaning dark-skinned, a reference to its inhabitants. Ancient Ethiopia, which roughly extended over the area now occupied by the republics of Sudan and Somalia and the modern empire of Ethiopia, shared borders in the north with another great power, the kingdom of Egypt.

Section of a mural from an Ethiopian tomb features what historian G. A. Hoskin believed to be white slaves being marched to the Egyptian king.

Although literally erased from historical accounts in current literature, ancient Ethiopia was accorded much deference and admiration by Herodotus, Diodorus and Homer, who described it as a place of revels for the gods.

Ethiopians, by virtue of their more creative past, considered themselves superior to their Egyptian neighbors, whom they viewed with a degree of condescension. "The Ethiopians," wrote Diodorus in the first century B.C., "conceive themselves to be of greater antiquity than any other nation; and it is probable that, born under the sun's path, its warmth may have ripened them earlier than other men. They supposed themselves to be the inventors of worship, of festivals, of solemn assemblies, of sacrifices, and every religious practice."

To classical writers, the general area south of Egypt was known as Ethiopia. In later years, several independent kingdoms, including Kush and the Ethiopian empire of Axum, developed in the section.

For more than five thousand years, and despite intermittent feuds which occasionally erupted into minor warfare, both Ethiopia and Egypt benefited from a unique coexistence which resulted in a cross-fertilization of their cultures through trade and a not inconsiderable amount of intermarrying. It is also important to remember that ancient Egypt was an African civilization and that blacks played an important role in its development as soldiers, laborers, officials, and rulers. Some scholars, for example, have said that Nefertari, wife of Ahmes, founder of the Eighteenth Dynasty, was a black woman. Numerous pictorial representations of the queen, all depicting her as a woman with black skin and marked

Marked Kushite features are apparent in this stone relief rendering of Egypt's Pharaoh Akhnaten and in the ushabti of Pharaoh Taharka (opposite page).

Negroid facial features, are generally accepted as evidence of her African ancestry. The two top court officials and closest confidantes of another queen, Hatsheput, were black. They were Sanmut or Senmut, her prime minister and chief chamberlain, and Nehesi (which is frequently translated as "Negro"), her admiral-in-chief. Sanmut is credited with being the architect who planned and built the queen's temple and tomb, the ruins of which still stand at Deir el-Bahri.

Around 1100 B.C., for reasons that are not clear today, Egypt's power declined while that of the kingdom of Kush increased. The result was that around the middle of the eighth century B.C., Kush's King Kashta declared his country an independent kingdom. Emboldened by Egypt's acquiescence in his declaration of independence, King Kashta rallied his armies and marched on Egypt, more than half of which he conquered after his first major encounter with the demoralized Egyptian army. Thus, Kush rule was extended to Thebes, upper Egypt's capital. King Kashta was succeeded by his son Piankhy. Instilled with his father's dream of Ethiopian greatness, Piankhy continued Kashta's conquest by occupying the remainder of Egypt up to the shores of the Mediterranean. King Piankhy's decisive victory over Kush's former masters re-

Ushabtis, representing servants of the monarchs, were entombed with their masters to serve them in the land of the dead.

sulted in the establishment of the largest and most powerful African state ever brought under one-man rule—an empire which covered nearly a fourth of the entire continent of Africa. Henceforth, Egypt's throne was occupied by the kings of Kush, who established the Twenty-fifth Dynasty of distinguished pharaohs.

During their rule, the Kushites replaced Egypt's ram god as chief deity with their own lion god, which is frequently depicted with three faces and four arms. They also established the elephant as a religious symbol, having trained the latter for war, work, and pageantry. Dr. William Leo Hansberry, one of the most distinguished black researchers of Africa's past, wrote of this period:

> Prior to Piankhy's conquest, Egypt's fortunes, under the rule of or misrule of a succession of weak, incapable kings, had been waning for well over three hundred years. Perhaps never before in historical times had the country's power and prestige ebbed to such a low tide . . .
>
> Under the aegis of her Kushite overlords, this condition was quickly and completely changed. In less than a generation, the arts of peace were caused to flourish anew, and ordered government, national security and individual well-being were again firmly re-established throughout the land. Her tombs were protected, her temples restored and the faded renown of her ancient name recovered its former luster in every civilized clime. In short, Egypt, as effete and decadent as she had become, was infused with new life when grafted upon the ancient but virile stock of the Kushite

A black Ethiopian princess, accompanied by a retinue of slaves and ladies-in-waiting, rides in an ox-drawn chariot in a painting from an ancient Egyptian tomb.

state; and, as an integral part of what was Africa's greatest commonwealth, the pharaonic kingdom soon found herself sharing with her imperial protector the prerogatives and prestige which came to the Kushite empire as a world power.

The successor to Piankhy was his brother Shabaka, an enlightened humanitarian who took great pains to restore Egypt to its former position of power and influence. Among his many innovations and governmental reforms was the abolition of the death penalty, which had been a common punishment for the most minor offenses, such as cheating and lying.

But the distinction of being the greatest of all black pharaohs was reserved for Shabaka's successor, Taharka (referred to in the Bible as Tirhaka) who ascended the throne in 690 B.C. at the age of forty-two. Pharaoh Taharka succeeded in building on the accomplishments of his predecessor by further unifying Ethiopia and Egypt, welding the two states into a single empire of unprecedented stability and prosperity. But peace and progress were of relatively short duration. Twelve years after Taharka took over the reigns of his empire, lower Egypt was attacked at its northwestern borders by the armies of the expansion-minded empire of Assyria. Taken by surprise, Taharka was forced to retreat south to the city of Memphis. After regrouping his forces for two years, Taharka launched a counterattack that drove the invaders from all Egyptian territories. Elated over his victory, Pharaoh Taharka proclaimed himself "Emperor of the World." Taharka's triumph was short-lived. When the Assyrians attacked again several years later, Taharka's forces were forced to flee to Napata, then the capital city of Kush. Taharka died in 663 B.C. His nephew Tanwetamani succeeded him and tried to drive the Assyrians out of Egypt. He got as far as Memphis, but a new Assyrian assault pushed him back once again, first to Thebes, then to Napata. Tanwetamani's defeat brought to an end Kush rule over Egypt, but Kushites continued to make history as rulers of their own empire.

Napata remained the capital city of Kush until about 540 B.C. when the royal family moved to Meroë to the south (some fifty miles east of Khartoum, capital of today's republic of Sudan). Even before Meroë became the new capital, it was well established as a religious center, as can be seen from its many ruins of temples and gathering places for religious worship. It has been suggested that the move was prompted by security considerations as well as by the fact that the immediate surroundings of Meroë, which was on the Nile River, provided better grazing opportunities for the royal herds of cattle and sheep than the arid wastelands around Napata. Another possible reason, researchers surmise, was that Meroë had emerged as an important city in its own right because of substantial iron ore discoveries and a flourishing iron industry.

The shift of Kushite power to Meroë was accompanied by the establishment of a new even more advanced culture and technology with well-constructed towns built of masonry, and with palaces and pyramids similar to those of Egypt, although considerably smaller and rising to a peak at a sharper angle. By the end of the third century B.C., Meroë had developed its own alphabet. Although much of Meroëitic writing has survived on tombs and temples, it has not yet been deciphered.

The end of Kush, which has been estimated to have occurred some 350 years after the birth of Christ, is as obscure as its early beginnings. Its last recorded ruler, King Malequerebar, the seventy-second monarch of his dynasty, was entombed in a small pyramid near Meroë around A.D. 320.

It is generally believed that the downfall of Kush and Meroë was hastened by invasions from the neighboring people of Axum. The forebears of modern-day Ethiopians, the Axumites had left their original homeland at the southern tip of Arabia and established the kingdom of Axum—now Ethiopia—on the western coast of the Red Sea. Officially, Axum became a Christian nation with the conversion to the faith of its King Ezana around A.D. 350, but it claims a Christian background that dates back to the biblical story of its Queen of Sheba and Jerusalem's King Solomon. Whether legend or history, the reported meeting of the two

Extensive excavation at El Kurru, just below the fourth Nile cataract, revealed the entrance to the tomb of Piankhy the Great.

monarchs, following a visit of the Queen to Jerusalem, constitutes a significant event in modern Ethiopian history. The reputed offspring of that union, King Melinik, is regarded as the founder of the royal line of the Lion of Judah from which Emperor Haile Selassie claims descent.

Although the ruins of Meroë, Napata, and other Kushite cities abound with evidence of ancient Africa's glorious past, such as the royal pyramids at El Kurru, Nuri, and Jebel Barkal in the northern part of the kingdom, much remains to be learned about the history of Kush.

One of the most important civilizations to emerge on the African continent during the post-Kush period was the ancient empire of Ghana, some one thousand miles northwest from the modern west coast republic of Ghana. Much of what we know about ancient Ghana today comes from the written accounts of Arab scholars who recorded their own impressions and those of other visitors to Ghana for posterity. Foremost among these accounts is that of Al Bakri, who was born in A.D. 1028 in Cordova, Spain, a member of a distinguished Arab family. By the time Al Bakri wrote his chronicles, in the year 1067, Ghana was already an ancient civilization, the result of its favorable location at a midway point on the trans-Saharan trade route that led from North Africa and the Nile Valley to the south and Africa's rain forest areas.

Much of Al Bakri's writings were concerned with Ghana's immense wealth (especially in gold), the great power of its ruling King Tankamanin and the splendor of life at the royal court. According to Al Bakri, Ghana's capital city Al Ghaba consisted of houses made of stone and acacia wood. "The king," he wrote, "has a palace and a number of dome-shaped dwellings, the whole surrounded by an enclosure like the defensive wall of a city. In the town where the king lives, and not far from the hall where he holds his court of justice, is a mosque where pray the Muslims who come on visiting diplomatic missions." Ghana's people, largely of Mande origin, were not Muslims themselves, but King Tankamanin, who was also their spiritual leader, permitted the establishment of a small settlement of Muslim merchants from the north.

Through Al Bakri's detailed reports we know that the people of Ghana shaved their beards and that the women shaved their heads, that they clothed themselves in cotton, silk, or brocade, according to their means and station in life. Al Bakri said that "the king adorns himself like a woman, wearing necklaces and bracelets" and that when he sits before the people,

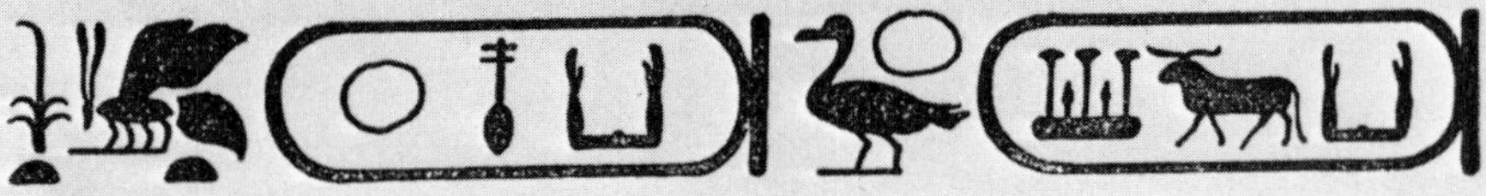

Shabaka, Piankhy's brother and successor, led an effete Egypt through a period of cultural revival.

"he puts on a high cap decorated with gold and wrapped in turbans of fine cotton. He sits in a pavilion around which stand his horses caparisoned in cloth of gold. Behind him stand ten pages holding shields and gold-mounted swords; and on his right hand are the sons of the princes of his empire, splendidly clad and with gold plaited into their hair. The governor of the city is seated on the ground in front of the king, and all around him are his vizirs in the same position. The gate of the chamber is guarded by dogs of an excellent breed, who never leave the king's seat. They wear collars of gold and silver."

Apparently, not all of the king's considerable financial resources were devoted to pomp and circumstance. A good portion was applied to maintaining and expanding his military might. "When the king of Ghana calls up his army," wrote Al Bakri, "he can put 200,000 men in the field, more than 40,000 of whom are bowmen."

Part of the king's wealth stemmed, so the chronicler explained, from his unique levy on imported and exported goods. For every donkey loaded with salt that entered Ghana, for instance, the king charged a duty of one golden dinar (approximately ⅛ oz. of gold) and for every one that left, the duty was two dinars.

Another noteworthy custom of ancient Ghana was the method of succession. Unlike the usual royal custom whereby succession to the throne passes from the king to his oldest son, ancient Ghana's monarchy provided for the succession from the king to his sister's oldest son.

While Al Bakri's accounts of Ghana,

The Temple of Taharka at Gibel El Birkel bears the name of its builder who reputedly was the greatest of all Ethiopian pharaohs. He ascended the throne in A.D. 690.

which he compiled in his *Book of Roads and Kingdoms*, comprise the most detailed descriptions of life in that ancient monarchy to have reached us today, they are by no means the only available documents to mention the existence of the ancient civilization. His reports are supported by numerous Muslim scholars, including Mahmud Al-Kati who, in 1519, almost a century before Al Bakri, made public his findings about Ghana and other African civilizations in a book entitled *Tarikh al-Fettah* (*Chronicles of the Researcher*) following years of extensive travel in the Sudan. Al-Kati, whose scholarly inquiries and wise counsel to King Askia Muhammad of Timbuktu had earned him an honorary degree of doctor of law, was as impressed as Al Bakri with the opulence of Ghana's royal court. The king of Ghana, he wrote, had one thousand horses, each of which had three grooms to attend to its needs.

Although some of the Arab scholars' accounts seem to have a legendary ring, the ruins of Ghana, discovered at the outset of World War I by Albert Bonnel de Mézières, a Frenchman in the colonial service of his country, bear out many of their claims. Subsequent excavations in 1953 of the ruins near Ghana's capital city, Kumbi Saleh, in what is now the republic of Mauritania, by two French archaeologists, Paul Thomassey and Raymond Mauny, leave no doubt about the accuracy of the Muslim scholars' accounts. Modern archeologists have concluded that Ghana's rise to prominence as a vital trade center in the western Sudan must

Massive sandstone columns are part of the ruins of an Ethiopian temple above the Nile's second cataract. The region abounds with monuments which rival those of Egypt in grandeur and beauty.

have occurred somewhere in the vicinity of A.D. 700 and that it maintained that position of importance until about 1076, when the Almoravids, a fanatical sect of Muslims from North Africa bent on spreading the faith of Islam throughout the rest of the continent, attacked Kumbi Saleh and put it to the torch. Although the Almoravids where obliged to release their grip on Ghana after ten years of occupation, Ghana was too weakened to recover and began to decline. The final blow came in 1203 when its neighbors, the Sosso, emboldened by Ghana's waning military might, launched an attack that brought the ailing colossus to its knees.

THE NATION WHICH succeeded Ghana as the most important center of culture, commerce, and political influence in the western Sudan region was the empire of Mali, whose rise to prominence in the thirteenth century roughly coincides with Ghana's decline. Mali's history goes back to the seventh century at which time it was an insignificant Mandingo community on the upper Niger River. But after centuries of steady growth, and after absorbing all of the territory once occupied by its vanquished predecessor, Mali not only surpassed Ghana in power and influence but grew to more than three times its size. Like Ghana, Mali owed much of its wealth to its strategic location on the trans-Saharan trade route and to two of the most coveted commodities of the time —gold and salt. Each day the long caravans, some of them consisting of hundreds of camels, streamed into Mali from the north, laden with salt that was readily exchanged for gold and then exported to the desalinated regions of the African interior.

The person credited with having transformed Mali from a powerless, insignificant state to an empire of international prominence was the Mandingo King Sundiata Keita, who ascended the throne in 1230. It is reported that Sosso King Sumanguru, after overpowering Ghana, attacked the Mandingos of Mali whom he considered his rivals. After capturing the infant Sundiata and his eleven brothers, all of whom were heirs to the Mali throne, he had all the brothers beheaded, sparing only Sundiata because he seemed too frail to be a threat. King Sumanguru lived long enough to regret his decision to spare Sundiata, for Sundiata grew stronger. After coming of age and taking over the reigns of his country, he led his people against the Sosso. In a bloody battle, fought in 1240, Sundiata defeated Sumanguru and, taking revenge for the murder of his brothers, had him put to death.

Sundiata's victory only whetted his appetite for further conquest. Within a few years, he had annexed all of Sosso territory, then continued his expansion westward up to the River Gambia, finally pushing through to the Atlantic coast. Unlike landlocked Ghana, Mali now had access to the sea, a fact which greatly enhanced its potential as a commercial power. Before the thirteenth century had come to a close, Mali was firmly established as the most powerful African state south of the Sahara and King Sundiata as the mightiest black ruler of his time.

While Sundiata's fame was largely confined to the Sudan and adjacent territories, that of his grandson Mansa (Sultan) Musa, who ascended the throne of Mali in 1307, spread throughout the African continent and beyond to Europe. Musa, who continued the expansion policies of his grandfather and extended the borders of the empire still further, is best remembered for the spectacular pilgrimage to Mecca which he undertook in the year 1324. Never before had pilgrims witnessed such a lavish display of wealth and power. The sultan, mounted on a resplendently decorated charger, arrived in Mecca with an entourage of some sixty thousand persons, including twelve thousand servants. Five hundred of the latter preceded the procession, each carrying a staff of gold weighing six pounds. Long trains of camels carried heavy loads of presents and gold which the sultan, in keeping with Muslim tradition, ordered distributed as alms among the poor he encountered on his way. It is reported that in this manner, the black monarch gave away twenty-four thousand pounds of gold. The effects of Musa's generosity were felt throughout the Arab world where the wide circulation of Sudanese gold forced down the value of the local dinar for more than a decade.

During the pilgrimage, Musa had befriended a fellow Muslim by the name of

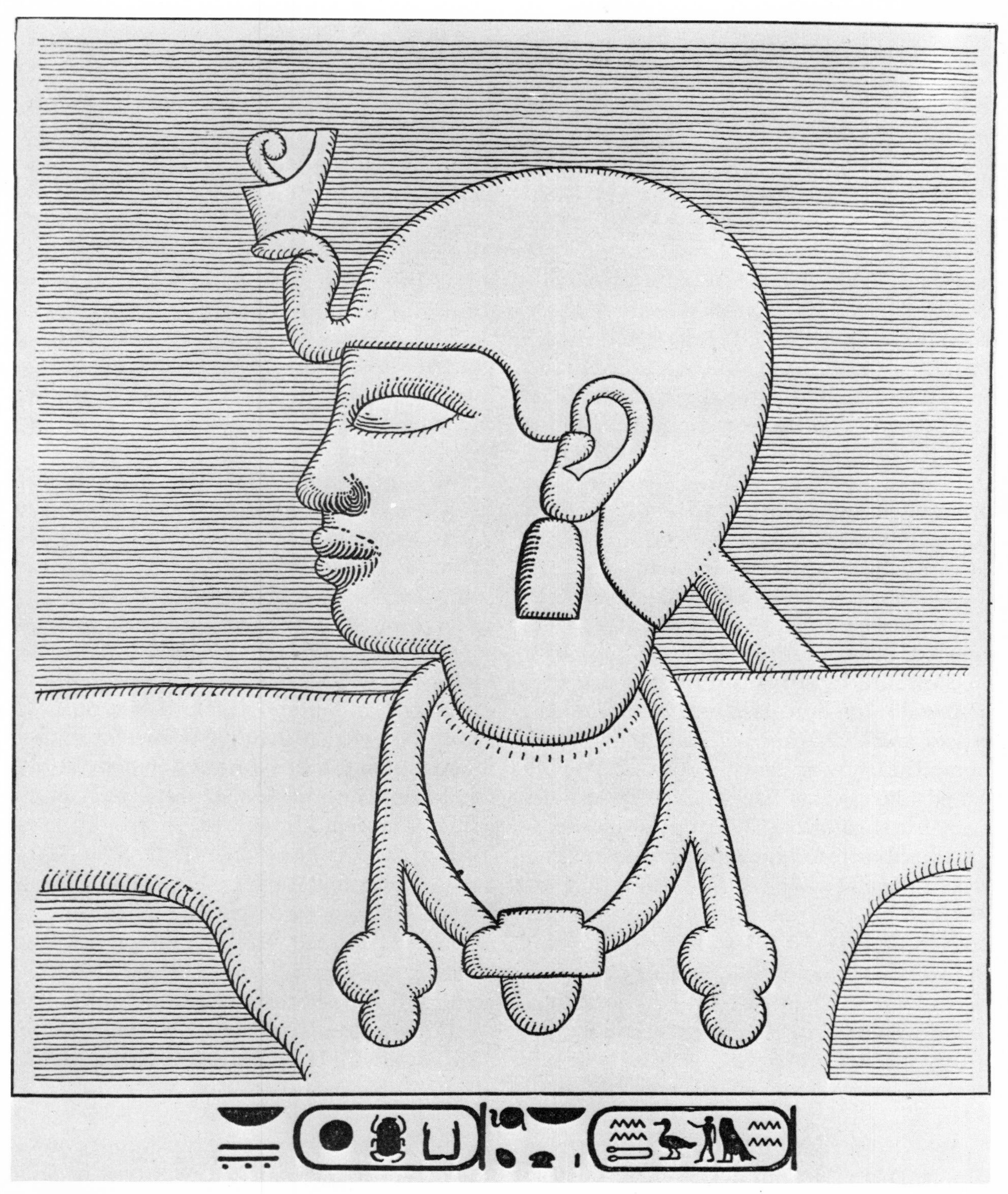

Contemporary portrait depicts King Netek-Amen of Meroë, capital city of Kush after 540 B.C.

Es-Saheli who was both an architect and a poet of considerable repute. Musa engaged Es-Saheli's services and upon their return to Mali, the latter designed many imposing buildings, among them the famed Great Mosque at Gao and the Sankor Mosque and University of Timbuktu.

When Musa died in 1332, he passed on to his son, Maghan, an impressive legacy. Mali had reached the zenith of its power. Its people were prosperous and it enjoyed an amicable relationship with its Arab neighbors to the north and black states to the east and south. Above all, it was respected around the world for the high caliber of its cultural and intellectual life. But, as is often the case with the children of great men, King Maghan did not have his father's skills. Inept in the art of governing, he was unable to arrest Mali's decline from greatness. When the Mossi people, a tribe from the upper Volta region, crossed Mali's borders and attacked Timbuktu, Maghan stood helplessly by while the most prestigious city of his empire was ransacked and ravished. Territory by territory the Mali empire fell apart as subject peoples rose in revolt. Even the more resolute Sultan Sulayman, Mansa Musa's brother, who took over the reigns of Mali from his hapless nephew Maghan, was unable to reverse the trend and revive Mali's power. He did, however, succeed in restoring a degree of internal stability in those parts of his empire that were still under Mandingo control. It is unfortunate that one of the most comprehensive eyewitness reports about the empire of Mali and its people was prepared during this period of general decline. It was written by a famous Arab writer named Ibn Battuta who had visited Mali in 1352.

Battuta was impressed with the Mali people's highly developed sense of fairness and the conspicuous absence of crime. "The Mandingos," he reported, "possess some admirable qualities. They are seldom unjust and have a greater abhorrence of injustice than any other people. The sultan shows no mercy to anyone who is guilty of the least act of it. There is complete and general safety throughout their country. Neither traveler nor inhabitant in it has anything to fear from robbers or men of violence. . . ."

Battuta found among the Mali people an unusual zeal for learning the Koran by heart. "They put their children in chains," he noted, "if they show any backwardness in memorizing it, and they are not set free until they have it by heart."

Ibn Battuta's general impression of Mali was still that of a great empire with considerable vitality. But Mali's days of greatness were in the past. Subject to repeated attacks by neighboring people, especially the Mossi and Tuareg, it continued to disintegrate until—around the

Typical Meroë pyramids are shown in sketches below. Portrait on opposite page is that of Meroë Queen Amani-Shakhatē.

middle of the fifteenth century—it was reduced to its former status of a tiny and obscure Mandingo state.

THE THIRD AND MOST POWERFUL of the great Sudanese civilizations was the kingdom of Songhay which began to form around the middle of the thirteenth century and which slowly usurped the territories of disintegrating Mali. In 1493, when Songhay's king, Sonni Ali, died, leaving the throne to an infant son, a disgruntled general of the king's army, Askia Mohammed, seized power and ascended the throne. King Askia, a Moslem, proved an able ruler, a brilliant military strategist, an efficient administrator, and an enlightened legislator. "In personal character," wrote Alexander Chamberlain, "in administrative ability, in devotion to the welfare of his subjects, in open-mindedness toward foreign influence, and in wisdom in the adoption of non-African ideas and institutions, King Askia was certainly the equal of the average European monarch of the time and superior to many of them."

There is ample evidence of Askia's abilities. During his nineteen-year reign, he extended Songhay's borders from the Atlantic Coast in the west to the border of what is now Nigeria in the east, and from the southern borders of modern Algeria to the tropical rain forest regions in the south. To ensure the proper administration of his unwieldy realm, which was larger than all of Europe, he divided it into manageable administrative provinces, each of which he put under the authority of a trustworthy governor. To facilitate trade, he standardized measures and weights throughout his kingdom. He created separate governmental agencies charged with specific functions such as the administration of finance, taxation, agriculture, justice, and defense. But most importantly, he infused the cities of Jenne, Walata and Timbuktu (the latter having been ravaged by the Sossi during the Mali era) with new vigor, and restored them to their former importance as the centers of intellectual life in Africa. Timbuktu, whose population under King Askia had grown to more than one hundred thousand, was especially honored by scholars who came to the city from Arabia, the Mediterranean, and central Europe. Many of the visiting foreign scholars were so impressed with what they found that they made Timbuktu their permanent home. The result was a lively exchange of European, Arabian, and African ideas, philosophies, and religious thoughts. The spirited exchange gave rise to a strong Sudanese literary movement. But although many books were written in Timbuktu, the demand for literature among its knowledge-thirsty citizens always exceeded the supply. Wrote Leo Africanus, a Moorish historian: "There is a big demand for books in manuscript, imported from Barbary. More profit is made from the book trade than from any other line of business." Notable among the books generated by Sudan's literary movement was the *Tarikh es Sudan* (*the History of Sudan*) by a Timbuktu scholar known as Es Sadi. Translated into many languages, the *Tarikh* included a chronicle of Timbuktu from its early beginnings up to 1655, the year of the author's death.

Askia's rule came to a sudden and inglorious end in 1512. Having become

Monolithic church, hewn out of solid rock, was built in Ethiopia's Lasta Mountains by King Amanuel who ruled Ethiopia from 1170 to 1220.

blind and infirm because of old age, he was unceremoniously deposed by his own son, Musa. From then on the throne passed through a succession of mediocre rulers who tried as best they could to keep the empire intact. In 1591, during the reign of Askia Ishak, a descendent of Askia Mohammed, the Songhay empire was attacked by the army of El Mansur of Morocco, a powerful ruler who had long cast a covetous eye on his prosperous neighbors to the south. El Mansur's General Judar crossed the Sahara with four thousand soldiers and nine thousand transport animals, mostly camels, a feat which took him six months and cost him the lives of three thousand men. Outside Gao, the Songhay capital city, Judar's reduced army was confronted by King Askia Ishak's army of eighteen thousand cavalry and nine thousand infantry. But General Judar was not worried. He knew he had something the Songhay forces lacked —gunpowder and firearms. Despite the Songhay warriors' bravery and numerical superiority, they were unable to withstand the Morrocans' fusillades. Many lost their lives and those who did not were either captured or fled across the Niger River to the south. A Sudanese poet captured the crumbling of one of the greatest social orders established by blacks since the birth of Christ in these words: "From that moment [Songhay's defeat] everything changed. Danger took the place of security; poverty of wealth. Peace gave way to distress, disaster and violence . . ." Songhay's military defeat spelled the beginning of the end of the last and greatest of the three Sudanese empires.

Although the disintegration of Songhay marked the beginning of the end of the great African empires, many smaller states continued to flourish and make important contributions to Africa's cultural, political, and economic development. Notable among them were the twin kingdoms of Kanem-Bornu in the central Sudan, to the east and somewhat south of the old empire sites. Originally two independent kingdoms, Kanem and Bornu were merged after Bornu's King Idris Aloma conquered and occupied Kanem around 1581. He did so by using firearms which he had introduced into his country after a Mecca pilgrimage.

A unique aspect of Bornu culture was the similarity of its warriors to European medieval knights. Unlike the lightly clad warriors in other parts of Africa, Bornu chieftains reportedly "were habited in coats of mail composed of iron chain, which covered them from the throat to the knee, dividing behind, and coming on each side of the horse. Some of them had helmets, or rather skullcaps, of the same metal, with chin-pea pieces, all sufficiently strong to ward off the shock of a spear. Their horses' heads were also defended by plates of iron, brass, and silver, just leaving sufficient room for the eyes of the animal."

Kanem-Bornu, whose origins date back to about A.D. 800, survived as an independent state until the early part of the nineteenth century when it fell prey, like many other African states, to the spreading colonization of Africa by European powers. Today, the ruins of Bornu's capital city, Gazargamo, built toward the end of the fifteenth century and destroyed by Fulani raiders in 1811, still speak eloquently of its former majesty. Located on the River Yobé on the border of Nigeria and the republic of Niger, the ruins are encircled by a huge twenty-foot-high earth wall that measures nearly two miles in diameter. Also surviving is the horsemanship that made Bornu's warriors the scourge of their enemies. Each year, modern Bornu horsemen, dressed much like their forefathers in chain mail and resplendent robes, dazzle visitors and countrymen alike with mounted war games and pageantry of bygone days.

With the Sudanese empires' decline a number of smaller black kingdoms, in-

The world-famous Great Monolith and a small obelisk are remnants which mark the site of Axum, the former capital city of Ethiopia which was destroyed by Moslem invaders in the sixteenth century.

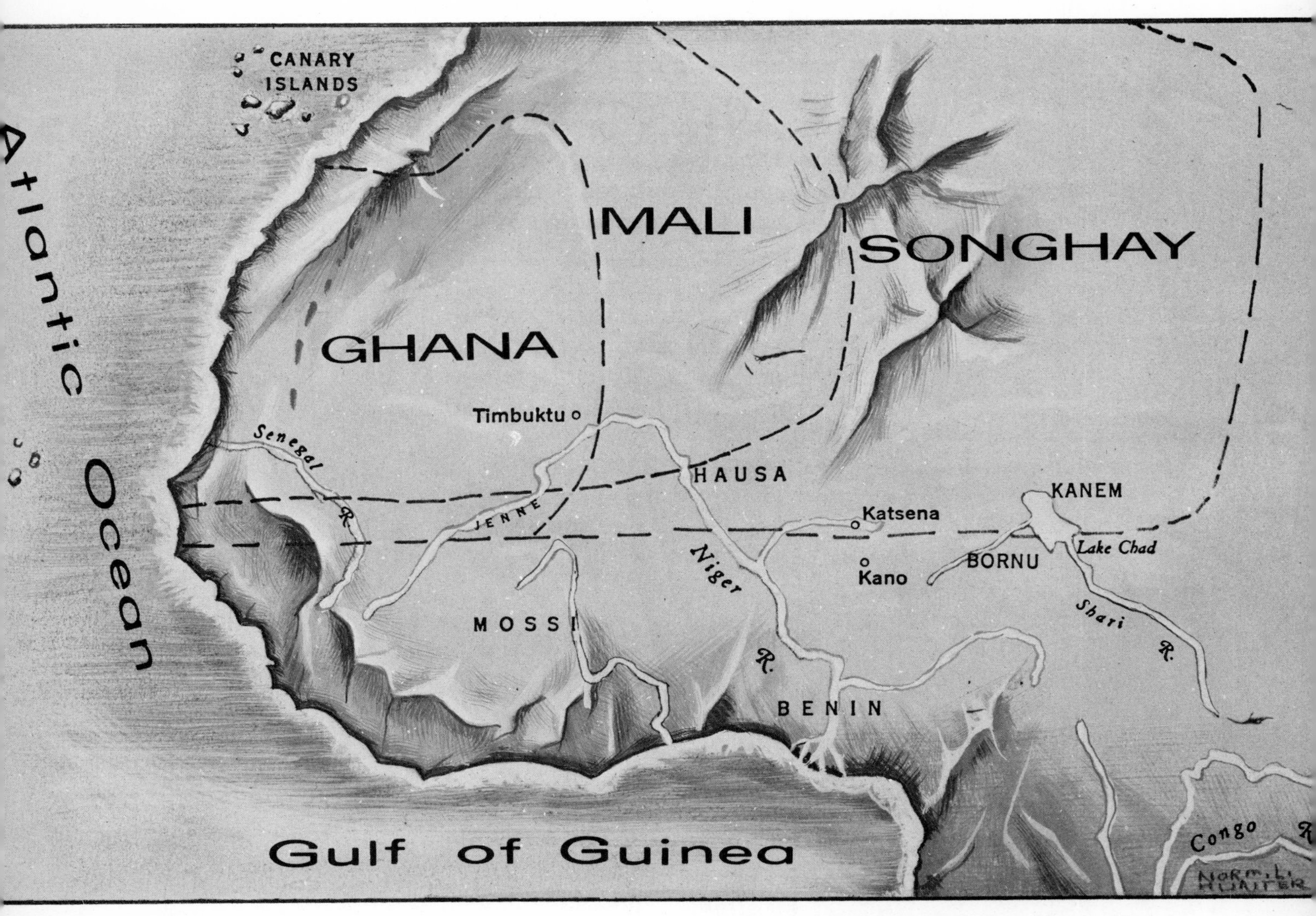

The ancient Sudanese empires, Ghana, Mali and Songhay, reached their peak of power during the Middle Ages. Ghana dominated the Sudan for almost three centuries. Mali rose in the thirteenth and survived until the seventeenth century. Songhay was a Sudan power in the fifteenth and sixteenth centuries.

cluding Benin, Oyo, Nok, Ife, Dahomey and Ashanti, emerged in the forest regions of West Africa. Their origins can be traced to the thirteenth century although they did not reach the zenith of their power until early in the sixteenth century. While not nearly as large or as influential as any of the great empires of the Sudan, the kingdom of Benin, largest of the forest nations, attained a measure of importance in its own right. Located in what today is the republic of Nigeria, it exchanged ambassadors with Portugal as early as 1485.

Without contact with the Sudanese cultures and the Muslim faith, Benin's people developed a religion of their own that centered largely on their king, whom they revered as a representative of ancestral spirits.

All of the forest kingdoms distinguished themselves as producers of beautiful art in brass, copper, bronze, gold, iron, ivory, and pottery. It was on the order of Oba (King) Ogula of Benin, who reigned toward the end of the thirteenth century, that the unique practice of making brass and bronze castings as devices for the recording of events for posterity was developed and perfected to a fine art.

Unfortunately the skill of bronze and brass casting did not survive and even modern casting techniques have failed to produce artifacts comparable in quality and artistry to the Benin masters.

When, toward the end of the fifteenth century, the Portuguese adventurer Vasco da Gama sailed around the Cape of Good Hope in search of unexplored lands, he was surprised to find flourishing towns and bustling sea ports along the coast of East Africa. To his further amazement he found that the people of the coast were living in many-storied stone houses, that their ships were built as well or better than his own, and that their sailors were sophisticated navigators who had sailed across oceans still unknown to the Portuguese. Above all, he marvelled at their prosperity and the disdain with which they regarded their Portuguese visitors. "When we had been there two or three days, two gentlemen of the country came to see us. They were very haughty, and valued nothing that we gave them," Da Gama complained.

Da Gama had come to the Land of Zanj, a name Arab travellers had given to the people on Africa's East Coast. Most of what is known today about the earlier history of the people of Zanj has been written by Abdul El Mas'udi, the author of *The Meadows of Gold and the Mines of Gems*, which has been compared in quality with the writings of another famous traveller, Marco Polo.

From El Mas'udi we learn that the Zanj of his time were "jet black" people who were skilled workers in metal, and who prized iron above gold; that they enjoyed a thriving trade with India, China, and Malaya, to which they shipped large cargoes of iron and ivory tusks, many weighing fifty pounds or more.

During the tenth century, the time of El Mas'udi's writings, large numbers of Islamic people from Oman settled along the Swahili coast and blended their culture with that of the original people of Zanj. The union was fruitful and resulted in the establishment of several prosperous coastal towns, including Mombasa, Kilwa, Sofala, Malindi and the off-shore island harbors of Zanzibar and Pemba. While the religion of the people became predominantly Moslem, their language remained Swahili, a basically African language showing strong Arabic influence.

"The Zanj," El Mas'udi informed us, "use the ox as a beast of burden, for their country has neither horses, nor mules nor camels, and they do not even know these animals." They were also "elegant speakers, and have orators in their own language. Often a devout man among them, entering a crowd, will make a speech inviting his listeners to conform to the ways of god and obey god's orders. . . ."

Mas'udi wrote of the election of a supreme king or Waqlimi, who "commands all the other kings of the Zanj." Unlike some African potentates, the Waqlimi did not have absolute powers and ruled only with the consent and at the discretion of the governed. "Waqlimi," explains El Mas'udi, "means 'son of the great god.' They [the Zanj] call him thus because they have chosen their king to govern them with equity. As soon as he exercises a tyrannical power and departs from the rules of justice, they kill him and exclude his posterity from royal succession, because they say that in acting thus he has ceased to be the son of the great god—that is, the king of heaven and earth."

The arrival of Portuguese on the Swahili coast spelled doom for the prosperous coastal towns. Spurred by greed, the Portuguese attacked with superior military might in order to force the towns' rulers to pay an annual tribute in the form of "a certain sum of money, or a rich jewel" to the king of Portugal. Any resistance on the part of the peace-loving, easy-going coastal people was met with brutality. Margaret Shinnie, in her book *Ancient African Kingdoms*, describes the event:

> Mombasa and many other fair and peaceful towns, with years of history behind them and great traditions of trade, were destroyed and their citizens massacred. The towns were seized; the trade routes altered to suit the new rulers; and later great forts, like Fort Jesus at Mombasa, were built to house garrisons to control the local populations.

Through the two-hundred-year Portuguese rule that followed, none of the coastal communities regained their former standing of importance and prosperity. Today, the only reminders of Zanj's

Timbuktu, a thriving city within the Mali and Songhay empires, was one of the world's leading centers of learning during the Middle Ages.

thriving coastal culture are contemporary writings, the ruined buildings, and broken pieces of precious Chinese porcelain.

A FEW HUNDRED MILES inland from the coastal town of Sofala, within the center of what today is Southern Rhodesia, stands a group of massive stone ruins unlike any others found on the continent of Africa. Rediscovered by chance by a European game hunter in 1868, they are the remains of the citadel of Zimbabwe (meaning royal court), estimated to have been built some time during the eleventh century. The ruins consist of two main groups a quarter of a mile apart, one known as the "Acropolis" and the other as the "Temple." It is assumed that the "Temple" was not, as its name suggests, a place of religious worship, but rather that it served as a residence for the king, while the Acropolis' hilltop location suggests its use as fortress for the defense of the settlement in the valley below.

Nothing definite is known about the early history of Zimbabwe and its people since no written accounts have survived. But archaeological investigation and written accounts by Portuguese who arrived at Zimbabwe during the beginning of the sixteenth century have helped to shed some light on Zimbabwe's obscure past. It is known today that Zimbabwe was part of the great kingdom of Shona people ruled by the powerful Monomatapa kings.

Remnants of objects of Persian, Chinese, Indian, Indonesian, and Arab origins found among Zimbabwe's ruins indicate that its people did not live in isolation but that, like their coastal neighbors, they were engaged in lively commerce with the outside world. It is assumed that Zimbabwe depended largely on the mining and export of gold, as indicated by thousands of mine workings and shallow diggings which have been discovered.

The Monomatapa's rule of Zimbabwe is believed to have come to an end toward the end of the fifteenth or the beginning of the sixteenth century. Some scholars believe that the rulers—their military power notwithstanding—were driven out by successive attacks from the Roswi people who established themselves for nearly two centuries as the rulers of the citadel. Another theory holds that the group relocated voluntarily because of an acute shortage of life-sustaining salt. It is known, however, that after the Monomapata rulers left Zimbabwe, their power declined steadily until the once extensive empire had dwindled into obscurity.

During the middle of the seventeenth century, a group of small and powerless groups made up of Twi-speaking Akan people, began to consolidate. The purpose of the consolidation was to offer resistance to the overlordship of the Denkyira, at the time the most powerful tribal group in the central forest lands of West Africa. The mainspring of the unification movement was King Osei Tutu who, after welding his Akan people into a single Ashanti nation, threw off the yoke of the hated Denkyira and established his nation as the region's greatest power.

King Osei Tutu, legend has it, derived his power and success directly from heaven. According to that legend, his court was visited one day by a celebrated

Under Mansa Musa, who ruled from 1307 until his death in 1332, the Mali empire reached the zenith of its power and influence.

magician named Anotchi who claimed to be an emissary of Onyame, the god of the sky. He told the king that he was sent to bring about the rise of the Ashanti nation. Then he proceeded to "draw from heaven" a golden stool which gradually descended amid thunderous noise until it came to rest on King Osei Tutu's lap. Anotchi explained that henceforth the fate of the Ashanti would be inextricably intertwined with that of the stool, that—in fact—it contained their souls and that it was the source of their power, honor and general welfare. Should the chair ever be taken from them or destroyed, he warned, the Ashanti nation would perish.

The stool became a symbol of central importance to the Ashanti. It has been established that as the prestige of the stool increased among the people, so did their fortunes and those of their king. Steadily, King Osei Tutu's domain increased in size until it extended to the coast, where the Dutch and British traders had established forts and trading posts.

King Osei Tutu died in 1712 at a ripe old age and his power passed on to King Opoko Ware who succeeded in extending the nation's boundaries even further. The only Africans to challenge the dominance of the Ashanti at the time were the coastal Fante, who had been leasing land to the Dutch and British for the establishment of trading facilities. Desirous of establishing their sovereignty and eager to become the collectors of the lease, the Ashanti in 1805 attacked their rivals, pursuing the latter's fleeing army to the British coastal Fort Abora where they sealed the Fante's defeat.

For several decades, the Ashanti lived in peaceful coexistence with the British traders, who were not strong enough to challenge the blacks' sovereignty. But this changed drastically in 1873. Having been refused permission by the Ashanti to set up further trading facilities on Ashanti inland territory, the British in that year sent heavily armed troops, headed by Sir Garnet Wolseley, on a "punitive expedition" to Kumasi, the Ashanti capital. The attack caught the Ashanti by surprise and they were defeated. After his troops had captured Kumasi, Sir Garnet ordered it burned to the ground and the king exiled.

Although now firmly in control, the British were still haunted by the legend of the golden chair since it inspired sporadic insurrections by unreconciled Ashanti tribes. In March, 1900, a British government representative, determined to get to the bottom of the legend, demanded from the Ashanti chieftains that they produce the chair and turn it over to him. He also told them that he intended to sit on the stool and that their exiled king would

African king prepares to lead his warriors into battle.

not be permitted to return should they refuse to comply with his requests. The chieftains, either unwilling or unable to meet his demands, but outraged by the insult, prepared for war. In the ensuing battle the British reportedly lost 1,007 men before they were able to subdue the stubborn Ashanti.

Much of the Ashanti people's distant past is shrouded in obscurity, but sufficient reliable evidence in the form of excavated material exists to create a picture of a civilization peopled with artisans, enterprising traders, and awesome warriors.

Apologists for the slave trade and European penetration of Africa are apt to point to the many "blessings" which white civilization bestowed on the "Dark Continent." The truth, which has gained increasing acceptance since the emergence of modern independent African states, stands in stark contradiction to the Peace Corps image which the colonial powers have tried to project. As unflattering as this truth may be to their collective egos, it is a fact that Europeans did not arrive in Africa as builders and healers but—quite to the contrary—as degraders and destroyers of human lives and cultural systems that were in many instances superior to their own.

In pre-European West Africa, the area from which came most of black Americans' ancestors, there were well-ordered, complex socioeconomic institutions that ranged from small village kinship groups to extensive empire states with established legal codes and governments. In most states or tribal communities, regardless of size, the fundamental political unit was the extended family made up of the descendants of a common ancestor. In nearly all of these family groupings, authority was vested in a village patriarch, a minor chieftain who had either inherited his rank from his father or had been chosen by the elders of the clan.

Agriculture formed the basis of most of West Africa's economic life. Tribes of the coastal regions and along the shores of large rivers were usually fishermen while in most of the grasslands the economy was based on herding, the livestock being cattle, goats, and sheep. Specialization was advanced. A tribe, for example, that concentrated its efforts on fishing would barter with another tribe that specialized in weaving or farming. Each tribal community had its skilled artisans, who included wood carvers, bronze- copper- and goldsmiths, pottery makers, weavers, and tailors. In some instances, artisans formed

Kanem-Bornu knights in the western Sudan, wore coats of mail like their European counterparts.

African art, such as this wooden Yoruba mask, has left an indelible impression on the "modern art" of the West.

special trade guilds. Iron was in extensive use from the Atlantic Ocean to Ethiopia.

With the exception of the ruling monarchs of large states, Africans did not own land as individuals but rather collectively as members of a tribe.

Polygamy—with one man having more than one wife—was a common practice. Usually, the number of wives a man would marry was determined by the number of wives he was able to support, a fact which caused most men of modest means to remain monogamous. Marriages were often arranged between the families of the bride and groom after an agreement had been reached over the size of a dowry—often a few head of cattle or sheep—which was payable to the parents of the bride.

Many social problems that have plagued the "civilized" countries of the West were unknown in pre-colonial Africa. The old, the sick, and the infirm were adequately cared for by the tribal groups or states. Prostitution did not exist, nor did the crime of robbery.

Some tribes were far advanced in the curing of diseases and there are indications that some Africans developed an effective vaccine against smallpox. Constantly plagued by malaria, Africans made considerable progress toward the discovery of a cure, having traced the cause of the disease to the mosquito. A European traveler in Ethiopia noted: "The natives hereabout say that Malaria is caused by the bite of the mosquito, but, of course, we know better—it is caused by misasmas of the swamps!"

Africans, without exception, were deeply religious people. Although scholars, to this day, condescendingly dismiss African religious expressions that fail to conform with "established" western theology as "animism," African religions lacked none of the philosophical complexities that characterize the "great religions" of the world. In the manner of advanced peoples everywhere, Africans struggled with the big questions: What is man? What is the purpose of life? What happens after death? What is man's relationship to the power or powers that created him? While the answers Africans gave varied from people to people, there were basic similarities. Most believed in a supreme deity who created the earth and in a host of lesser gods often associated with natural phenomena such as the sun, the wind, rain, and thunder. Further down in the divine hierarchy were a vast number of spirits, some of them ancestral but most of them embodied in various objects that surrounded the Africans in their daily lives.

Art was closely interwoven with African religion, especially the masks and statuettes of wood, ivory, terra cotta, brass, and bronze that found extensive use in the performance of religious rites. It is well known that Pablo Picasso and other modernists turned their backs on the Greco-Roman and Renaissance masters to absorb and incorporate in their own works the rich traditions of West Africa. There were no art museums in pre-European Africa, for aesthetic expression was a collective experience in which the people participated. Art, as far as the Africans were concerned, was not for art's sake but for life's sake.

Like art, music was collectively expressed. It was grounded in two basic techniques which survived in the New World —polyrhythmic percussion and the alternating call-and-response pattern between leader and chorus. Wherever there was music in Africa there was dance. Men and women danced because dancing had both social and religious meaning. Any event in the life of Africans, from birth to death, was celebrated by rhythmic movement because dancing, to the African, was life itself.

Africans were not only a people made up of a wide variety of racial stocks, they also spoke over eight hundred languages. Contrary to a popular myth, these languages were far from simple. Giving a classic description of an African language, Mario Pei wrote:

> Swahili is a complete refutation of the rather general belief that languages of "primitive" peoples are necessarily primitive, and consist largely of grunts, groans and mixed-up ideas. Swahili has a euphony that is comparable to Italian, with clear, distinct sounds, vowel endings, and a most pleasing arrangement of syllables that consist for the most part of consonant-plus-vowel. It is capable of such absolute precision that the Swahili version of the Pentateuch contains fewer words than the Hebrew original, without the slightest loss or distortion of meaning. Its grammatical and syntactical

Wooden stool was carved by Baluba artisans in the Congo.

structure is logical, almost to the point of being philosophical. . . . Using Swahili roots, prefixes and suffixes, it would be as easy to construct the vocabulary of nuclear fission (or of any other science or philosophy) as it is in languages like the modernized Irish of Eire or the modernized Hebrew of Israel. . . .

African literature was primarily oral. This oral literature fell into two basic types—professional and popular. In the former, the tribal traditions, customs, laws, and important events were disseminated and passed on by word of mouth from generation to generation by men whose sole occupation was to commit such information to memory. Popular literature, on the other hand, consisted of the folklore, narratives, and proverbs with which amateur story tellers, usually older members of the tribe, regaled the young.

Much of Africa's flourishing culture was debased or totally destroyed through the ruthless exploitation of the continent by Europeans. But much has survived, enough to give modern-day scholars in the fields of history, anthropology, archeology, and linguistics a more accurate view of Africa and its rich contribution to the total human culture than that which prevailed in the past. There is little doubt today that as a result of the massive importation of African slaves, many African cultural components have grown new roots in the New World, especially in the United States. Often suppressed and denied, Afro-Americans are celebrating a rebirth of African culture through a newly awakened sense of black awareness and pride in their African heritage.

Delicately carved head is part of the ornamentation of a chief's baton used by the Lunda tribes of the former Belgian Congo's Kasai district.

2

Slave Trade

One of the most important events in shaping modern history was the African slave trade. The institution of slavery, which has existed throughout the ages in one form or another among peoples of all races, reached unprecedented dimensions following the penetration of Africa by Europeans in the fifteenth century.

It was a period marked by the decline of the great Sudanese empires which were locked in a life-and-death struggle with Arab invaders and various African tribes. Exploiting the conflict for their own ends, European traders hastened the process of disintegration by supplying the warring factions with muskets for which they charged a high price in gold and slaves.

Initially, the customers of the European slave traders were the planters of the newly established Portuguese and Spanish colonies in South and Central America and the sugar farmers in the Caribbean islands. Eventually, they were joined by the cotton and tobacco plantation owners in North America. As Europeans opened territory after territory in the New World, the demand for cheap labor increased and with it the skill of those who derived huge profits from supplying that demand.

Spain, which had been given possession of most of the New World by a papal bull, but which at the same time was prohibited from directly dealing in slaves, entered the slave business anyway, although in a rather oblique way. King Charles V, the successor of King Raymond and Queen Isabella, issued the asiento, a license which gave its holder the exclusive right to import annually four thousand slaves into the Spanish colonies in the New World.

The first to acquire the asiento were the Portuguese, who had long since become skilled in the capturing and marketing of

To make maximum use of ship space and reap maximum profit from each trip, slave ships were loaded according to carefully designed plans.

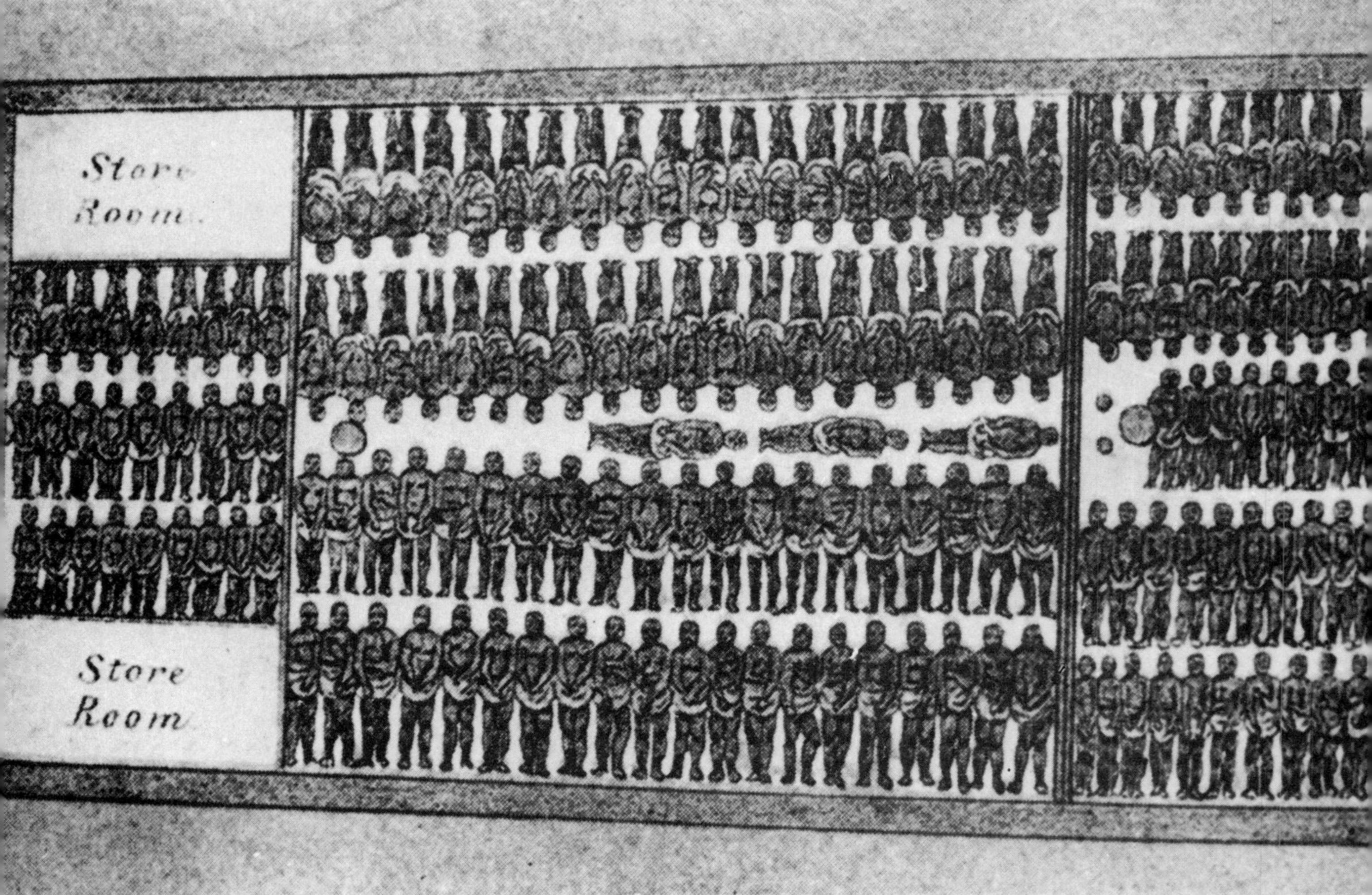

African slaves. Portugal had entered Africa under Prince Henry the Navigator. As early as 1441, Prince Henry dispatched a ship to Africa's West Coast with orders to secure a cargo of skins, oils, spices, and gold. Captain Antonio Gonsalves, the young master of the ship, landed near Cape Bojador in what is today the republic of Senegal. Over-zealous, Gonsalves not only filled the ship with the cargo he was ordered to obtain but—for good measure—added ten Africans whom, upon return, he presented to his sovereign as a gift. Prince Henry thought highly of the present, so much so that he passed on some of the slaves to the Pope who promptly

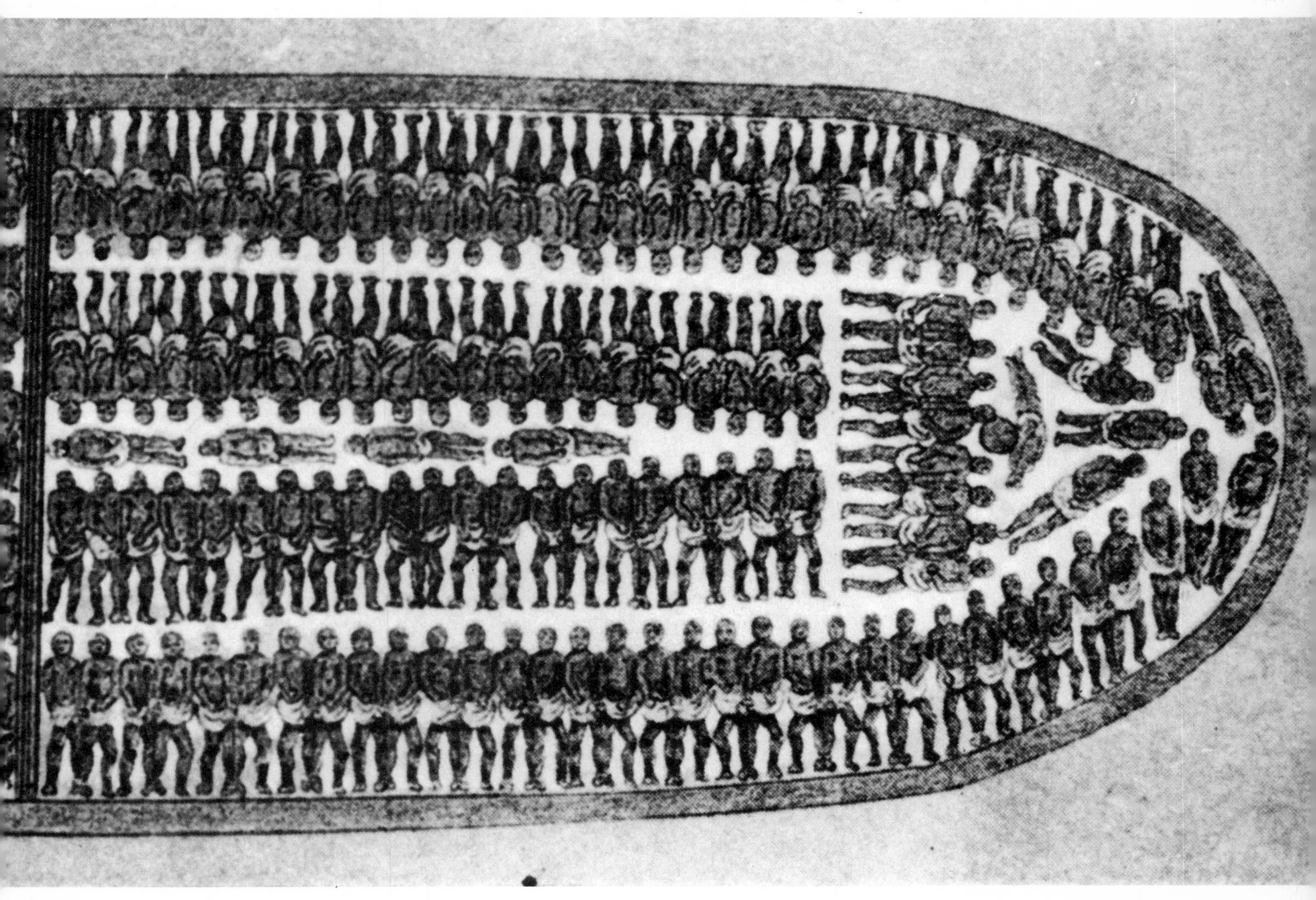

conferred upon the prince full possession of all West Africa's coastal regions.

The Pope's edict set the stage for a long succession of Portuguese expeditions aimed at the exploration and exploitation of the gold-rich Gulf of Guinea area. In 1481 Portugal established the first European outpost in Africa, Fort Elmina.

For more than a century, the Portuguese led the rest of Europe in the slave trade. During that time Portugal not only supplied the New World's plantations with African slaves but imported some one thousand Africans each year for domestic and other work. Gradually, the Portuguese population began to take on Negroid

This illustration is from an 1860 *Harper's Weekly* account of the capture of the slave bark *Wildfire* by the U.S. steamer *"Mohawk."* The bark carried 510 captured Africans.

characteristics as more and more blacks were absorbed.

A similar black influx, although not quite such a large one, occurred in Spain. Many of these Portuguese and Spanish blacks, notably Estevanico, played a crucial role during the exploration of the New World alongside such men as Columbus, Balboa, De Soto, Pizarro, Cortez, and Mendez.

By the end of the fifteenth century, Portugal's monopoly in Africa was being challenged as the Dutch, English, French, Swedes, Danes, and Prussians established slave trading posts of their own. While the Portuguese were the first to enter the slave trade on a massive scale, the British became the innovators of the trade and made it into a highly specialized industry.

In 1713, the British acquired the coveted asiento, and Liverpool soon became the center of the British slave trade. The profits from buying and selling black human beings were so enormous (up to 50 percent on the initial investment) that even small tradesmen, such as ropers, candlemakers and barbers, formed syndicates through which they pooled their savings in order to send ships to Africa.

It has been recorded that ships sailing from Liverpool alone sold 303,737 slaves between 1783 and 1793. Their net profit during that period was three million pound sterling. Like the Portuguese and the Dutch, the British established a system of slave bases on the West Coast of Africa.

There were several methods of obtaining slaves. One method was the purchasing of prisoners of tribal wars. In time, Europeans became skilled in promoting enmity between tribes, even to the point of aiding one of the warring parties by supplying them with firearms. Slave agents would assist the European and

Arab slavers in chaining the captive men, women, and children together in coffles, then herding them to the coast. There they would be prepared for overseas shipment in one of the many receiving forts. Some slavers obtained their merchandise by organizing raiding parties. Others realized their objective by using a combination of trickery, bribes, whisky, and violence.

The bulk of the slaves were captured within a narrow, two-hundred-mile wide, three-thousand-mile long strip of coastal land that stretched from the Senegal River to the southern border of what is now Angola.

On arrival at the fort and factory, the slaves were inspected for diseases and other defects and sorted out accordingly. Those who were sold at the fort were branded on their chests and rowed to the waiting slave ship for the dreaded "Middle Passage," which derived its name from the fact that it was the second leg of the ship's triangular travel route from its European home port to Africa, then to the West Indies and, finally, back home.

It is estimated that 30 percent of the slaves did not survive the five-to-eight-week sea voyage across the Atlantic. Most of these died, suffocating in the foul air of the ships' holds in which they were literally packed like sardines, often with less than eighteen inches between ceiling and floor.

Some slaves died from disease; some committed suicide by crashing their heads against a wall, by cutting their wrists, or by jumping overboard into the shark-infested waters whenever an opportunity presented itself. Some mothers even strangled their babies to spare them further suffering.

It has been estimated that during the height of the slave-trading period—which began in the fifteenth century and lasted until the second half of the nineteenth century—between fifty and one hundred thousand African slaves crossed the Atlantic each year. Nobody knows, or is likely to find out, the exact total of Africans who were forcibly taken from their homeland and pressed into bondage. Some historians set that figure at twenty million while others believe that fifty million would be more accurate. North America received an estimated one million slaves—one of the smallest, though historically the most significant portions of the slave trade.

All of these estimates apply only to slaves who actually reached the slave auction blocks of the New World. They do not include the estimated 30 percent of slaves who did not survive the Middle Passage, nor the countless numbers that perished in slave coffles during forced marches from the site of their capture to the coast. If one adds to these figures the undetermined millions of Africans who were killed in slave-trade-inspired tribal wars, the enormity of "the largest migration in human history" comes into focus.

Low ceilings on each cargo deck forced slaves to remain in a crouched position throughout the five-to-eight-week Atlantic crossing.

If it is difficult to make numerical estimates of Africa's population loss as a direct result of the slave trade, the task of assessing the total impact of the traffic in "black gold" on Africa and the Western world in general is all but impossible. It is clear that, besides having robbed Africa of about a fourth of its population, the slave trade contributed to the disintegration of its social systems by pitting tribe against tribe, brother against brother. Moreover, slavery brought about the doctrine of white racism which alleges the mental, moral, and cultural inferiority of blacks and other nonwhite peoples in order to justify the latter's systematic exploitation and abuse by whites. Finally, by supplying entire continents with vast populations of cheap labor, it hastened the development of European-controlled overseas possessions in the Western Hemisphere, stimulated the emergence of the Industrial Revolution, strengthened the economies of European nations and thus spurred the development of the socioeconomic concept of capitalism.

Reluctant captives are subdued upon their arrival in Florida early in the nineteenth century.

3

Arrival

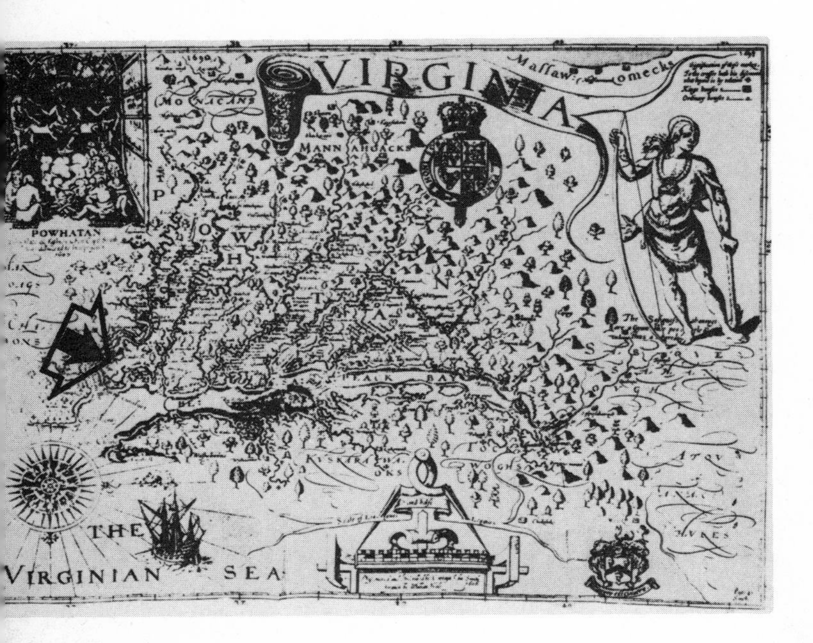

THE HISTORY of the black man in British America began—harmlessly enough—with the unscheduled arrival of a Dutch man-of-war at the newly established settlement of Jamestown, Virginia, in 1619, a year before the *Mayflower* dropped anchor at Plymouth Rock. Among its cargo were twenty blacks of undetermined origin and status whom the captain turned over to the colonists in exchange for food and other necessities.

Reportedly, the twenty blacks fared relatively well in their new environment. Although they were put to work as indentured servants—a fate they shared with countless whites—some attained full freedom and some even acquired land, were baptized and obtained the right to vote. Several became affluent and masters of servants of their own. And one is said to have risen to become the master of a white servant.

Few of the million-odd blacks who were to follow the initial twenty during the next two centuries were so fortunate. Most of them arrived in chains and died in chains.

During Colonial days, slavery was as firmly rooted in New York as in the other colonies. Sketch shows New York City's slave market at the foot of Wall Street.

One of the reasons for the Jamestown group's fate was that at the time of their arrival the plantation system was yet to emerge. From that moment, which established cotton as the undisputed king of the United States economy, the demand for cheap labor soared to unprecedented levels. But initially, race played only an incidental role in the gradually emerging institution of mainland slavery: a black skin per se did not yet confer slave status on its owner. Few planters of the time were concerned with the race of their work force. In fact, many had tried from time to time to meet the growing demand for plantation hands with white indentured servants—mostly impoverished Europeans who, voluntarily or under duress, had left their homelands and who had contracted to finance their passage to the New World with a set number of years of their labor. The disadvantages of using white indentured servants for plantation work were many. Indentured whites were difficult to obtain in large numbers. They could not be treated too badly without arousing the displeasure of free whites. Their condition of servitude expired after a certain period, at which time they were freed and given a small sum of money for a new start in life.

Indigenous Indians, too, had been tried and found wanting. Unlike blacks, who arrived as aliens in the colonies, Indians were familiar with the terrain and could run away from their masters and rejoin their tribes. Those Indians who were unable to escape frequently fell ill or died under the stresses of plantation life.

The Indians' reputation for being "unfit for slavery" dates back to the early sixteenth century. At that time, thousands of

Indian slaves died in Haiti's mines and sugar fields. The tragedy caused Bishop Bartolomé de las Casas, the "Apostle of the Indies," to appeal to King Ferdinand and Queen Isabella of Spain to spare the Indians from further slavery "as an act of mercy" and to use African blacks in their place. The bishop's plea, made in 1517, was granted. Shortly before his death in 1566, after witnessing the suffering his one-sided humanitarianism had unleashed among the black race, Las Casas denounced his earlier stand. "It is as unjust," he wrote, "to enslave Negroes as it is to enslave Indians—and for the same reason."

The bishop's change of heart came much too late. The trade in black flesh had already become the backbone of international commerce and was to reach even greater magnitude in the centuries to come.

It was believed by many cotton planters that "one black could do the work of four Indians." Moreover, being easily identifiable because of their dark skin and having no place of refuge, blacks could not escape. Consequently, the burden of slavery fell on their backs.

In the end, God-fearing white Puritans, throwing scruples to the wind, concentrated on solidifying the slave status of blacks. Virginia and Maryland took the lead. In the 1660s, these states passed laws which made blacks servants for life. From that moment, blacks were ruled bond or free depending on the status of their mothers. A subsequent law, passed in 1667 by Virginia, held that even the baptism of a black—heretofore a freedom-bestowing act—did not alter his status as a slave. A rash of subsequent laws, designed to plug legal loopholes, completed the job of reducing blacks to lifetime servitude.

Not all whites approved of slavery. Among the early voices raised to protest the practice were those of Massachussets Judge Samuel Sewall and Cotton Mather, two prominent Puritans. Motivated more by concern for the slaves' spiritual well-being than by indignation over their condition of involuntary servitude, both men concentrated their efforts on the establishment of Bible schools for slaves. In 1701, Judge Sewall published a pamphlet, *The Selling of Joseph,* in which he urged slavemasters to join his effort. Although New England, unlike the rest of the colonies, had no laws prohibiting the teaching of reading and writing to slaves, the Puritans' appeal fell largely on deaf ears. One of the reasons for this was that baptism and church membership entailed such privileges as voting and officeholding—privileges which would have undermined the slavemasters' authority. It was also feared that literacy would bring about discontent and the desire to be free, sentiments which could spark uprisings among the slaves. In the plantation states, resistance to instructing blacks in the Christian faith was, for obvious reasons, even greater, as Judge Sewall pointed out: "Talk to Planters of the South of a Negro, and He'll be apt to tell ye (or at least his actions speak it loudly) that the Body of one of them may be worth twenty pounds; but the Souls of an hundred of them would yield him one Farthing . . ."

Despite such opposition, subsequent efforts by other men met with modest success. In 1705, the London-based Society for the Propagation of the Gospel in Foreign Parts, sponsored by the Anglican Church, established a black school in New York City. Other schools followed in Charleston, Philadelphia, Williamsburg, and Newport.

The first broadside attack on the institution of slavery in British America was delivered on February 18, 1688, by a group of Quakers at Germantown, Pennsylvania. During the first half of the eighteenth century, thanks to the efforts of such Quakers as John Woolman and Anthony Benezet, the antislavery movement gained momentum, although it was mainly confined to Quaker circles. The antislavery cause received an unexpected boost from three interrelated developments: the widening gulf between the colonies and the English motherland, white citizens' growing antagonism toward the unlimited importation of blacks and the mounting determi-

Newly landed slaves are checked off a manifest before being transported to Colonial slave markets.

nation of slaves to be free. The growing sentiment against further importation of slaves had little to do with moral considerations but was largely based on fear. The growing slave population was increasingly viewed as a threat to the peace, a notion reinforced by the slave revolts in the Caribbean. The discontent over continued slave importation resulted in a rash of Colonial legislation aimed either at impeding the practice by the levying of a heavy duty on each imported slave or at forbidding it outright. The subsequent vetoing of such legislation by the British government, which yielded to pressure from influential British slaveship owners, only strengthened the colonies' resolve to have their own way. On April 6, 1776, three months before the signing of the Declaration of Independence, the Continental Congress voted unanimously to prohibit the importation of slaves into any of the colonies. The slave trade was banned in America in 1807 and in the British Empire in 1834.

More and more blacks fell prey to the slavers' greed as the slave trade became one of the most lucrative industries in the colonies.

4

Revolutionary War

G.R.Hall

THE CONTRADICTION OF SLAVERY within a nation preparing to wage war in defense of "the unalienable right" of "all men" to "Life, Liberty, and the Pursuit of Happiness," was not lost on the country's great patriots, nor—for that matter—on the slaves. Thomas Jefferson, himself a slave-owner with second thoughts, wrote a paragraph into one of the early drafts of the Declaration of Independence, denouncing England's King George III for promoting slavery. The paragraph read in part:

> He [King George] has waged cruel war against human nature itself, violating its most sacred rights of life and liberty in the persons of a distant people who never offended him, captivating and carrying them into slavery in another hemisphere, or to incur miserable death in their transport thither. This piratical warfare, the opprobrium of *infidel* powers, is the warfare of the Christian king of Great Britain. Determined to keep open a market where MEN should be bought and sold, he has prostituted his negative for suppressing every legislative attempt to prohibit or restrain this execrable commerce; and that this assemblage of horror might want no face of distinguished die, he is now exciting those very people to rise in arms among us, and to purchase that liberty of which *He* deprived them, by murdering the people upon whom He also obtruded them; plus paying off former crimes committed against the liberty of one people, with crimes which he urges them to commit against the lives of another.

George Washington worked as a surveyor before entering public life. That the "father of the Revolution" owned slaves is one of the paradoxes of the American Revolution.

The paragraph did not survive. It was omitted from the final draft of the historic document in order to keep the Southern delegation, made up largely of wealthy plantation owners, from opposing its acceptance.

Other famous patriots who went on record as being in principle opposed to slavery, despite the fact that most of them had engaged in the practice themselves, were George Washington, James Madison, John Adams, Tom Paine, Patrick Henry, and Benjamin Franklin.

The spread of libertarian ideas throughout the colonies during pre-Revolution days had not been without effect on the slaves. Especially in New England, slaves began to take the initiative in protesting their condition of lifetime servitude. In 1773 and 1774, a group of slaves sent two petitions to the Massachusetts legislature demanding their freedom. Both petitions were promptly tabled.

The efforts of individual slaves to obtain their freedom through legal means met with greater success. One of the more prominent "freedom suits" involved a woman slave, Jenny Slew, who in 1766 sued her master, John Whipple of Ipswich, Massachusetts, charging him with restraining her liberty. Jenny Slew not only won her freedom, but in addition, the court awarded her "the sum of four pounds" in damages.

Jenny Slew's victory led to a large number of individual freedom suits throughout the North. Although most of them were successful, the legal route toward freedom was no panacea for the problem of slavery. In the first place, litigation was time-consuming. (Some suits dragged on for several years.) Secondly, it was expensive, with legal fees and related expenses exceeding the means of the average slave.

With the escalation of hostilities between the colonies and England, another opportunity for freedom presented itself to the slaves—enlistment in the Revolutionary Army against the British Crown. Black involvement and participation in the conflict had preceeded the actual outbreak of the war by several years. On March 5, 1770, a long feud between Boston citizens and garrisoned soldiers of the British army culminated in a massacre in which the citizens' spokesman and leader, a forty-seven-year-old black sailor named Crispus Attucks, was the first to be killed.

Twenty years earlier, the six-foot-two Attucks had run away from his master, William Brown of Framingham, Massachusetts, who promptly had the following description of his escaped property inserted in the *Boston Gazette:*

> Short, curly hair, his knees nearer together than common; had on a light colored bearskin coat, plain brown fustian jacket, or brown wool one, new buckskin breeches, blue yarn stockings and a checked woolen shirt. Whoever shall take up said runaway, convey him to above said master, shall receive ten pounds, old tenor reward, and all necessary charges paid. And all masters of vessels, or others, are hereby cautioned against concealing or carrying off said servant on penalty of law.

The announcement did not achieve its purpose. Attucks disappeared and presumably went to sea. There is no record of his whereabouts until twenty years later when, on that fateful evening of March 5, history placed him on Boston's Dock Square. There he heard reports of an altercation between a barber's apprentice and a British sentry, in which the latter had clubbed the youth with the butt of his musket. Instilled with the revolutionary fervor of the times, Attucks urged the Dock Square crowd to get rid of the hated British soldiers. Within minutes, he led a crowd of stick-wielding and cursing Bostonians to the Custom House on King Street where they confronted the sentry. Just as the crowd began to move in on the sentry with curses and threats, seven ad-

Crispus Attucks, a runaway slave who became a sailor, was the first person to be killed in the struggle between the colonies and the British.

Attucks (arrow) and four compatriots were killed in the Boston Massacre on March 5, 1770.

ditional Redcoats, led by Captain Thomas Preston, arrived on the scene.

"Don't be afraid," shouted Attucks. "They dare not fire." For a moment Attucks and the crowd faced the menacing bayonets of the soldiers. Suddenly someone threw a stick that hit Private Hugh Montgomery. As the soldier fell back, he raised his musket and fired, hitting Attucks in the chest. The crowd surged forward and more shots were fired. When the noise of the shots had subsided, five citizens lay bleeding on the ground, two mortally wounded and three dead—one of them Crispus Attucks.

Thus Attucks became not only the first black but the first American to give his life for the colonists' cause. The incident, which entered the pages of American history as the Boston Massacre, had far-reaching consequences for the colonies. Said John Adams, second United States president: "Not the Battle of Lexington or Bunker Hill, not the surrender of Burgoyne or Cornwallis were more important events in American history than the battle of King Street on the 5th of March, 1770."

The participation of black patriots in the revolutionary agitation was extensive. Black Minutemen joined whites who answered Paul Revere's summons to arms. There were blacks among the famous Green Mountain Boys and at such prominent historical junctures as the battles of Lexington, Concord, and Bunker Hill. At Lexington and Concord, black militiamen

Pomp Blackman and Prince Esterbrook made the heroes' honor roll, Blackman paying for his patriotism with his life. During the Battle of Bunker Hill, which was actually fought on nearby Breed's Hill, black patriots, including Peter Salem, Barzillai Lew and Salem Poor, distinguished themselves as heroes.

Although many blacks had served with distinction in Colonial militias, there was increasing reluctance to permit black enlistment in the newly formed Continental Army, which initially had admitted free blacks on a limited scale. Opposition to black enlistment came largely from the South; and since the Continental Army, unlike the militias, depended on the financial support of each of the thirteen colonies, great care was taken at General Washington's headquarters not to offend white reactionaries. There were other reasons for opposition to black soldiers. Many felt that the opening of the Continental Army ranks to blacks would provide a sanctuary for runaway slaves and jeopardize the "property" of slave owners. But, above all, they felt that blacks with guns spelled trouble, especially since the fear of slave uprisings in the South had reached the point of hysteria.

Consequently, on July 10, 1775, the adjutant general of the American army, Horatio Gates, obviously acting with the consent of newly commissioned Commander-in-Chief George Washington, issued an order to his recruiting officers, forbidding them to enlist, among others, "any deserter from the Ministerial army, stroller, Negro, or vagabond." For a short period the Continental Congress wavered in approving this new policy, but within a few months the policy of exclusion from the army for both free blacks and slaves was reaffirmed.

Outraged by the decision, free black soldiers carried their protest to Washington's headquarters at Cambridge where, on December 30, 1775, the general modified the decision by ordering recruiting officers to re-enlist free blacks, pending a final decision by Congress. On January 16, a congressional committee recommended that free blacks who had already served should be permitted to re-enlist, but that slaves or free blacks without service records should be barred.

On November 7, 1775, aboard the "William" in Norfolk harbor, John Murray, Earl of Dunmore and deposed royal governor of Virginia, had issued a proclamation declaring martial law in order to stave off "treasonable purposes." Included

Black patriots fought valiantly at the Battle of Bunker Hill.

in that proclamation was the statement: ". . . and I do hereby further declare all indentured servants, Negroes, or others, free, that are able and willing to bear arms, they joining His Majesty's Troops, as soon as may be, for the more speedily reducing the Colony to a proper sense of their duty, to His Majesty's crown and dignity."

Lord Dunmore's proclamation, especially his promise of freedom to all slaves who would take up arms against the Americans, was regarded by the colonists as the most singular act of British villainy. Moreover, it spread panic among white colonists because they were well aware of its effect on the already restive slaves. The colonists' apprehensions were not unfounded. Faced with the alternative of continued slavery under the Colonial banner and freedom under the British, thousands of slaves threw off the yoke of their masters to join the forces of the Crown.

The Continental Army's black exclusion policy was shortlived. But the change was prompted not by a sense of fairness but by military expediency.

In December, 1777, General Washington's nine-thousand-man army suffered through the ordeal of Valley Forge, resulting in the desertion of more than three thousand men. Faced with a pressing manpower shortage, Washington was left no other choice but to reverse his original order and admit all blacks—free men and slaves—to his depleted ranks. The measure gained increased acceptance because of the "substitution system" which permitted draft eligibles to avoid conscription by producing a substitute person to take their place.

Not all states permitted the substitution of slaves for whites. Massachussetts barred the system, as did all of the Southern states except Maryland. When in 1779 South

Peter Salem, cited for extraordinary valor at the Battle of Bunker Hill, is shown shooting the commander of a British unit.

BY HIS EXCELLENCY

GEORGE WASHINGTON, Esq;

General and Commander in Chief of the Forces of the United States of America.

THESE are to CERTIFY that the Bearer hereof *Brister Baker Soldier* in the *Second Connecticut* Regiment, having faithfully ſerved the United States *from April 8th 1777 to June 8th 1783* and being inliſted for the War only, is hereby DISCHARGED from the American Army.

GIVEN at HEAD-QUARTERS the *8th of June*

G. Washington

By HIS EXCELLENCY'S
Command,

J Trumbull Jun Secy

REGISTERED in the Books
of the Regiment,

G. Curtiss Adjutant,

THE above *Baker* has been honored with the BADGE of MERIT for *Six* Years faithful Service. *H Swift Col*

HEAD-QUARTERS, June *8th* 1783.

THE within CERTIFICATE ſhall not avail the Bearer as a Diſcharge, until the Ratification of the definitive Treaty of Peace; previous to which Time, and until Proclamation thereof ſhall be made, He is to be conſidered as being on Furlough.

GEORGE WASHINGTON.

Carolina and Georgia were urged by Congress to raise an army of three thousand slaves, for each of whom their owners were to be compensated with a sum up to one thousand dollars, the legislators of the two states balked and the idea was dismissed. Despite the fact that blacks fought in the military contingents of every state the official position of the Southern states regarding the enlistment of blacks remained negative. The exception was Virginia, which openly permitted the enlistment of free blacks while barring slaves.

Washington never had reason to regret his decision to admit blacks to military duty. By the end of the Revolutionary War, some five thousand blacks, both slaves and freemen, had fought valiantly, some with great distinction, for the right of men (white men, as it were) to be free. For the most part, blacks served in integrated units, side by side with whites, although few were permitted to rise above enlisted rank. They fought in literally every major battle of the war—Monmouth, Red Bank, Saratoga, Savannah, Princeton, Yorktown, Eutaw Springs, and Fort Griswold. At least two blacks, Oliver Cromwell and Prince Whipple, crossed the Delaware with General Washington. During the Battle of Rhode Island, an all-black Rhode Island regiment found itself under attack by the Hessian forces which had established a reputation as formidable fighters. The Hessians, confident in their own prowess and in the knowledge that the black unit consisted largely of unseasoned recruits, prepared for an easy victory. Instead, they met with stubborn resistance. The black troops counterattacked and inflicted many casualties, turning the encounter into a victory.

Black participation in the war was not confined to the battlefield. Black sailors served gallantly in the tiny United States Navy. One of the black naval heroes was Caesar Terrant, who piloted the *Patriot*, a Virginia-based vessel. Another was Mark Starlin, a runaway slave who rose to become the only black naval captain in Virginia's history. He was credited with daring night raids on British vessels in Hampton Roads.

An especially daring chapter of the Revolutionary War was written by black operatives whose spying on the enemy helped the Colonial forces win crucial victories. One of them, a slave named Pompey, has been credited with making possible the capture of a vital British outpost at Stony Point, New York, by Anthony Wayne's forces. After obtaining the enemy password, Pompey led a detachment of Americans through enemy lines in preparation for a surprise attack on the fort. Undoubtedly the most daring black spy was James Armistead, a double agent spying for the Americans. It was largely because of the deliberate misinformation he carried to the enemy and the factual

Facsimile of an honorable discharge of a black soldier of the American Army.

intelligence he supplied to General Lafayette that the latter was able to trap his nemesis—Britain's General Cornwallis.

Most Americans know that foreign volunteers, such as France's Marquis de Lafayette, Poland's Thaddeus Kosciusko and Prussia's Baron von Steuben fought on the American side. But few know that black volunteers aided the revolutionary cause. The Fontages Legion, a unit of Haitian fighters, distinguished itself during the siege of Savannah by preventing the collapse of the American lines.

It has been estimated that more than twenty-five thousand blacks served on the side of the British against the Americans. Lured by the promise of freedom, many slaves braved hardships and even risked death while making their way to the British lines. Only a relatively small number (approximately 1,000) of slaves were actually used by the British for combat duty. Most of them served in various military related capacities such as repairmen, blacksmiths, wagon drivers, road construction workers, demolition men, sawyers, carpenters, cooks, quartermasters, sailors, and spies. The reasons for this were the growing need for military work crews and the reluctance of the British to put arms into the hands of too many slaves.

To offset the slave drain created by the British army's readiness to augment its troop strength with blacks, Southern states —which were beginning to feel the loss— instituted a number of emergency measures. North Carolina, in an effort to recruit more whites for the patrolling of plantation areas, passed a law exempting men who volunteered for patrol duty from military service. Georgia attempted to abort any "wicked attempts of slaves" to defect, with a law providing that no more than one third of the troops in each county could be sent out of the county. South Carolina went a step further by instituting the death penalty for any bondsman who joined the British forces.

None of these measures deterred slaves, who continued to defect in large numbers until the end of the war in 1783. When the defeated British army sailed for home, it took along some fourteen thousand blacks despite American protests.

It has been estimated that more than one hundred thousand slaves received their freedom as a direct result of the war. This figure included slaves who ran away, especially to Canada and Florida. Quite a few slaves hid in swamps and waged guerrilla warfare against slaveowners along the Savannah River in Georgia and South Carolina.

Additional thousands were granted freedom by masters who, affected by the spirit of the time, had come to regard slave

Prince Whipple was a bodyguard of one of George Washington's aides.

ownership as incompatible with American ideals.

By the end of the war, more and more men and women, white and black, were taking a stand against slavery, either as individuals or as members of antislavery groups. Composed largely of men of means and considerable social standing, the pioneer antislavery societies used a wide variety of approaches, including the purchasing of slaves in order to set them free. Some groups organized boycotts of slave-produced products; others helped freed slaves find jobs.

The Quakers, who sparked the prewar antislavery movement continued their struggle. As a result, Pennsylvania in 1780 abolished slavery. During this same period, both Baptists and Methodists joined the battle against human bondage.

As the antislavery movement gained strength, state after state enacted gradual emancipation legislation. Connecticut in 1784 provided that no person, whatever his status at birth, could be kept in slavery after having reached the age of twenty-five. In the same year, Rhode Island decreed that all offspring born to slave mothers after March, 1784, would be free. New York, in order to encourage slave masters to manumit their slaves, waived the masters' bonded responsibility for slaves they set free.

Several Southern states joined the abolition bandwagon with limited antislavery bills. Virginia, for example, permitted a master to manumit his slaves without first obtaining permission from the state legislature. Three years later, in

Famous painting of the Delaware crossing shows two blacks, Prince Whipple and Oliver Cromwell, manning oars in General Washington's boat.

After Valley Forge, 3,000 Continental troops deserted, and Washington reversed his black exclusion policy, admitting all blacks, freedmen as well as slaves.

1785, Virginia followed up with a law that granted freedom to any slave imported into the state and kept there for a year.

Mushrooming abolitionist sentiment expressed in laws and deeds led to the death of slavery in the North.

Many abolitionists looked with great expectation toward the first Constitutional Convention in Philadelphia in 1787, confident that it would declare the end of slavery throughout the land and for all times. Their optimism proved unfounded. In the give and take of political compromise, the Northern lawmakers placated the slave interest by agreeing, in effect, that Congress could not prevent any state from importing slaves for twenty years.

In a further concession to slave owners, the framers of the Constitution provided for the return of runaway slaves. Article IV, Section 2, states:

> No person held to Service or Labour [meaning slaves] in one State, under the Laws thereof, escaping into another, shall . . . be discharged from such Service or Labour, but shall be delivered up on Claim of the Party to whom such Service or Labour may be due [the slave master].

Perhaps the most crucial Constitutional compromise was the ruling which, in effect, gave national sanction to the inferior status of slaves by setting their political weight at three-fifths of that of whites. "Representatives and direct taxes shall be apportioned among the several States . . . ," the Constitutional provision read, "according to their respective numbers, which shall be determined by adding to the whole number of free persons . . . three fifths of all other persons [meaning slaves]."

Most of the white founding fathers found the idea of confiscating the slaves and setting them free distasteful. "As a property," said Jefferson, who had yet to set free the hundred-odd slaves he held at his Monticello estate, "they [slaves] are lawfully vested and cannot be taken away."

Though committed to the gradual ending of slavery, Jefferson was not at all inclined to "retain and incorporate the blacks into the state." To do so, he considered the "height of folly." He regarded amalgamation as both revolting and socially impossible.

Despite the snail-pace of the slave liberation movement, and despite the many obstacles encountered by newly freed slaves, the post-Revolutionary period produced a number of outstanding blacks whose contribution to the cultural growth of the young republic merits the highest acclaim. Among them was Benjamin Banneker who was born in 1731 near Baltimore, Maryland. He was the grandson of an Englishwoman, Molly Welsh, who arrived in America as an indentured servant, paid off her obligation, bought a farm and two slaves, one of whom—Banneker's grandfather—she married. Banneker's mother, Mary, was one of four children born to this marriage. His father, like his grandfather, was a freed slave from Africa.

Before attending an integrated school in Baltimore, young Benjamin learned to read and write from his English grandmother. Early in life he showed an interest in astronomy and mathematics. By the time he was forty years old, he had attained such distinction in these sciences that he was appointed to serve on the commission which surveyed and laid out the newly planned city of Washington, D.C. His service on that committee led the *Georgetown Weekly Ledger* to refer to him as "an Ethiopian whose abilities as surveyor and astronomer already prove that Mr. Jefferson's concluding that that race of men [the black race] were void of mental endowment was without foundation."

Following the completion of his work on the nation's capital, Banneker retired to a farm near Baltimore where he devoted his time to astronomical and other scientific research, as well as to writing an annual almanac in which he published his ideas and findings. He also found time to build what is believed to be the first clock made in America. His deep concern about the horrors of war caused him to devise a plan for the establishment of a "Peace-Office for the United States" in which he suggested that a secretary of peace be appointed and that military titles, ranks, and uniforms be abolished.

But Banneker's major interest was the ending of slavery. The scientist's exalted position as perhaps the best-known black man of his time enabled him to enter into a dialogue with Jefferson, then secretary of state in George Washington's cabinet, in which he took Jefferson to task for reneging on his earlier stated principles regarding freedom and the equality of man. In a letter to Jefferson, dated August 19, 1791, Banneker wrote:

> Sir, suffer me to recall to your mind that time, in which the arms and tyranny of the British crown were exerted, with every powerful effort, in order to reduce you to a state of servitude; look back, I entreat you, on the variety of dangers to which you were exposed; reflect on that time, in which every human aid appeared unavailable and you cannot but be led to a serious and grateful sense of your miraculous and providential preservation . . . .
>
> . . . how pitiable it is to reflect that although you were so fully convinced of the benevolence of the Father of Mankind, and of His equal and impartial distribution of these rights and privileges, which he hath conferred upon them, that you should at the same time counteract His mercies,

Fraunces's Tavern in New York City, a major black-owned and operated business in the pioneer period, was among George Washington's favorite restaurants.

in detaining by fraud and violence, so numerous a part of my brethren under groaning captivity, and cruel oppression, that you should at the same time be found guilty of that most criminal act, which you professedly detest in others, with respect to yourselves . . .

Banneker's letter, which drew a polite reply from Jefferson, became the talk of the time in high and low circles on both sides of the slavery issue. But it failed to halt the spread of a new conservatism that was beginning to permeate the United States, a conservatism which looked at slavery in the South as a regrettable, but perhaps unavoidable necessity.

Banneker was not the only black man who rose above adversity and parlayed his prominence into a weapon against slavery. His contemporary, Prince Hall, made history by becoming the most effective black activist of his time. Born around 1748 in Barbados, the son of an Englishman and a free black woman, Hall worked his way to Boston on a ship in 1765. For nearly seven years he moved about quietly, observing the unfolding of events as the rift between the colonies and England widened. He worked as a laborer during the day, but his night hours were devoted to the study of libertarian philosophies, especially those contained in the Declaration of Independence.

Hall's careful preparation paid dividends. Within three years he rose from obscurity to become "one of the leading lights of the first freedom movement" in the Colonies.

It was Hall who led the protest of free black soldiers who were dismissed from the Continental Army under General Washington's black exclusion policy and who wrote and boldly signed his name to one of the first slave petitions sent to the Massachussetts legislature. Filed in the General Court of Massachusetts on January 13, 1777, the petition read in part:

[The petitioners] cannot but express astonishment that it has never been considered, that every principle from which America has acted, in the course of her unhappy difficulties with Great Britain, bears stronger than a thousand arguments in favor of your humble petitioners. They therefore humbly beseech Your Honors to give their petition its due weight and consideration, and cause an act of the legislature to be passed, whereby they may be restored to the enjoyment of that freedom, which is the natural right of all men, and their children (who were born in the land of liberty) may not be held as slaves after they arrive at the age of twenty-one years. So may the inhabitants of this State (no longer chargeable with the inconsistency of acting themselves the part which they condemn and oppose in others) be prospered in their glorious struggle for liberty, and have those blessings secured to them by Heaven, of which benevolent minds cannot wish to deprive their fellowmen.

African-born Phillis Wheatley was an internationally known poet during the Revolutionary period.

And your petitioners, as in duty bound, shall ever pray:—

LANCASTER HILL,
PETER BESS,
BRISTEN SLENFEN,
PRINCE HALL,
JACK PIERPONT, [his X mark]
NERO FUNELO, [his X mark]
NEWPORT SUMNER, [his X mark]

An organizer par excellence, Hall made his major contribution by setting up the first black Masonic lodge, African Lodge No. 1, one of the first secular black organizations in America. Earlier, he had attempted to join a lodge of the white American Masons. When he was turned down, he tried his luck with a lodge attached to a British regiment stationed near Boston. This time he succeeded. On March 6, 1775, Hall and fourteen other black men were initiated into a British military lodge. After the British army had withdrawn from Boston, Hall and his black fellow Masons formed their own lodge under a limited charter. After the war, Hall's lodge received formal recognition when it was chartered as African Lodge No. 459 by the Grand Lodge of England. In time, Hall helped organize Masonic lodges in Philadelphia and Providence, Rhode Island, making freemasonry the first black organization to link several states.

Hall's interest in freedom was not confined to the protest of slavery. Despite the fact that he was black, he considered himself an American patriot and felt as indignant about British tyranny toward the colonies as he did about slavery practiced by the colonists. Consequently, in April, 1778, he enlisted in the army to aid the revolutionary cause.

After the war, Hall once more moved into the public limelight. Again making use of the public petition, he demanded equal education for black children, having come to regard education as one of the main sources of power. "We . . . must fear for our rising offspring," he said, "to see them in ignorance in a land of gospel light, when there is provision made for them as well as others and [they] can't enjoy them, and [no other reason] can be given [than that] they are black. . . ."

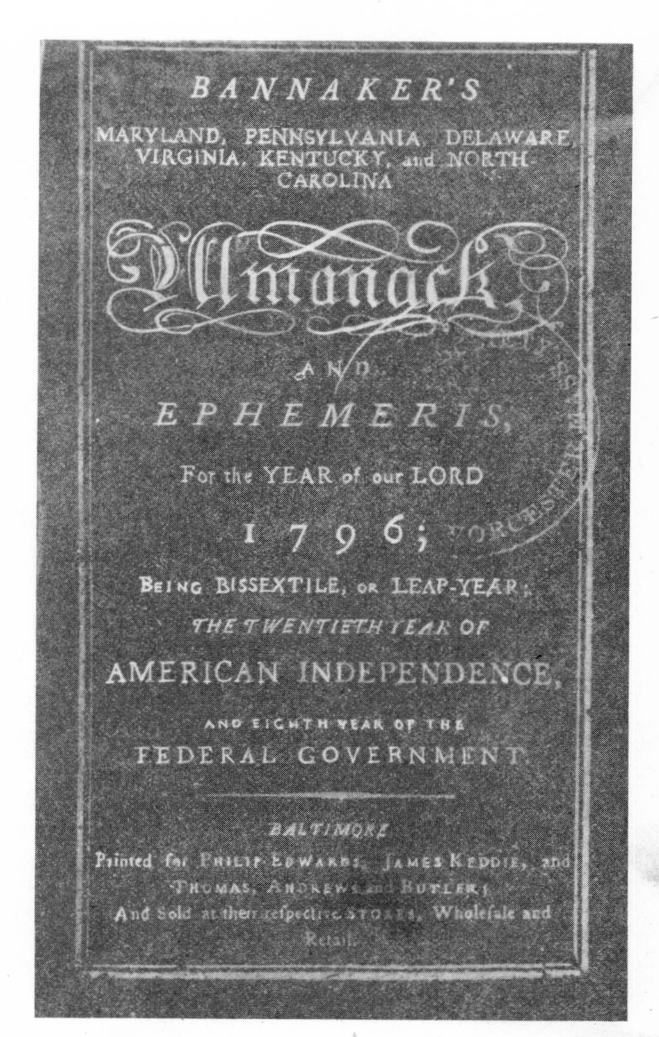
BANNAKER'S
MARYLAND, PENNSYLVANIA, DELAWARE, VIRGINIA, KENTUCKY, and NORTH-CAROLINA
Almanack,
AND
EPHEMERIS,
For the YEAR of our LORD
1796;
BEING BISSEXTILE, OR LEAP-YEAR;
THE TWENTIETH YEAR OF
AMERICAN INDEPENDENCE,
AND EIGHTH YEAR OF THE
FEDERAL GOVERNMENT.
BALTIMORE:
Printed for PHILIP EDWARDS, JAMES KEDDIE, and THOMAS, ANDREWS and BUTLER;
And Sold at their respective STORES, Wholesale and Retail.

Benjamin Banneker, a multitalented scientist, helped plan the nation's capital. He compiled an *Almanack* (above) in which he published many of his observations.

Hall died on November 4, 1807, a fairly wealthy man, known and respected throughout the state of Massachusetts and beyond. His lifelong efforts in behalf of black brotherhood and collective black action put him among the leaders of the black protest pioneers.

One of the most remarkable black men of the post-revolutionary period was Paul Cuffe, the son of an African-born former slave and a mother of Indian extraction. Cuffe was born in 1759 on Cutterhunker, one of the Elizabeth Islands near Bedford, Massachusetts. When he was sixteen years old, two years after his father's death, he went to sea as a deck hand on a ship bound for the Gulf of Mexico. During the war years he continued to sail and on one occasion was captured and imprisoned for three months in New York.

In 1780, barely twenty-one years old, Cuffe incurred the wrath of the Massachusetts authorities by refusing to pay his personal tax. Inspired by the battle cry of the Revolution—"No taxation without representation"—Cuffe insisted that blacks should be exempted from taxation. The tax collector was not swayed by his reasoning and threatened Cuffe with jail. Since only a nominal sum was involved, Cuffe paid, but immediately sent a petition, signed by several blacks, to the Massachusetts legislature, appealing his case and demanding immunity for blacks from tax laws since they had "no voice or influence in the election of those who tax us." The appeal was heard and a law was enacted granting blacks the privileges of all other citizens of Massachusetts.

Cuffe's stature in the community rose. Having inherited some land from his father, Cuffe converted it into cash and bought a seagoing ship which he captained himself. Within a few years he owned a small fleet of ships and was part owner of several others. In time he acquired a shipyard and built his own ships.

Captain Cuffe's enterprises, which made him a wealthy man, did not distract him from his ideals. In the 1790s he built a school house at his own expense and allowed anyone with an interest in learning to attend.

Captain Cuffe continued his interest in furthering the cause of blacks and spent considerable effort encouraging blacks to emigrate to Sierra Leone. Toward that end, he corresponded with prominent friends in Great Britain and Africa, even visiting the colony himself to determine the practicality of his plan. In 1815, two

Prince Hall, a staunch advocate of black brotherhood, formed the first black Masonic lodge.

PAUL
CAPTAIN
CUFFEE
1812.

years before his death, he personally carried thirty-eight black immigrants to Sierra Leone, most of them at his own expense. On arrival, he furnished them with the necessities for a new start in life.

Another black person to win wide acclaim during the Revolutionary and post-Revolutionary periods was Phillis Wheatley, an African-born poetess whose *Poems on Various Subjects, Religious and Moral*, was the first book by a black woman to be published in America and the second to be written by an American woman. Although she did not use her poetic talents to attack the system of slavery, she cannot be dismissed as inconsequential to the black cause. The fact that she was successful in a field considered totally outside the capabilities of blacks served as a heavy counterweight to the forces which had assigned blacks to a role of mental and cultural inferiority.

She was born at a place in Africa she was unable to recall. It is a matter of record that she arrived in Boston in 1761 on a slave ship when she was about seven or eight years old and that she was bought off the slave block by a wealthy merchant and tailor named John Wheatley. Wheatley and his wife Susannah took a liking to the little girl and reared her more as a daughter than as a slave. Soon, young Phillis—as they had named her—astonished everybody by speaking, reading, and writing fluent English. Her first poem was published while she was still in her teens. It was a blank verse eulogy of Harvard University. By the time she was about twenty years old, she was acclaimed a prodigy, not only in America but also in Europe. Voltaire, who had heard of her, praised her for her "very good English verse." In 1773 she visited England where her volume of poetry was published.

Phillis Wheatley's poetry was totally devoid of militancy and rarely reflected the hardships and suffering of slaves. In fact, in one poem she praised the circumstances that brought her to America because they helped her to learn of the existence of Christ.

In 1776, when George Washington received his commission as commander-in-chief of the United States military forces, Miss Wheatley expressed her delight over the event in a tribute she sent to the general.

Washington thanked her in a letter addressed to "Miss Phillis." His letter ended with an invitation to visit him at his headquarters should she ever come to Cambridge, Massachusetts. Miss Wheatley ac-

Captain Paul Cuffe rose from deckhand to wealthy shipowner. He was the mainspring of efforts aimed at resettling freed American slaves in Sierra Leone.

cepted the invitation and reportedly was entertained by the "father of the nation" and his staff.

Upon the death of old Mrs. Susannah Wheatley, in whose State Street house she had lived, the black poetess was forced for the first time in her adult life to face racial reality. She married a black grocer by the name of John Peters who soon alienated her white friends. Poor and often ill, the couple drifted from place to place and their two children died in quick succession. In December, 1784, Phillis Wheatly died within hours of the death of her infant child.

If the rise to fame, and even wealth, of a handful of black men and women during the post-Revolution era seemed to foreshadow the possibility of massive black participation in the American Dream, it was at best a fleeting illusion. Within a few years, owing largely to economic realities brought on by greed and the cotton gin's insatiable appetite for cheap labor, the oppression of blacks reached unprecedented levels. Thus, the slaves' dream of freedom, nurtured in the libertarian atmosphere of the Revolution, became Langston Hughes' "dream deferred."

5

Blacks and Indians

FEW ASPECTS OF AMERICAN HISTORY are more deserving of historians' attention—yet few have been more neglected by them—than the encounters of the black man and the Indian, the two major victims in the monumental tragedy perpetrated by the white man during his conquest of North America. In this encounter, blacks and Indians interacted in a multitude of ways—most frequently as allies and collaborators against the common oppressor, but occasionally as adversaries, the often unwitting agents of the white man's power politics.

Some scholars believe that the blacks' contact with Indians not only predated the arrival of the pilgrims' *Mayflower*, but also that of Columbus' *Santa Maria*. Even in conservative scholarly circles, the idea that blacks set foot on the North American continent and met Indians long before the arrival of the first English settlers is generally accepted. Estevanico took part in the Navarez expedition to Florida during the days of the Spanish conquistadors and is widely hailed as the first non-Indian to discover the Southwest.

A common bond between black slaves and Indians developed almost with the establishment of the first British colonies. Among the more spectacular manifestations of this bond was the fact that Indians frequently spared blacks during "massacres." Reporting on one of the earliest Indian raids on a British settlement, John H. Russell observes: ". . . it is significant that in the massacre of 1622 not an African perished at the hands of the Indians, although there were at the time of the massacre more than twenty Negroes scattered throughout the little colony."

Unity between African slaves and Indians was further strengthened by the colonists' attempts to press captured Indians into slavery. In most of these cases, the enslaved Indians were reduced to the same level as the black slaves and were subject to the same Slave Code. Consequently, racial lines between the two groups of slaves were soon obliterated. They not only lived together, plotted together, and helped one another to escape, but also intermarried.

The attraction between blacks and In-

In 1784, Jean Baptiste Pointe DuSable (right) built the first house on the site of present-day Chicago (above). The bill of sale (below) documents the purchase of the DuSable house by a white trader in 1800.

dians was not based solely on empathy and their common plight. Many Indians, for their own special reasons, regarded blacks as "good medicine" capable of superhuman feats. Others valued Africans for their knowledge of the white man's "medicine," especially in the areas of agriculture and technology.

To discourage Indians from assisting black fugitives, virtually every Indian treaty contained a standard clause requiring Indians to help recover runaway slaves. Most tribal chiefs paid lip service to the clause, but few complied.

The Indian reservations were not only magnets for runaway slaves but for free blacks as well. In the Northern colonies especially, where there was a general shortage of black women, free black men made a common practice of marrying Indian women.

Many blacks—both free and slave—chose to live with Indian tribes and adopted Indian customs. They married Indian women and reared their children in the Indian tradition. Some rose to positions of influence in the tribal hierarchy. Outstanding among them was James Beckwourth, a former slave, born in 1789, who attained the rank of chief among the Crows. One of the leading black figures in

Black chief of the Crow Indians James Beckwourth (left) discovered the Sierra pass named for him. Abraham (right), a runaway slave, played a key role in the Seminole war triggered by a slave-catcher's capture of the black wife of Seminole chief Osceola (below, right).

the Westward movement, Beckwourth has been credited with discovering the pass through the Sierra Mountains which still bears his name.

Another slave who rose to prominence during the exploration of the West was York (see p. 101), one of the most important participants in the Lewis and Clark expedition of 1803–1806.

Because of the preferential treatment accorded them by the Indians, blacks were frequently cast in the role of mediator between whites and the Indians. As a result, blacks played a crucial part in the opening of the West as trappers, traders, scouts, and interpreters. George Bush, for example, a sought-after black scout, led an expedition through the hazardous Oregon Trail and thus was instrumental in the settling of the state of Washington. George Bonga of Duluth, a black trader of considerable wealth, served as interpreter at the signing of the Chippewa Treaty of 1837.

Jean Baptiste Pointe DuSable, a fur trader with considerable influence over the Indians in the Lake Michigan area, founded the settlement that was to become the city of Chicago. In addition, countless black men participated in the saga of the West as stagecoach drivers, cowboys, Pony Express riders, lawmen, and even as members of notorious outlaw gangs that terrorized the frontier towns.

As a result of the massive intermingling of blacks and Indians, entire tribes vanished into the African-American population. It is known that many black historical figures of the Revolutionary War pe-

Indian villages were refuges for runaway slaves. Frontiersman Nat Love (below) was nicknamed Dead-Eye Dick.

riod, including Crispus Attucks, Captain Paul Cuffee, and Salem Poor, were part Indian. In 1926, Melville Herskovits examined 1,551 blacks and found that one-third claimed partial Indian ancestry.

The solidarity between blacks and Indians became a growing source of anxiety for whites as black-led or black-inspired Indian insurrections increased in intensity and frequency. Indian-black military cooperation reached its climax in the bloodiest, most protracted, and most costly of all Indian wars, the so-called Seminole Wars of 1817–18 and 1835–42 which, because of the extensive participation and leadership of blacks, might have been more aptly named "Seminole-African Wars." Triggered by the capture and enslavement of Seminole Chief Osceola's black wife Che-Cho-Ter (Morning Dew), the seven-year war had as its root cause the Seminoles' resistance to the Indian Removal Act, which called for the transfer of all Indians to territories west of the Mississippi. It cost the U.S. government thirty million dollars and countless casualties to bring the Seminoles and their African allies to heel.

Some Indian tribes, following the example of the settlers, established a black slavery system of their own. It has been reported that at the outset of the Civil War, "the Seminoles had a thousand slaves; the Cherokees and Chickasaws had each about three thousand slaves," and that "in these nations there were less than fourteen thousand full-blooded Indians to ten thousand Negro slaves." Although slavery practiced by the Indians varied widely from tribe to tribe, it contrasted sharply with slavery among whites. For the most part, Indians intermarried with their slaves and rarely required more of them than the annual payment of a portion of their crops.

6

Slavery

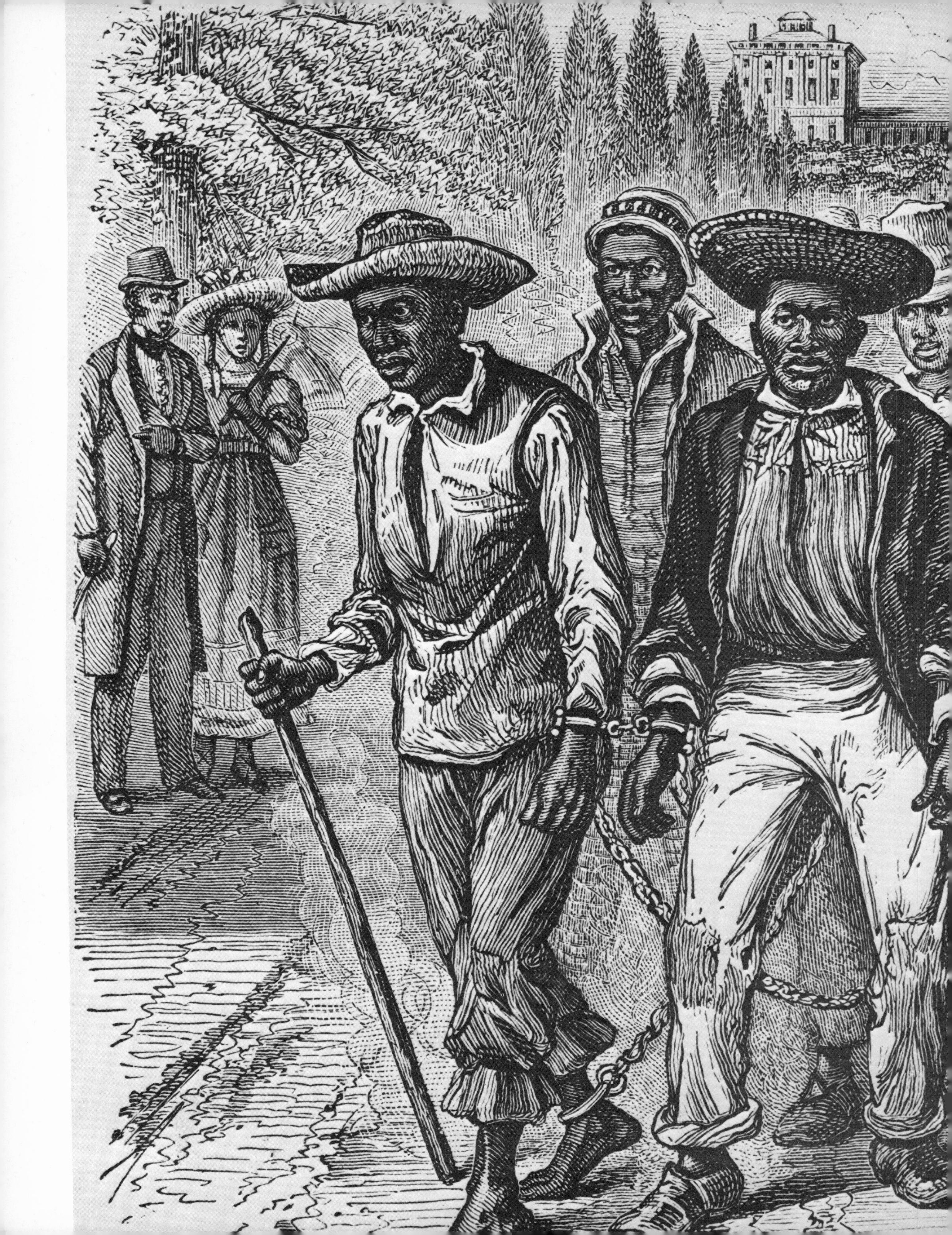

WITH THE INVENTION of the cotton gin by Eli Whitney in 1793, the stage was set for the establishment of the most exploitative and degrading social system ever forced upon one race by another. This system, whose purpose was to ensure whites the unencumbered enjoyment of vast profits, depended for its smooth operation on the total suppression and denial of black people's humanity. Toward this end, an elaborate set of legal codes was adopted by the various state legislatures and individual cities and communities, each designed to impress upon the slaves the utter futility of any thought—not to mention attempt—of ever rising above their status as powerless and voiceless pieces of merchandise.

While the Slave Codes and their application differed slightly from state to state, they were basically the same since each new state had patterned its codes after the older states. Another factor which accounted for a high degree of uniformity of the codes was the fact that the maintenance of the slave system confronted whites with the same basic problems, regardless of location, and thus called for similar solutions.

Because of considerable intermingling of blacks and whites despite existing taboos, some of the most important codes defined who was a slave and who was free. These codes were by far the most widely varying and most confusing pieces of legislation of the ante-bellum period. Unless they could produce "freedom papers," blacks were generally presumed to be slaves. In the case of mulattos, the mother's status usually determined that of her child. Thus if the mother was a slave

—whether Negro, mulatto, quadroon, or octoroon—and the father was white, the child was considered a slave. Conversely, if the mother was white and the father a slave, the child was free-born. In Alabama, a mulatto was any "person of mixed blood, descended, on the part of the mother or father, from Negro ancestors, to the third generation inclusive, though one ancestor of each generation may have been a white person." In Virginia, on the other hand, a law decreed that "every person who has one-fourth part or more of Negro blood shall be deemed a mulatto as well as Negro." And in Kentucky, possessing less than a fourth of African blood, was "*prima facie* evidence of freedom."

As chattel or property, slaves could be sold, rented, mortgaged, bartered, given away, deeded and used as collateral in business transactions. Not infrequently, they were prizes at raffles and lotteries or the objects of wagers between planters. Because of their intrinsic value, slaves were favored commodities for speculators who bought and sold them in the fluctuating slave market like stocks and bonds.

In numerous cases, slaves were earmarked as gifts even before they were born. In Georgia, for example, the owner of a slave woman bequeathed to his granddaughter "the first child to whom Harriet gives birth."

Since slaves could not enter into any binding contract, including marriage, a slave father had no legal status and his family could be broken up by the sale of one or all of its members at the convenience of the owner. This happened frequently, especially at the death of an owner, at which time slaves, who formed part of the deceased's estate, were divided among the heirs. Regretting the "inconvenience to the slaves," a North Carolina court ruled that slave families must be broken up "if the executor [of the will] discovers that the interest of the estate requires it; for he is not to indulge his charities at the expense of others [the heirs]."

Although slaves did not possess civil or legal rights, they were held legally accountable and were subject to punishment for any violations of the codes. Invariably, the laws dealt more severely with slaves than with whites for the commission of the same misdemeanor or felony. Basic to all disciplinary slave codes was the requirement that slaves submit unquestioningly to their masters and respect all whites with whom they came in contact. Louisiana formalized this requirement by decreeing that ". . . he [the slave] owes to his master, and to all his family, a respect without bounds, and absolute obedience, and he is consequently to execute all the orders which he receives from him, his said master, or from them." No act of cruelty inflicted by a master on his slave was ever permitted to serve as a mitigating circumstance if it provoked the slave to slay his master. A Tennessee court ruled that the slaying of a master who mistreats his slave was murder and punishable by death "because the law cannot recognize the violence of the master as a legitimate cause of provocation." Thus, the plea of self-defense, one of the most fundamental concepts in English and American law, was not available to the slave.

President Washington watches slaves stack hay on his Mount Vernon estate.

Under the codes, a slave could not point a finger at a white person, use insulting or abusive language, strike back when hit by a white man, beat drums, blow a horn, possess guns or liquor, administer drugs to whites, practice medicine, swear, smoke, walk with a cane, gamble with whites, raise animals or crops for himself, ride in a carriage (except as part of his duties), and attend a gathering of more than five (himself included) unattended slaves. A slave's willful or unintentional failure to step out of the way of whites was considered "insolent" and could draw harsh punishment. To make their escape more difficult, slaves were not allowed to be "at large" without a pass, which they were obliged to show to any white man upon demand. The forging of such a pass or of "free papers" was a felony, subject to severe penalties. If a slave failed to heed a white man's order to stop, the white man had the legal right—and in some states the obligation—to shoot him.

Slaves were not allowed to acquire property, nor could they testify in court against whites, or become a party to a suit, except indirectly when represented by a white person in their own "freedom suit." Only when the case involved another slave were slaves regarded as competent witnesses.

Most cities and towns supplemented the state slave codes with codes designed to meet their particular "needs" and customs. Under such city codes, a large number of communities prohibited slaves from being on the streets after curfew hour or after dark. In Natchez, Mississippi, all "strange slaves" had to leave the city limits by four o'clock on Sunday afternoons.

All code enforcement was handled by local magistrates, sheriffs, or constables who dealt out swift "justice" in special "Negro courts" which were noted for their capriciousness. The most common punishment for code violations by slaves was flogging in public, a practice that was regarded as an effective deterrent to other slaves. Some states, in a feeble attempt to make the punishment of slaves more humane, imposed a limit on the number of lashes allowed during one flogging. The most commonly sanctioned maximum number was thirty-nine. Additional lashes, however, were permissible if the flogging was administered in separate doses that extended over several days. Alabama established a record of sorts by permitting "up to 100 stripes" in one flogging.

Another form of legal punishment was imprisonment, but this was seldom applied because it deprived the slaveowner of his slave's labor and was therefore considered uneconomical. Occasionally, in the case of a particularly stubborn slave, the court would order him branded or mutilated in various ways that would not interfere with his effectiveness as a laborer. The "cropping" of a slave's ears or "burning in the hand or face" met this requirement.

In the case of capital offenses such as murder of any degree, manslaughter,

Slaves were frequently raffled off. In the announcement (r.), a horse was given top billing over a year-old female slave.

RAFFLE

Mr. Joseph Jennings respectfully informs his friends and the public that, at the request of many acquaintances, he has been induced to purchase from Mr. Osborne, of Missouri, the celebrated

DARK BAY HORSE, "STAR,"

Aged five years, square trotter and warranted sound; with a new light Trotting Buggy and Harness also, the dark, stout

MULATTO GIRL, "SARAH,"

Aged about twenty years, general house servant, valued at *nine hundred dollars*, and guaranteed, and

Will be Raffled for

At 4 o'clock P. M., February first, at the selection hotel of the subscribers. The above is as represented and those persons who may wish to engage in the usual practice of raffling, will, I assure them, be perfectly satisfied with their destiny in this affair.

The whole is valued at its just worth, fifteen hundred dollars; fifteen hundred

CHANCES AT ONE DOLLAR EACH.

The Raffle will be conducted by gentlemen selected by the interested subscribers present. Five night will be allowed to complete the Raffle. BOTH OF THE ABOVE DESCRIBED CAN BE SEEN AT MY STORE, No. 78 Common St., second door from Camp, at from 9 o'clock A. M. to 2 P. M

Highest throw to take the first choice; the lowest throw the remaining prize, and the fortunate winners will pay twenty dollars each for the refreshments furnished on the occasion.

N. B. No chances recognized unless paid for previous to the commencement.

JOSEPH JENNINGS.

rape and attempted rape of white women, rebellion or attempted rebellion, beating a master or his family with the result of bruises or bloodshed, robbery, or arson, the death penalty was mandatory. It was usually carried out by public hanging, but on occasion a felon was publicly burned at the stake in keeping with a Carolina code which directed that a slave convicted of a capital offense should be put to death by means that would be "most effectual to deter others from offending in the like manner." If a slave was executed for a capital crime, his owner was entitled to a partial compensation from the state "for the destruction of his property."

Only a fraction of Black Code violations reached the "Negro courts." Most of the disciplining of slaves was done by their masters, overseers, and foremen, the most common tool of punishment being the cowskin whip.

Frederick Law Olmsted, a white Northerner who in 1852 made an extensive journey through the South, reports an incident of slave flogging. Olmsted had been riding across a plantation with its white overseer and a young member of the plantation owner's family when they found a young slave woman hiding in the brush.

> He [the overseer] got off his horse, and holding the horse with his left hand, struck her thirty or forty blows across the shoulders with his tough, flexible raw-hide whip (a terrible instrument for the purpose). . . .

A slave who proved incorrigibly uncooperative or who was a habitual runaway was entrusted by his master to a profes-

Men, women, and children were bought and sold like cattle in the infamous slave pen in Alexandria, Virginia.

PRICE, BIRCH & CO
DEALERS IN SLAVES

sional "slave breaker" who, with cowskin whip, branding irons, and other pain-inflicting instruments, would attempt to transform him into a docile worker. Slave breakers, for the most part, were so efficient in their work that many masters found it expedient to send them their newly acquired slaves in order "to get them off to a good start." If a slave had escaped, a master could hire the services of a slave catcher whose "Negro dogs" were especially trained to track blacks. Invariably, dogs were permitted to maul the captured slave severely in order to teach him a lesson.

In addition to the cowskin whip, the master had at his disposal an arsenal of time-tested punishments for dealing with "insolent" slaves. They included incarceration in the stocks, the cutting of food rations, selling the slave away from his family, putting the slave in "chains and irons," and the brutal "gelding" of slaves. There were punishments which attested not only to the cruelty, but also to the inventiveness of some slavemasters. Kenneth M. Stampp, in his book *The Peculiar Institution*, writes about a Maryland tobacco grower who forced a slave "to eat the worms he failed to pick off the tobacco leaves," and of a Louisiana planter who humiliated disobedient male field hands by dressing them in women's clothing and by giving them "women's work."

While slaves were without legal rights, except the right to be tried by a (white) jury, every state went through the motion of enacting laws ostensibly aimed at protecting the slave. In practice, these laws did little to ease the slaves' plight. Although the wanton killing of a slave by a white man carried stiff penalties, only a handful of whites were ever convicted.

All slave owners were required by law to properly feed and clothe their slaves. If they failed to do so, they could be fined and their slaves could be ordered sold. Yet, prosecution under these statutes was rare since slaves abused in this manner were not allowed to bring suit against their masters, and few whites would take it upon themselves to sue in behalf of a slave.

To prevent slaves from becoming exposed to revolutionary ideas, no person, not even their master, was permitted to teach them to read and write or to supply them with printed material of any type, including the Bible. For the same reason, it was unlawful to employ a slave in a print shop or newspaper.

The all-encompassing codes for the reg-

This typical announcement of a slave bargain appeared in New Orleans in 1835.

BY

HEWLETT & BRIGHT.

SALE OF

VALUABLE

SLAVES,

(On account of departure)

The Owner of the following named and valuable Slaves, being on the eve of departure for Europe, will cause the same to be offered for sale, at the NEW EXCHANGE, corner of St. Louis and Chartres streets, on *Saturday*, May 16, at Twelve o'Clock, *viz.*

1. **SARAH**, a mulatress, aged 45 years, a good cook and accustomed to house work in general, is an excellent and faithful nurse for sick persons, and in every respect a first rate character.

2. **DENNIS**, her son, a mulatto, aged 24 years, a first rate cook and steward for a vessel, having been in that capacity for many years on board one of the Mobile packets; is strictly honest, temperate, and a first rate subject.

3. **CHOLE**, a mulatress, aged 36 years, she is, without exception, one of the most competent servants in the country, a first rate washer and ironer, does up lace, a good cook, and for a bachelor who wishes a house-keeper she would be invaluable; she is also a good ladies' maid, having travelled to the North in that capacity.

4. **FANNY**, her daughter, a mulatress, aged 16 years, speaks French and English, is a superior hair-dresser, (pupil of Guilliac,) a good seamstress and ladies' maid, is smart, intelligent, and a first rate character.

5. **DANDRIDGE**, a mulatoo, aged 26 years, a first rate dining-room servant, a good painter and rough carpenter, and has but few equals for honesty and sobriety.

6. **NANCY**, his wife, aged about 24 years, a confidential house servant, good seamstress, mantuamaker and tailoress, a good cook, washer and ironer, etc.

7. **MARY ANN**, her child, a creole, aged 7 years, speaks French and English, is smart, active and intelligent.

8. **FANNY or FRANCES**, a mulatress, aged 22 years, is a first rate washer and ironer, good cook and house servant, and has an excellent character.

9. **EMMA**, an orphan, aged 10 or 11 years, speaks French and English, has been in the country 7 years, has been accustomed to waiting on table, sewing etc.; is intelligent and active.

10. **FRANK**, a mulatto, aged about 32 years speaks French and English, is a first rate hostler and coachman, understands perfectly well the management of horses, and is, in every respect, a first rate character, with the exception that he will occasionally drink, though not an habitual drunkard.

☞ All the above named Slaves are acclimated and excellent subjects; they were purchased by their present vendor many years ago, and will, therefore, be severally warranted against all vices and maladies prescribed by law, save and except FRANK, who is fully guaranteed in every other respect but the one above mentioned.

TERMS:—One-half Cash, and the other half in notes at Six months, drawn and endorsed to the satisfaction of the Vendor, with special mortgage on the Slaves until final payment. The Acts of Sale to be passed before WILLIAM BOSWELL, *Notary Public*, at the expense of the Purchaser.

***New-Orleans, May* 13, 1835.**

ulation of black life in the South did not apply to slaves alone. "Free blacks," too, faced serious restrictions. The purpose of special codes for freedmen was twofold: to maintain white supremacy over blacks whatever their status and to make freedom through escape or other means an unattractive prospect.

TOWARD THE END of the ante-bellum period in 1860, the slave population of the South had grown to approximately four million. More than half of that number lived in the seven Deep South states with the heaviest concentration in the big cotton plantations in the Alabama–Mississippi Black Belt and South Carolina. Only about five hundred thousand slaves worked in cities and towns. Contrary to popular belief, the "typical" Southerner of the ante-bellum era was not a wealthy slave-owning planter. In fact, nearly three-fourths of the South's five and a half million whites had no connection with slave ownership whatsoever and, of the remaining fourth, 50 percent owned fewer than five.

Work routines on the big plantations were highly organized, with each slave assigned to a special task, either as an individual or as a member of the field gang. Like most organizations, the plantation structure, too, developed a clearly defined hierarchy or pecking order in which each slave knew his place. At the top of this order was the foreman or "driver," usually an imposing looking, powerfully built slave who had distinguished himself as a stern disciplinarian. Appropriately named, the driver was charged with the responsibility of keeping up the field hands' work pace, if necessary with the aid of the cowskin whip. As the overseer's right-hand man, he was authorized to make work assignments, distribute food

A young slave couple and their infant child are auctioned off in Virginia.

allotments, settle disputes among the slaves, blow the horn that signalled the beginning and end of the work periods, and in general enforce plantation discipline. In return, the driver enjoyed certain privileges. He was exempted from manual labor in the field, had considerable freedom of movement on the plantation, received bigger food rations and was usually better dressed and housed than the rest of the slaves.

Somewhat on a par with the foreman, and occasionally even above him in the plantation class structure, were the house slaves, a category which included the butler, the coachman, the nursemaid or "mammy," the seamstress, the cook, and other domestic help. Receiving their instructions directly from the master or mistress, they were not subject to the overseer's authority. House slaves lived either in servants' quarters in the "big house" or in cabins adjacent to it. They were often hand-picked for their light complexion or for their demonstrated ability to adopt "white ways." Some of them identified with their owners and looked down on the slaves in the field. Because of their close, day-to-day contact with plantation masters, some house slaves took an active part in the latter's family affairs and were sometimes their most trusted confidantes.

Also ranking above the ordinary field slaves were slaves who possessed special skills, such as carpenters, blacksmiths and harnessmakers. Since the smooth operation of the plantation depended to a considerable extent on their resourcefulness and cooperation in keeping plantation equipment in good repair, slave artisans were accorded special consideration and usually enjoyed a degree of independence.

Most of the slaves on large plantations, with the exception of the house slaves, lived near the "big house" in an aggregate of small, often windowless, cabins generally referred to as "the quarters" or "slave row." Depending on the financial capabilities or humane inclinations of the plantation owner, slave quarters varied widely in quality and construction and were usually built either of logs, clapboard or brick. Slave housing comprised three basic types—multiple units for married slaves and their families, one-room cabins for unmarried slaves who held positions of some prestige, and dormitory-like dwellings for the unmarried rank and

The selling of slaves required notarized bills of sale such as the one at right.

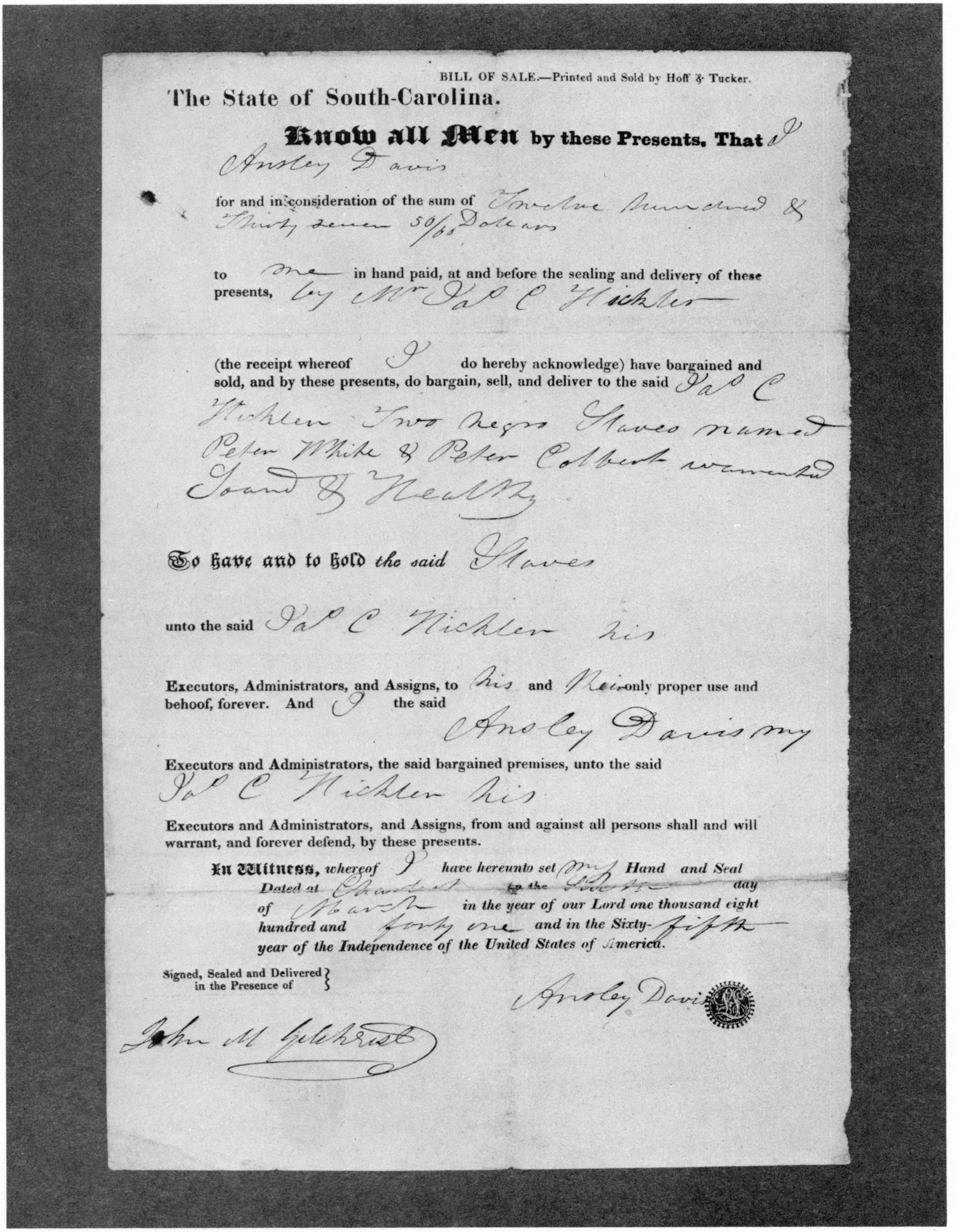

BILL OF SALE.—Printed and Sold by Hoff & Tucker.

The State of South-Carolina.

Know all Men by these Presents, That I Ansley Davis

for and in consideration of the sum of Twelve hundred & Thirty seven 50/100 Dollars

to me in hand paid, at and before the sealing and delivery of these presents, by Mr Jas C Hickler

(the receipt whereof I do hereby acknowledge) have bargained and sold, and by these presents, do bargain, sell, and deliver to the said Jas C Hickler Two negro Slaves named Peter White & Peter Colbert warranted Sound & Healthy

To have and to hold *the said* Slaves

unto the said Jas C Hickler his

Executors, Administrators, and Assigns, to his and their only proper use and behoof, forever. And I the said Ansley Davis my

Executors and Administrators, the said bargained premises, unto the said Jas C Hickler his

Executors and Administrators, and Assigns, from and against all persons shall and will warrant, and forever defend, by these presents.

In Witness, *whereof* I *have hereunto set* my *Hand and Seal Dated at* Charleston *the* [illegible] *day of* March *in the year of our Lord one thousand eight hundred and* forty one *and in the Sixty-* fifth *year of the Independence of the United States of America.*

Signed, Sealed and Delivered in the Presence of

Ansley Davis (L.S.)

John M Gilchrist

file. With a few notable exceptions, slave quarters for the most part were drab and uncomfortable places, designed mainly as refuges for the night and during inclement weather and not as centers of family life. Consequently, they were equipped with only the absolute necessities, such as a fireplace or stove or hearth and crudely made cots. In many cases, slaves simply slept on the floor.

Once a week, slaves received their food rations which consisted of "a peck of corn and three or four pounds of bacon or salt pork" and were generally lacking in balance and variety. Since food rations were rarely sufficient, it was a common practice among slaves to raid the master's corn cribs and chicken coops. There was a difference between "taking" and "stealing," as far as the slaves' mores were concerned. "Taking" applied to things that belonged to whites and was considered condonable behavior. "Stealing," on the other hand, involved things that belonged to other slaves and was regarded as a cardinal sin. An additional source of food was wild game. Since slaves were forbidden to own guns, they became quite expert in designing and building traps, their most common quarry being 'coons, 'possums and rabbits.

Twice a year, plantation slaves were issued their clothing supply. A typical allowance was described as follows in the plantation manual of a South Carolina planter:

> Each man gets in the fall 2 shirts of cotton drilling, a pair of woolen pants and a woolen jacket.

Prison-like lockup in Virginia, with individual cells, served as slave storage facility.

In the spring 2 shirts of cotton shirting and 2 pr. of cotton pants . . . Each woman gets in the fall 6 yds. of woolen cloth, 6 yds. of cotton drilling and needle, skein of thread and ½ dozen buttons. In the spring 6 yds. of cotton shirting and 6 yds. of cotton cloth similar to that for men's pants, needle thread and buttons. Each worker gets a stout pr. of shoes every fall, and heavy blanket every third year.

Unlike the highly systematized and structured routines on big plantations, small agricultural units with fewer than five slaves—which made up more than half of the South's slaveholding estates—were loosely organized, marginal enterprises. On such farms, the master not only supervised his bondsmen himself but frequently toiled, and even ate, alongside them. In many instances, the master's standard of living was not much—if at all—higher than that of his slaves, and although the relationship between such masters and slaves was never allowed to become that of fellow workers, social distinctions were less pronounced than on the large plantations.

The undisputed "aristocrats" among the slaves were those who lived in cities and towns, approximately 10 percent of the South's four million slaves.

Many urban slaves served either as housekeeper, cook, butler, coachman, maid, gardener, or caretaker, occupations which, because of their heavy concentration of slaves, carried a stigma and, therefore, were all but abandoned by whites. But not all urban slaves did domestic work. In fact, town slaves worked in practically every skilled and unskilled occupation, to the chagrin of free laborers who resented the competition.

Belying the widespread contention that slaves were incapable of creative or imaginative work, many town slaves worked at artistic crafts such as stone cutting, engraving and the making of musical instruments. Most of the artful wrought-iron work of the famed balconies in the French Quarter of New Orleans was done by slaves.

UNDOUBTEDLY THE MOST dehumanizing aspect of slavery—apart from its reduction of human beings to salable commodities—was the practice of "breeding" slaves. Although the reticence of slavers regarding this subject accounts for a scarcity of written records, ample evidence exists—in the form of personal accounts of slaves and newspaper advertisement references to the child-bearing potentials of slave women offered for sale—that the practice of raising slaves for the specific purpose of marketing was widespread.

The myth of the slave who willingly accepted his lot and even found a degree of contentment as the loyal servant of a humane white master dies hard, in spite of abundant evidence to the contrary. First

Black people were sometimes offered for public sale in "miscellaneous lots" (r.)

Public Sale of Negroes,

By RICHARD CLAGETT.

On Tuesday, March 5th, 1833 at 1:00 P. M. the following Slaves will be sold at Potters Mart, in Charleston, S. C.

Miscellaneous Lots of Negroes, mostly house servants, some for field work.

Conditions:* ½ cash, balance by bond, bearing interest from date of sale. Payable in one to two years to be secured by a mortgage of the *Negroes,* and appraised personal security. *Auctioneer will pay for the papers.

A valuable Negro woman, accustomed to all kinds of house work. Is a good plain cook, and excellent dairy maid, washes and irons. She has four children, one a girl about 13 years of age, another 7, a boy about 5, and an infant 11 months old. 2 of the children will be sold with mother, the others separately, if it best suits the purchaser.

A very valuable Blacksmith, wife and daughters; the Smith is in the prime of life, and a perfect master at his trade. His wife about 27 years old, and his daughters 12 and 10 years old have been brought up as house servants, and as such are very valuable. Also for sale 2 likely young negro wenches, one of whom is 16 the other 13, both of whom have been taught and accustomed to the duties of house servants. The 16 year old wench has one eye.

A likely yellow girl about 17 or 18 years old, has been accustomed to all kinds of house and garden work. She is sold for no fault. Sound as a dollar.

House servants: The owner of a family described herein, would sell them for a good price only, they are offered for no fault whatever, but because they can be done without, and money is needed. He has been offered $1250. They consist of a man 30 to 33 years old, who has been raised in a genteel Virginia family as house servant, Carriage driver etc., in all which he excels. His wife a likely wench of 25 to 30 raised in like manner, as chamber maid, seamstress, nurse etc., their two children, girls of 12 and 4 or 5. They are bright mulattoes, of mild tractable dispositions, unassuming manners, and of genteel appearance and well worthy the notice of a gentleman of fortune needing such.

Also 14 Negro Wenches ranging from 16 to 25 years of age, all sound and capable of doing a good days work in the house or field.

of all, slaveowners, by definition, were not humane. Secondly, slaves were not contented with their lot although the lack of practical alternatives caused most of them to submit to their masters' authority. To be sure, only a small minority of slaves took an active part in bloody insurrections. But rare was the slave who did not at one time or another during his servitude give vent to his yearning for freedom through some form of passive or active resistance. It was the ever-present awareness of this indomitable spirit of the slave that kept whites in a perpetual state of terror from which they found no escape since it was merely compounded by each additional act of cruelty to their human property.

Because of their integral position within the South's economy, slaves found many opportunities for impressing upon their masters that slavery had its serious drawbacks. Among the most common and subtle forms of slave protest was doing a job poorly, very slowly or, whenever possible, not at all.

Many slaveholders learned the hard way that forcing a slave to perform beyond the limits of production he had set for himself only invited additional resistance. Such resistance often took the form of feigned illness. Slaves became ingenious in faking symptoms and simulating virtually every disabling condition, including pregnancy, paralysis, dysentery, smallpox, broken limbs, insanity, deafness, and blindness.

Some determined slaves did not rely on merely faking symptoms of illness. They resorted to self-mutilations, such as chopping off their fingers or an entire hand or foot, in order to reduce their usefulness to their masters. In more extreme cases, slaves excaped bondage by committing suicide, usually by hanging or drowning.

Despite slaveowners' awesome legal authority over their slaves, the management of bondsmen was a frustrating, often unprofitable business at best. Slaves were keen observers of their managers' personality, quickly seizing on any weak spot they might detect. Occasionally, when faced with an indecisive overseer, slaves would press their advantage until there was a complete collapse of discipline which the owner could only restore by selling the most unruly members of the gang.

It was an accepted axiom among bondsmen that "the slave who is whipped easiest gets whipped most." Frederick Douglass wrote of an experience which supports that conclusion. At the age of sixteen

Before daybreak, the horn of the slave foreman or "driver" summoned the slaves from their cabins.

he was sent for a year of "seasoning" to a slave-breaker who for six months beat and mistreated him unmercifully. One day, acting on an unexplainable impulse, Douglass fought back. "Whence came the daring spirit necessary to grapple with a man who, eight-and-forty hours before, could, with his slightest word have made me tremble like a leaf in a storm, I do not know," he wrote. Douglass not only won the fight; he even drew some blood. "After this transaction," wrote Douglass, "he [the slave-breaker] never laid on me the weight of his finger in anger. He would, occasionally, say he did not want to have to get hold of me again—a declaration which I had no difficulty in believing; and I had a secret feeling, which answered, 'You need not wish to get hold of me again, for you will be likely to come off worse in a second fight than you did in the first.' "

Each year, planters lost vast sums of money as a result of damage by slave saboteurs. No matter how vigilant, they were unable to prevent slaves from setting fires to buildings, crops, and gins. Arson by slaves was not limited to rural areas.

One of the most widespread forms of slave protest was escape. Most slaves ran away on the spur of the moment—often after a particularly cruel beating—without any particular geographic knowledge of where they had been and where they were going. They were usually caught, or returned voluntarily after a few days of starving and after recognizing the futility of their undertaking. But there were also numerous slaves who spent years carefully planning an escape and who waited patiently for the most propitious moment to carry out their plan. Many of them succeeded, some by relying on their own resourcefulness, others by linking up with the Underground Railroad—a widely cast network of aid stations set up by white and black abolitionists for the specific purpose of helping slaves to escape. Estimates regarding the number of slaves who reached freedom through various manners of escape vary widely, ranging from forty thousand to one hundred thousand.

The history of slavery is not only studded with acts of violence committed by white slavers against the slaves but also by violence committed in retaliation against whites. Beating and working slaves beyond endurance was a common way of provoking violence. Ante-bellum news accounts and court records are filled with testimonies of slaves who confessed that they killed their masters because the latter had been "too hard" on them. They poisoned their masters and mistresses with arsenic, ground glass, and spiders beaten up in buttermilk. They clubbed or shot them to death or chopped them to pieces with axes. Some set the "big house" on fire and gleefully watched the occupants perish in the flames. Yet, in the end, when the massive power of the slave system was brought to bear on them, the rebellious slaves were captured and killed. Thus, as Kenneth Stampp points out, the usual reward of slave violence "was not liberty but death."

Under the watchful eyes of a mounted overseer, male and female slaves plough the soil for a new crop.

Such was the fate of Nat Turner, a slave whose name struck terror in the hearts of whites throughout the South. The mastermind and executioner of the bloodiest, most daring slave insurrection in the history of the United States, Turner was born in 1800 on a plantation in Southampton County, Virginia. A devout Baptist with strong leanings toward the mystical, Turner had become convinced early in life that he had been chosen by God to lead his people out of bondage. The "spirit," he said, had instructed him that on the appearance of a sign "I should arise and prepare myself and slay my enemies with their own weapons." In due time, he succeeded in convincing other slaves of his divine mission, an accomplishment which earned him a position of considerable influence and respect among them and acknowledgement as a prophet.

The "sign" Turner had patiently awaited for years appeared in February, 1831, in the form of a solar eclipse. After nightfall on Sunday, August 21, the prophet and seven followers—armed with hatchets and broadaxes—entered the home of Joseph Travis, Turner's master. Within minutes they had killed every member of the Travis family. From the Turner home, the insurrectionists continued on their mission of vengeance. Moving stealthily from plantation to plantation, they killed every white man, woman, and child in sight while gathering additional recruits from among the now masterless slaves.

The insurrection lasted only forty-eight hours. By the time it was crushed by a hastily mobilized force of some three thousand army, navy, and militia men, Turner's rebels numbered about seventy and they had killed nearly sixty whites. While his tiny army was dispersed or captured, Turner escaped. Predictably, the insurrection triggered a massacre in which enraged whites killed not only the rebels but scores of innocent slaves who happened to cross their path. Reported the Richmond *Whig:* "Men were tortured to death, burned, maimed and subjected to nameless atrocities. The overseers were called upon to point out any slaves whom they distrusted; and if any tried to escape, they were shot down."

For almost two months, Turner eluded capture. During that time, panic seized large parts of Virginia, North Carolina, and Maryland as whites feared that Turner might reassemble his group and mount other surprise attacks.

On October 30, Nat Turner was captured. It was an event that was celebrated with the firing of guns throughout Southampton County. Turner was taken in chains to Jerusalem, the county seat, where he was brought to trial on November 5. The same day he was convicted and sentenced to be hanged. Six days later, "between the hours of ten A.M. and two P.M.," the unremorseful prophet was executed, sustained to the end by the biblical parallel ". . . that he [Jesus] must go onto

Jerusalem, and suffer many things of the elders and chief priests, and scribes, and be killed."

THE HISTORY OF VIOLENT RESISTANCE to slavery did not begin with Nat Turner, nor did the fear in which whites beheld their slaves. Despite the myth of the docile slave—an invention of hindsighted historians—there was never a period when slaveholders were free of apprehension about their "troublesome property." The terrible price in lost peace of mind the slaves exacted is apparent from the comments of a planter who wrote during a period of slave restiveness:

Slaves worked from sunrise till sundown tilling the soil of big plantations.

These insurrections have alarmed my wife so as really to endanger her health, and I have not slept without anxiety in three months. Our nights are sometimes spent in listening to noises. A corn song, or a hog call, has often been the subject of nervous terror, and a cat, in the dining room, will banish sleep for the night. There has been and there still is a panic in all this country. I am beginning to lose my courage about the melioration of the South. Our revivals produce no preachers; churches are like buildings in which they worship, gone in a few years. There is no principle of life. Death is autocrat of slave regions.

No other personality in history quickened American slaves' hope for freedom through resistance more than a small black man named Pierre Dominique Toussaint L'Ouverture, the father of the Haitian Revolution of 1791 which began when more than one hundred thousand slaves killed their masters and burned down several thousand coffee and sugar plantations in a rampage that lasted three weeks. At the time of the uprising, L'Ouverture, nearly fifty years old, was an obscure slave who had obediently served as a carriage driver on a large plantation in the northern part of the island. Realizing that one massacre does not make a revolution, the heretofore moderate carriage driver joined and soon seized control of the slaves and within a relatively short time forged them into a disciplined, well-trained army. Taking advantage of the rivalry between Britain, France, and Spain over the control of the island, L'Ouverture took to the field, first as an ally of Spain against France, then as an ally of France against England and Spain. Thus, through a combination of military genius and shrewd diplomacy, General L'Ouverture forced the withdrawal of all foreign troops. The last to withdraw were the British, whose abortive attempt to wrest the island from the black general cost them some forty thousand men.

Though Haiti was still considered a French colony and L'Ouverture ruled nominally in the name of Napoleon Bonaparte, he was the *de facto* ruler of Haiti, a fact which displeased the ambitious and egocentric Corsican. In time, Napoleon dispatched his brother-in-law, General Charles Victor Emmanuel Leclerc, with an army of French troops to subdue the haughty Haitian. Through a letter, inviting L'Ouverture to a parley, General Brunet, an aide of Leclerc, lured the usually cautious black statesman into the French army's headquarters. As soon as L'Ouverture arrived, he was arrested and taken aboard a ship which promptly sailed for France where Napoleon had him imprisoned in a dark cell of a medieval fortress near the Swiss border. There, in April, 1803, the great liberator died.

L'Ouverture's death was a setback, but not the end of Haitian liberty, for a young Haitian officer and former aide to L'Ouverture, General Jean-Jacques Dessalines, who as a slave had learned to hate the French, took over where his mentor left off. Under the defiant motto, "war for war, crime for crime, atrocity for atrocity," Dessalines rallied the Haitian army, forced the advancing French troops to a standstill and then to retreat. He turned next to lead the systematic extinction of the island's white population which, under the more moderate policies of L'Ouverture, had been permitted to remain in Haiti. The French, having lost some sixty thousand men, left the island for good, while Dessalines "ripped the white from the French tricolor, joined the red and blue and proclaimed the second republic in the Western Hemisphere."

The seeds of Haitian freedom sown by L'Ouverture and reaped by Dessalines had far-reaching consequences for the United States. Napoleon, disgusted with the loss of his colony, became increasingly disenchanted with all his possessions in the Western Hemisphere and, in 1803, sold the Louisiana Territory to America for four cents an acre—"the biggest real estate bargain," according to some historians, "in history."

Men, women and children use hoes to cultivate, weed, and loosen the earth around plants.

Thus [wrote De Witt Talmadge] all of Indian Territory, all of Kansas and Nebraska, Iowa and Wyoming, Montana and the Dakotas, and most of Colorado and Minnesota, and all of Washington and Oregon states, came to us as the indirect work of a despised Negro. Praise, if you will the work of Robert Livingston or a Jefferson, but today let us not forget our debt to Toussaint L'Ouverture, who was indirectly the means of America's expansion by the Louisiana Purchase of 1803.

During L'Ouverture's spectacular victories over the European powers, his fame spread to every part of the world where slavery was practiced, especially to the United States, where his name was clandestinely celebrated in many slave cabins. Among his greatest admirers was a twenty-four-year-old Virginian slave named Gabriel Prosser. A powerfully built, six-foot-two-inch bondsman who wore his hair long in imitation of his biblical idol, Samson, Prosser meditated on the Old Testament, particularly the passages dealing with blood and doom. Like L'Ouverture, he had dreams of a black state—not in the Caribbean but in his homestate Virginia.

In the spring of 1800, Prosser began careful preparations for the realization of his plan, a task in which he was assisted by his two brothers, Martin and Solomon, and his wife, Nanny. For several months, the four went about recruiting followers and at every opportunity slipped away from their plantation chores to study strategic points and the locations of arms and ammunition in Richmond.

By early August, Prosser and his close associates had completed the task of recruiting a potential force of several thousand slaves (estimates vary widely, ranging from two thousand to fifty thousand) who had pledged their participation in Prosser's undertaking. Next came the planning of the details of the takeover. "Three columns would attack Richmond," Lerone Bennett wrote, "the right wing would grab the arsenal and seize the guns; the left wing would take the powder house; the key, central wing would enter the town at both ends simultaneously and would cut down every white person, except Frenchmen, Methodists and Quakers." Following the capture of Richmond, Prosser planned similar surprise attacks on other Virginia cities until the entire state was in control of the slaves. At that point, Prosser intended to climax his victory by proclaiming himself king of Virginia. If something should go wrong, Gabriel Prosser's army was to retreat to the mountains and conduct a guerrilla war against the slavemasters.

Something did go wrong. On August 30, the day Prosser had selected for the attack, two slaves who were privy to the conspiracy informed their masters who, in turn, notified Richmond authorities. The information, because of its importance, was relayed to the governor who immediately made arrangements for the secret mobilization of the state's militia forces and for the reinforcement of the guards at all vital military installations.

Another misfortune befell the slaves. Without it, some historians believe, they might yet have succeeded in their undertaking, despite the betrayal of the two slaves. Prosser, who had been unaware of the betrayal, had assembled some thousand slaves, armed with scythe swords, pikes, and what few hand guns they were able to steal from careless masters, at a rendezvous six miles outside Richmond. But before the group could launch its attack, torrents of rain began to pour down,

Vast numbers of slaves worked in the rice fields.

washing away bridges and inundating roads, making it impossible for the slaves to enter Richmond. Reluctantly, Prosser ordered the postponement of the invasion and dismissed his army. The postponement proved fatal. Before he had an opportunity to reassemble his men, the Virginia forces struck. Prosser and thirty-four of his closest followers were arrested and, after a swift trial, convicted and hanged. At the trial, one of the defendants, believed to be Prosser, declared defiantly:

I have nothing more to offer [in my defense], than what General Washington would have had to offer, had he been taken by the British and put to trial by them. I have adventured my life in endeavoring to obtain the liberty of my countrymen, and am a willing sacrifice to their cause; and I beg, as a favour, that I may be immediately led to execution. I know that you have pre-determined to shed my blood, why then all this mockery of a trial?

accumulating money and some property, and rose to a position of respect among both blacks and whites, he was consumed with concern for other blacks still in bondage. He turned down an opportunity to emigrate to Africa, because he wanted "to stay in America and see what he could do for his fellow creatures."

The South's cotton-dominated economy was the backbone of the slavery system.

The spirit of Prosser and L'Ouverture did not die with them but inspired other slaves to risk their lives for the cause of freedom. One of them was Denmark Vesey, who in the year of Prosser's demise won a lottery and purchased his freedom. For twenty-two years he worked as a carpenter in Charleston, South Carolina. Although he succeeded during that period in

While a slave, Vesey had been in the service of a slave trader, a position which afforded him many opportunities for travel and for broadening his knowledge of people. Drawing on this extensive experience, he embarked on a careful plan of agitation. For four years, he impressed upon slaves that they were so miserable that even death would be an improvement of their lot. Relentlessly he drove home his message that God helped those who helped themselves. What kind of help he had in mind, he explained by quoting Joshua: "And they utterly destroyed all that was in the city, both man and woman, young and old, and ox, and sheep, and ass, with the edge of the sword." In addition to quoting from the Bible, he quoted L'Ouverture and constantly read to the slaves newspaper accounts of progress made by the black people of Haiti.

Uncompromising in his hatred for whites, whose very presence he found increasingly difficult to bear, Vesey sternly rebuked, taunted or ridiculed any slaves who, in his opinion, displayed too much deference toward whites. "You deserve to be a slave," he told bondsmen whom he considered too obsequious.

Vesey's constant badgering of the slaves gained him their respect and in many instances their fear. Some slaves feared the firebrand more than their own masters and at least one slave admitted that he feared Vesey more than he feared God. But more important, Vesey's ideas began to take root in the minds of the Charleston slaves and from it grew a willingness to translate the ideas into deeds. Vesey decided that the time for action had arrived. Around Christmas of 1821, Vesey—a robust man in his early fifties—began building his organization with the careful selection of his chief lieutenants: Gullah Jack, an African-born sorcerer who had a

Below, slaves perform the classic slave chore of picking cotton.

reputation of being invulnerable, Blind Phillip who reportedly could see ghosts and other invisible phenomena, and Peter Poyas, a skilled carpenter and an ingenious organizer.

In order to avoid repeating Prosser's mistake and to prevent the betrayal of the conspiracy by slave informers, Vesey built a cell-like organization in which only the most trusted leaders of each cell were apprised of the details of the plot while the rank and file were kept largely in the dark. In this way, even if a slave were arrested or voluntarily turned informer, he could not jeopardize the entire plan. For nearly half a year, Vesey and his conspirators recruited slaves. His years as an agitator had been well spent. Throughout the Charleston area, volunteers answered his appeal. In many cases, entire plantations were signed up. It has been estimated that some nine thousand slaves followed Vesey's call. Meanwhile, weapons were constructed and collected.

On July 16, Vesey called the cell leaders to his house and explained to them his plan, but not before warning them that any traitor would be killed on the spot. The attack, he explained, would begin by setting the governor's mills and several houses in the vicinity on fire. Simultaneously with the attack on the mills, the main body of the slave army was to strike at six points, taking possession of arsenals, guardhouses, powder magazines, and naval stores. All whites were to be killed. In conclusion, Vesey pointed out that their plan could not fail if they only acted in as united and as courageous a manner as the people of Haiti.

Little did Vesey know that treason—the one eventuality he had taken such pains to prevent—had already taken place. Two months earlier, an eager slave named William Paul attempted, without authorization from Vesey, to recruit a house servant. The recruitment of house slaves had been reserved to Vesey's top aide, Peter Poyas, who had proceeded in this task with the utmost caution since house slaves, because of their close relationships with their masters, were suspect as potential informers.

But the damage had already been done. Within five days after Paul's recruitment attempt, the authorities were in possession of the bare outlines of the plan, though not of the details. Sealing the insurrectionists' fate, another slave defected three days before the planned attack. This time the informer was one of the plot leaders who had intimate knowledge of the plans. In the days that followed, history repeated itself. Like Gabriel Prosser and his men, Vesey and his followers were arrested, quickly tried and hanged. Only one of the leaders confessed to the conspiracy; the rest went to the gallows in silence, having withstood torture, threats, and promises of leniency. Because of their silence, hundreds of slaves who had taken an active part in the conspiracy remained anonymous and were thus saved from certain death.

After filling their baskets, the slaves carried the freshly picked cotton to horse-driven presses where it was compressed into bales.

So ended the second of the two largest slave conspiracies in the United States. Although both failed to accomplish their objective, they established precedents for a long string of slave insurrections and slave conspiracies, including the Nat Turner uprising of 1831. Herbert Aptheker, author of *American Negro Slave Revolts*, identified some 250 slave rebellions and conspiracies in the area of the continental United States, the first of which dated back to ninety-four years before the *Mayflower*. Many historians are convinced that the widespread fear of slave revolts among whites played an important part in precipitating the Civil War and that an understanding of this fear constitutes one of the most important prerequisites for the understanding of racial attitudes in the United States today.

STUDENTS OF SLAVERY in America are amazed by the fact that slaves in the face of indescribable physical and mental abuse were able not only to survive but to develop within the narrow confines of their existence a rich culture system of their own. Scholars are divided over the extent to which the slaves' culture was transplanted from their rich heritage in Africa. Some believe that the African cultural legacy was considerable. Among them are Melville J. Herskovits, Lorenzo Turner, and John Hope Franklin, who have identified a number of modern-day Afro-American traits in the areas of family life, language, religion, music, dance and motor habits as being of African origin. Turner found "in fairly general use . . . especially in the South," such African words as goober (peanut), gumbo (okra), ninny (female breast), tote (to carry) and yam (sweet potato). Historian Franklin warns against the misinterpretation of "the survival of varying degrees of African culture in America," which, he insists, "does not suggest that there has been only a limited adjustment of the Negro to the New World situation. To the contrary, it merely points up the fact that he came out of an experience that was sufficiently entrenched to make possible the persistence of some customs and traditions. . . . After all, perhaps the survival of Africanisms in the New World was as great as it was because of the refusal of the members of the dominant group in America to extend, without reservations, their own culture to the Negroes whom they brought over."

Be this as it may, few scholars disagree that the slaves were eager exponents of a unique culture of survival that not only helped sustain their humanity during bondage but which to this day provides Afro-Americans with the psychic strength necessary to survive as a minority within a largely hostile white majority. Furthermore, it is generally conceded today, however grudgingly, that this unique "slave culture" has immeasurably enriched the general culture of white America.

By far the most important aspect of slave culture was religion. Having become largely fatalistic in outlook because of the seeming inevitability of their condition,

The invention of the cotton gin in 1793, which mechanically separates cotton fibers from seeds, stepped up the textile industry and with it the need for cheap slave labor.

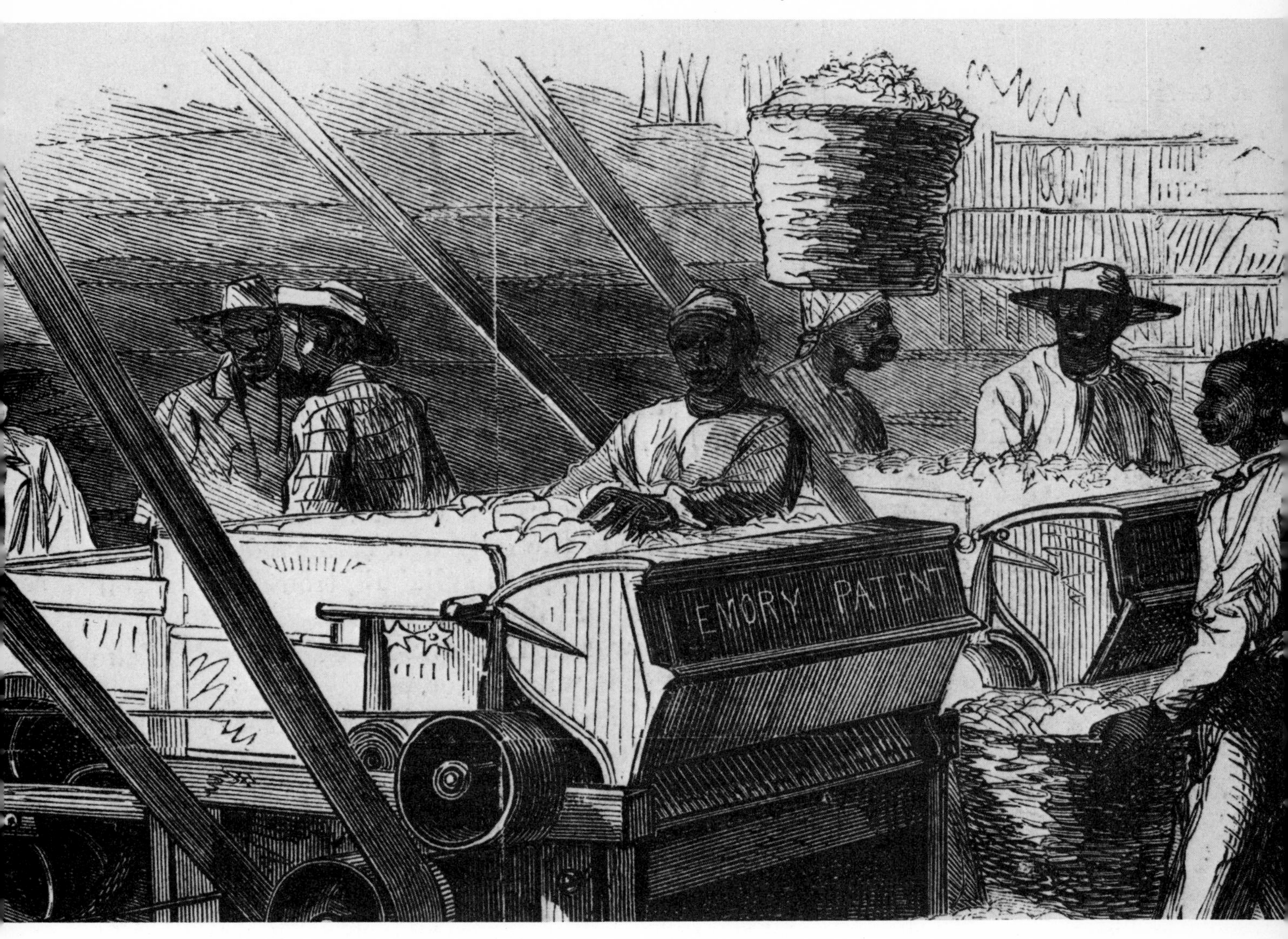

slaves eagerly embraced Christ and his promise of a better life hereafter. This trend was encouraged by some whites who tried to inculcate the slaves with the idea that whites' "right" to rule came from God. Proselytizing slaves, however, had its drawbacks. One Mississippi slaveholder objected to the manner in which slaves conducted their religious services. "They would be singing and dancing every night in their cabins," he complained, "till dawn of day, and utterly unfit themselves for work." Even more ironic was the fact that the Christian faith, al-

A major event in the life of slaves on big plantations was ration day when periodic allotments of food, clothing, utensils, and tobacco were distributed.

though handed to the slaves in order to make them docile, produced some of the most uncompromising slave rebels, as we have seen earlier in the cases of Toussaint L'Ouverture, Gabriel Prosser, Denmark Vesey and Nat Turner. Slaves interpreted the gospel, worshipped Christ and built "their" church to meet their own peculiar needs. In the process, the black church became one of the major institutions for black survival and black resistance—a position it maintained up to the era of Dr. Martin Luther King Jr.

CLOSELY RELATED to and often indistinguishably interwoven with the slaves' religious expression was their music, which not only was a part of their religious worship, but of their work day in the fields and virtually any other tasks they performed in groups or as individuals. The blues of W. C. Handy, Louis Armstrong's jazz, Lionel Hampton's swing, Charlie Parker's bop, Miles Davis's "cool" sounds and Aretha Franklin's "soul" and its many derivatives, all can be traced to the slaves' spirituals, gospel songs, funeral dirges, work chants, "devil songs" and shouts and—as Lerone Bennett Jr. points out—"even farther, back to the polyrhythmic complexity of the forgotten land—West Africa."

The uniqueness of "slave music" lies in its harmonious blending of "Africanisms" with Protestant hymns and revival songs for the expression of a wide range of emotions—sorrow, joy, pain, pleasure, anguish, love, hatred, resignation, defiance, frustration etc.—that encompassed the experience of human bondage. Cut off from most other avenues of self-expression, slaves poured their very souls into their music, making it the most spontaneous, most cathartic art form developed in the United States, "The Negro," wrote Kenneth Stampp, in *The Peculiar Institution* "had a repertory of songs for almost every occasion, and they not only sang them with innumerable variations but constantly improvised new ones besides. They sang spirituals which revealed their conceptions of Christianity and professed their religious faith. They sang work songs (usually slow in tempo) to break the monotony of toil in the tobacco factories, in the sugar houses, on the river boats, and in the fields. They sang whimsical songs which told little stories or ridiculed human frailties."

LeRoi Jones, in his book *Blues People*, shows that the development of black music was a key factor in the development of black Americans themselves. He suggests that the blues—a term which he uses

collectively for all black-created music in the United States—reflects the slaves' adaptation of their African heritage to new situations which called for reinterpretation. Consequently, he sees the changes undergone in this musical development as reflective of the transmutation of the African who did not believe he would be in America forever into the black American who knew he was trapped and, therefore, had to find new ways of coping with his oppressive environment. In creating his particular kind of music, Jones believes, the black man found an answer to his plight.

Among the many persistent myths about the slaves and black Americans in general is the notion that they contributed little, if anything, to the literature of the New World. Nothing could be farther from the truth. Though slave immigrants did not write and read, they carried in their minds and hearts a vast treasure of folktales. These, their creative genius adapted to the new realities of servitude.

In this adaptive process, slaves took the main ingredients of African fables, modifying them with different experiences, local color, and new animals. Thus, folktales served not only to preserve the slaves' African past, they also became the vehicle through which they were able to express with impunity their innermost thoughts and hostilities. "The animal tales told by Negro slaves with Brer Rabbit as the hero," explains J. Mason Brewer in his book, *American Negro Folklore*, "had a meaning far deeper than mere entertainment. The rabbit actually symbolized the slave himself. Whenever the rabbit succeeded in proving himself smarter than another animal, the slave rejoiced secretly, imagining himself smarter than his master." How a basically helpless and frightened creature like Brer Rabbit could serve similarly helpless and frequently frightened slaves as a hero symbol is explained by Arna Bontemps: "No hero-animals in Africa or elsewhere were so completely lacking in strength. But the slaves took pains to give Brer Rabbit other significant qualities. He became in their stories by turn a practical joker, a braggart, a wit, a glutton, a lady's man, and a trickster. But his essential characteristic was his ability to get the better of bigger and stronger animals. To the slave in his condition the theme of weakness overcoming strength through cunning proved endlessly fascinating."

It was not until after the Civil War that slave folklore was captured in print and accorded a place in American literature. The first volume of slave tales was *Uncle Remus: His Songs and His Sayings*, collected by Joel Chandler Harris and published in 1880. Other important collections of slave folklore include Charles C. Jones' *Negro Myths from the Georgia Coast*, told in the Gullah dialect and pub-

Out of plantation prayer meetings and slave-quarter wakes came the spirituals and other unique expressions of the African-American personality.

lished in 1888, and, among contemporary collections, *The Book of Negro Folklore* by Langston Hughes and Arna Bontemps.

The slaves' contributions to the literary life of the United States were not confined to folktales but included the enrichment of the English language itself. Whether in speech, songs, poems, prayers, rhymes, or lore, they coined their own words and phrases whenever the English equivalents did not suit their specific purpose or were unavailable to them. Thus, like no other immigrant group, slaves gave rise to the emergence of the "American" language through the massive infusion of their own colorful expressions that reflected their remarkable sense of irony in the face of adversity.

Exploitation by the slavemasters was ever-present on the slave's mind and consequently was a recurring theme in slave rhymes and poems. The recital of such rhymes to the accompaniment of the "juba" beater formed one of the most popular forms of entertainment in the slave quarters during holidays. Frederick Douglass cites the following example:

> We raise de wheat,
> Dey gib us de corn;
> We bake de bread,
> Dey gib us de cruss;
> We sif de meal,
> Dey gib us de huss;
> We peel de meat,
> Dey gib us de skin,
> And dat's de way
> Dey takes us in.
> We skim de pot,
> Dey gib us de liquor,
> And say dat's good enough for
> nigger.

On Sundays, the slave quarters of large plantations bustled with activity as slaves looked after their personal affairs.

A slave woman on a shopping errand carries her load in time-tested African fashion. The drawing below depicts a typical plantation graveyard.

Walk over! walk over!
Tom butter and de fat;
Poor nigger you can't get
over dat;
Walk over!

"Nature," Frederick Douglass once wrote, "had done almost nothing to prepare men and women to be either slaves or slaveholders. Nothing but rigid training, long persisted in, can perfect the character of the one or the other." Implied in

To prevent escapes, guards frequently checked passes or slave tags (above and below) of slaves found off the plantation after curfew.

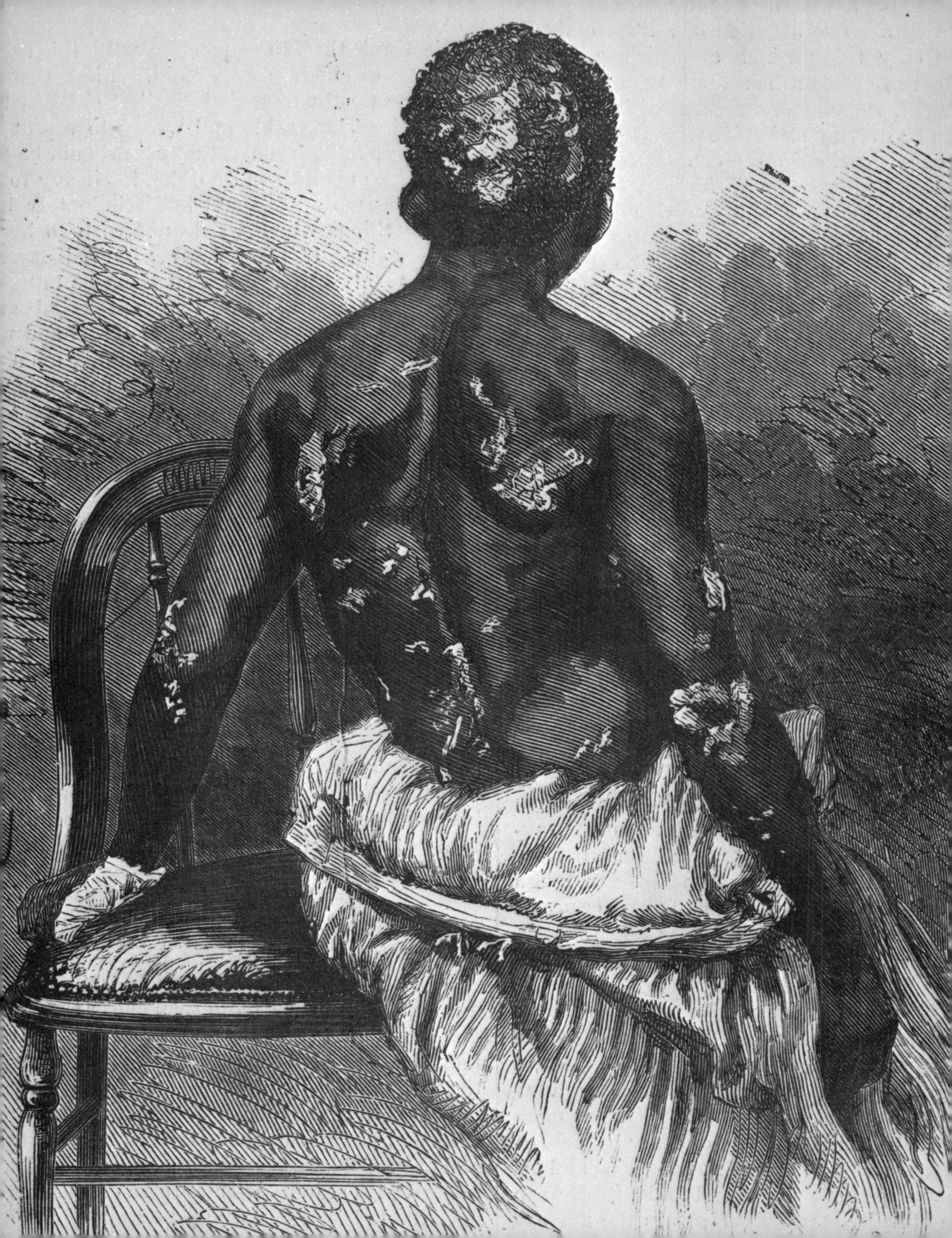

Douglass's statement is the enormous toll in terms of stunted human and social development which the slave system exacted from both master and slave. No matter how hard they tried, whites could not escape the fact that slavery degrades the slaver as well as the slave. This fact was recognized early by Thomas Jefferson, who expressed his concern over the evil influence of slavery upon white youth in these words:

> The whole commerce between master and slave is a perpetual exercise of the most boisterous passions, the most unremitting despotism on the other. Our children see this, and learn to imitate it; for man is an imitative animal . . . . The child . . . puts on the same airs in the circles of smaller slaves . . . and thus nursed, educated, and daily exercised in tyranny, cannot but be stamped by it with odious peculiarities.

Jefferson's warning was disregarded, not only by slaveowners of the South but also by non-slaveowning Southerners and Northerners. In fact, poor Southerners, who derived no direct economic benefits from the slave system, were among its staunchest supporters. For slavery was more than a system of economic exploitation; it was also a social caste system that made the poorest white a racist with a built-in sense of superiority.

Nonslavers jealously guarded their "superior" position in the racial pecking order and were ever ready to defend it by joining mobs which dealt out summary justice to "insolent" slaves, or by cruelly punishing those whites—especially "outsiders" from the North—who had committed the cardinal sin of "tampering" with slaves. Anything, from expressing abolitionist sentiments to inciting slave insurrections, was "tampering."

The price of white supremacy was high. Imperceptibly, the maintenance of the slavery system turned the Southern regions into a totalitarian police state as all political power was usurped by a handful

Brutal punishment, such as the one that left the marks on this Virginia slave woman's back, arms, and head, was a common practice among plantation slavers.

After the Slave Insurrection Panic of 1741 in New York City, slaves, who were not represented by counsel, were tried and convicted upon insufficient evidence.

of planters whose sole interest in politics was the perpetuation and increase of their power. They enacted laws that virtually suspended all civil liberties and ruthlessly crushed any opposition to "our cherished institutions." Heavily armed patrols—made up largely of poor whites—roamed the countryside to prevent slave revolts. Garrisons were reinforced and a state of quasi-martial law was proclaimed as countermeasures to the paralyzing fear of slave insurrections.

As in the case of most totalitarian states, all intellectual life died out as scholars and writers who refused to accept the role of apologists for the slavery system either withdrew in silence or left the South. In this climate of absolute moral bankruptcy, religious worship became a mockery as preachers searched frantically in the scriptures for passages to reconcile the enslavement of human beings with Christ's message of universal brotherhood.

On a purely personal level, the two-edged sword of slavery cut deep into the psyches of whites, exposing some of the most base perversions ever to afflict mankind. "Absolute and arbitrary power," Douglass said, "can never be maintained by one man over the body and soul of another man, without brutal chastisement and enormous cruelty." Southern whites were more than equal to the task. They raped, flogged, castrated, burned, branded, hunted, sold, bought, bred, prostituted, hanged, lynched, and starved slaves at will. Moreover, they did so without a sense of shame or remorse.

Slavery was similarly costly in economic terms since only a relatively small number of Southerners owned and profited from slaves. "There is no legislation except for the benefit of slavery and slave holders," wrote Hinton R. Helper, a poor white Carolinian, in his book *The Impending Crisis of the South*, which was published in 1857 and which exposed the exploitation of poor whites by the cotton aristocrats. Helper attributed the general economic backwardness of the slave states and the poverty of a vast majority of whites to the maintenance of the bondage system. To prove his point, he quoted government statistics pertaining to mass starvation brought on by the exhaustion of the land through single-crop farming and the absence of a diversified economy. "Never," charged Helper, "were the poor classes of people . . . so basely duped, so

Public burnings of "troublesome" slaves accused of having attacked and injured their masters were justified as deterrents.

adroitly swindled or so damnably outraged." Helper's words struck home, for immediately upon publication of his book, it was banned in all slave states, a fact which prompted Helper to predict: "The South can never have a literature of her own until after slavery shall have been abolished."

The South did not care. Faced with the choice between slavery on the one hand and literature, civil liberties, human decency, peace and tranquillity, and Christian virtues on the other, the South chose slavery. If white supremacy was a luxury the South could ill afford, it was a luxury most Southerners—rich or poor—felt they could not live without. Consequently, they were willing to pay, if necessary with their lives.

Whatever the cost in human and economic terms to whites, it was insignificant in comparison with the price paid by the slave system's key victim—the slave. Be-

A slave revolt led by Nat Turner (left) in 1831 left a trail of some sixty dead whites in Virginia (below).

Shortly after his capture (above), an unrepentant Nat Turner was hanged. Below are news accounts of the insurrection.

SLAVERY RECORD.

INSURRECTION IN VIRGINIA!

Extract of a letter from a gentleman to his friend in Baltimore, dated

'RICHMOND, August 23d.

An express reached the governor this morning, informing him that an insurrection had broken out in Southampton, and that, by the last accounts, there were seventy whites massacred, and the militia retreating. Another express to Petersburg says that the blacks were continuing their destruction; that three hundred militia were retreating in a body, before six or eight hundred blacks. A shower of rain coming up as the militia were making an attack, wet the powder so much that they were compelled to retreat, being armed only with shot-guns. The negroes are armed with muskets, scythes, axes, &c. &c. Our volunteers are marching to the scene of action. A troop of cavalry left at four o'clock, P. M. The artillery, with four field pieces, start in the steam boat Norfolk, at 6 o'clock, to land at Smithfield. Southampton county lies 80 miles south of us, below Petersburg.'

From the Richmond Whig, of Tuesday.

Disagreeable rumors have reached this city of an insurrection of the slaves in Southampton County, with loss of life. In order to correct exaggeration, and at the same time to induce all salutary caution, we state the following particulars:

An express from the Hon. James Trezvant states that an insurrection had broken out, that several families had been murdered, and that the negroes were embodied, requiring a considerable military force to reduce them.

The names and precise numbers of the families are not mentioned. A letter to the Post Master corroborates the intelligence. Prompt and efficient

yond indescribable physical abuse, the slave was subjected to perhaps the most monstrous of all atrocities—the crushing of his dignity and self-respect as a member of the human race.

Despite the eroding influences of slavery, slaves exhibited remarkable loyalty to one another and frequently helped some of their fellow slaves to escape, even when family ties prevented them from joining the flight. In the face of overwhelming odds, many slaves managed to preserve a semblance of family life. There are countless stories of slaves who bought their freedom, then labored for the rest of their lives in order to purchase the freedom of their relatives.

If slaves and slavers suffered irreparable consequences from slavery, so did the nation as a whole. On the national level, ante-bellum slavery become the most divisive issue and the most embarrassing stain on the honor of the United States in its dealings with other nations. This latter fact was eloquently stated by Frederick Douglass after his return from an extended stay in England:

> While slavery exists, and the union of these states endures, every American citizen must bear the chagrin of hearing his country branded before the world as a nation of liars and hypocrites; and behold his cherished flag pointed at with the utmost scorn and derision. . . .
>
> Slavery blunts the edge of all our rebukes of tyranny abroad—the criticisms that we make upon other nations, only call forth ridicule, contempt, and scorn. In a word, we are made a reproach and a by-word to a mocking earth, and we must continue to be so made, so long as slavery continues to pollute our soil.

Torn internally and mocked and despised by the world, the United States, because of slavery, was on a collision course with destiny.

Joseph Cinque was the principal figure in the *Amistad* slave mutiny of 1839 in which he and some fifty blacks seized command of the vessel.

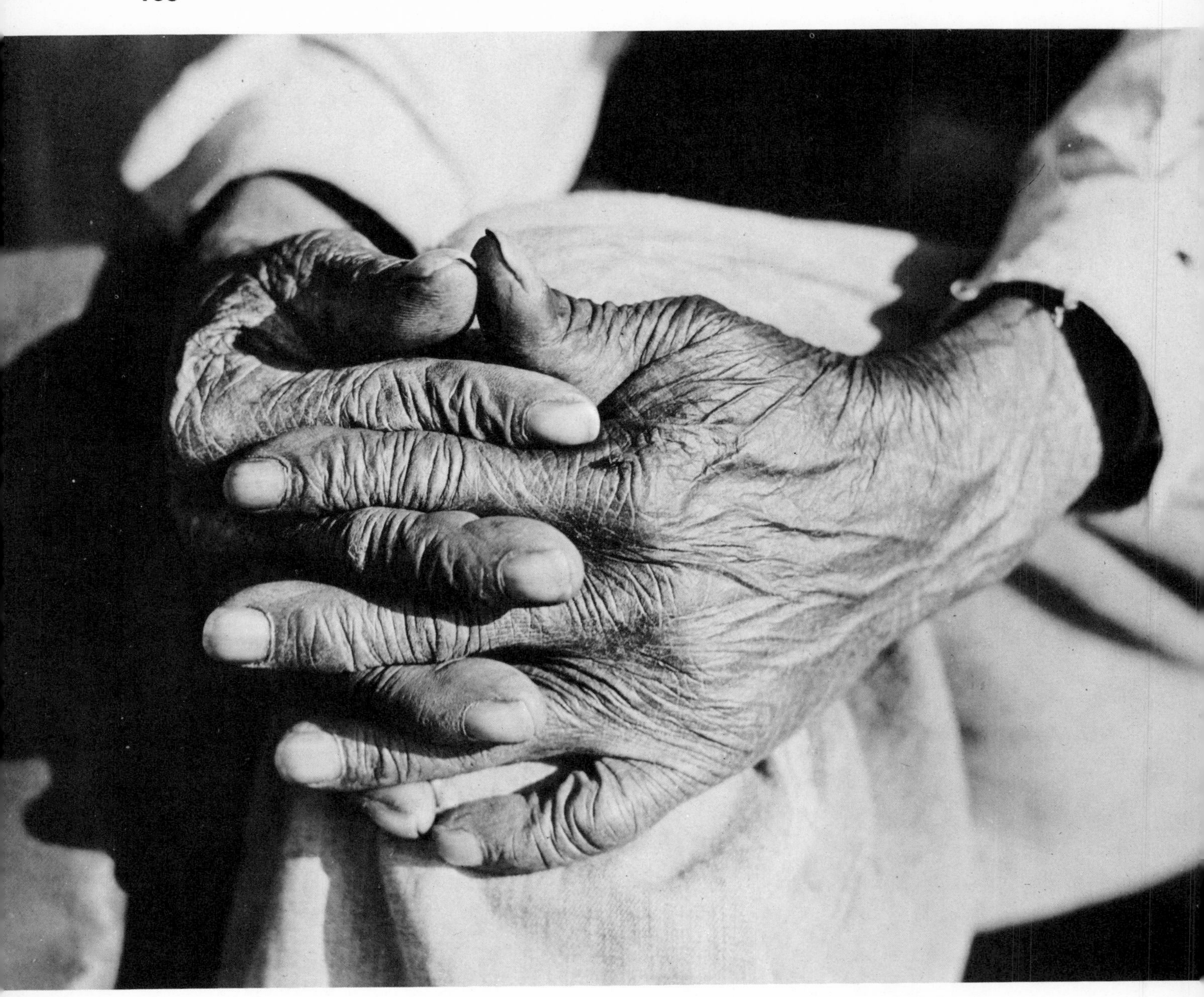

7

Free Blacks

ALTHOUGH SLAVERY was the pervasive and overpowering force affecting the black population up to the Civil War, there existed from early Colonial times a small and increasing population of free blacks. Most of these people lived in a social no-man's-land far superior to the bondage of the slaves, but inferior to the status of whites.

When the first U.S. census was taken in 1790, fourteen years after the Declaration of Independence, there were fifty-nine thousand free blacks in the nation. About twenty-seven thousand were in the Northern states, and thirty-two thousand in the Southern. In the following ten years the number increased by 82 percent, and in the next ten by 71 percent. After this the number continued to increase, but more slowly. During the early years of the nation the growth of the free black population was about three times that of the slave population. After 1830 the increase was largely due to the gradual emancipation in the North. By 1840, the rate of increase of the free black population had fallen behind that of the slaves, and it continued to drop until the Civil War.

During the first half of the nineteenth century the increasing difficulty of life for free blacks in the South and the spread of antislavery activity in the North resulted in a northward shift of the free black population. By 1860, when the Civil War began, more free blacks were living in the North than in the South. Of the 488,000 blacks in the U.S. in that year, 44 percent lived in the South Atlantic states, and 46 percent in the North. The rest were in the South Central states and in what was then the West. Maryland, however, continued to lead in the number of free blacks. That state's slave population only slightly outnumbered the 83,900 free blacks who lived there. Virginia was second in the number of free blacks, with 58,000, and Pennsylvania was third. In that state in 1860 there were no slaves; all 56,000 blacks were free.

Free blacks tended to live in cities, because it was in urban areas that they had the best chance for employment, education, and social mobility. In 1860 there were 25,600 free blacks in Baltimore, 22,000 in Philadelphia, 12,500 in New York, 10,000 in New Orleans and 3,200 in Charleston, South Carolina. In the rural western areas there were few free Negroes.

Free blacks were not evenly distributed in the nation's population. They tended to concentrate in areas where their fore-

FREEDOM'S JOURNAL.

" RIGHTEOUSNESS EXALTETH A NATION."

CORNISH & RUSSWURM, Editors & Proprietors.

NEW-YORK, FRIDAY, MARCH 30, 1827. [VOL. I. No. 3.

MEMOIRS OF CAPT. PAUL CUFFEE.

Being now master of a small covered boat of about 12 tons burthen, he hired a person to assist as a seaman, and made many advantageous voyages to different parts of the state of Connecticut and when about 25 years old married a native of the country, a descendant of the tribe to which his mother belonged.—For some time after his marriage he attended chiefly to his agricultural concerns, but from an increase of family he at length deemed it necessary to pursue his commercial plans more extensively than he had before done.—He arranged his affairs for a new expedition and hired a small house on West-Port river to which he removed his family. A boat of 18 tons was now procured in which he sailed to the banks of St. George in quest of Codfish and returned home with a valuable cargo. This important adventure was the foundation of an extensive & profitable fishing establishment from Westport river, which continued for a considerable time and was the source of an honest and comfortable living to many of the inhabitants of that district.

At this period Paul formed a connexion with his brother-in-law Michael Warner, who had several sons well qualified for the sea service, four of whom have since laudably filled responsible situations as Captains and first mates. A vessel of 25 tons was built, and in two voyages to the Straits of Belisle and Newfoundland he met with such success as enabled him, in conjunction with another person, to build another vessel of 41 tons burthen in which he made several profitable voyages. Paul had experienced too many disadvantages of his very limited education, and he resolved, as far as it was practicable, to relieve his children from similar embarrassments. The neighborhood had neither a tutor nor a school-house. Many of the citizens were desirous that a school-house should be erected. About 1797 Paul proposed a meeting of the inhabitants for the purpose of making such arrangements as should accomplish the desired object. The collision of opinion respecting mode and place occasioned the meeting to separate without coming to a conclusion; several meetings of the same nature were held, but all were unsuccessful in their issue. Perceiving that all efforts to procure a union of sentiment were fruitless, Paul set himself to work in earnest and had a suitable house built on his own ground, which he freely gave up to the use of the public, and the school was open to all who pleased to send their children. How gratifying to humanity is this anecdote! and who that justly appreciates the human character would not prefer Paul Cuffee, the offspring of an African slave, to the proudest statesman, that ever dealt out destruction among mankind?—About this time Paul proceeded on a whaling voyage to the straits of Belisle, where he found four other vessels completely equipped with boats and harpoons, for catching what Paul discovered that he had not made proper preparations for the business, having only ten hands on board and … which was old and alm… the masters of the … situation they … practice of … with his cr… solved t… at leng… prud… the… ra… f…

ral good. It is not so much a right of property, as it is a legal relation; and it ought to be treated as such.

The second object was, to relieve slave-holders from a charge, or an apprehension of criminality, where in fact, there is no offence. There can be no palliation for the conduct of those who first brought the curse of slavery upon poor Africa, and poor America too.—But the body of the present generation are not liable to this charge. Posterity are not answerable for the sins of their fathers, unless they approve their deeds. They found the blacks among them, in a degraded state, incapable either of appreciating or enjoying liberty. They have, therefore, nothing to answer for on this score, because they have no other alternative, *at present*, but to keep them in subjection. There is nothing so de- [illegible] by our principles, to the acknowledgment of guilt, in that which we at the same time believe to be absolutely unavoidable, and in which therefore, it is impossible really to feel self-reproach. Our southern brethren have high ideas of liberty.

There is nothing so calculated to make men restive under command, as a habit and love of commanding others. Upon their own principles, they have been forced to acknowledge even the existence of slavery, in any shape, as criminal. They have therefore concluded that as heavy a curse hung over the present generation for continuing slavery, even when it is plainly unavoidable, as over the last for introducing it. The consequence has been, that those who seriously bewailed the evil, have folded their arms in despair; and those who regarded only their own gratification, expecting to hear the curse at any rate, have taken the desperate resolution, "Let us eat and drink, for to-morrow we die." But the principle is preposterous, and the conclusion incorrect. A Christian *may* hold slaves, and exact their services, without any occasion to feel a pang of self-reproach *merely on account* of his holding slaves.

The third object aimed at, was to fasten the charge of criminality on the very spot where such a charge will be; and where it ought to be felt; and where alone reformation is practicable. There are no duties, without corresponding rights, and no rights without corresponding duties. While it is the duty of the slave to submit him… so long as the laws … a slave, it is his … *laws*, in the enj… good name, a… enjoy consi… And on t… tors sho… best cir… and tha… as pos… tate … ne…

ance. We may hope to enjoy the favor of our merciful heavenly Father. But this is not done. I think I may venture to assert, that most of the slave-holding states, neither the laws, nor public opinion, secure to the slaves any of the privileges of humanity. Nothing more is done for them, in *kind*, than is done for the domestic beasts; and nothing more in *degree*, except as they are a more valuable species of property, and are recognised, to some extent, as possessing rational faculties. Let the contrary be shown. I say that of all that kind of provision, which goes to purify and elevate the character, and to create in the subject affection and confidence towards the government, every trace and track is completely excluded. The culture of their minds, the preservation of their morals, their instruction in the only religion which can make them good servants, happy neighbors, and hopeful heirs of eternal life, every thing of the kind is guarded against, by the *laws* at least, even more studiously than the abuse of their persons, and the destruction of their lives. Whatever is attempted for their improvement, is done by individual effort, and in direct violation of the laws. Here is our guilt; our full, dark, unmitigated guilt. It is the guilt of our nation.

We in the non-slave holding states, do not feel it as we ought. But we cannot wash our hands, until we can safely declare, that we have done every thing we can, by public and private efforts, to remove the injustice. We have not done this. Comparatively speaking nothing has been done. The Colonization Society has indeed made a beginning, and done as well as could be expected. But I ask how long it will probably be, before that institution can dispose of 30,000 blacks in a year, which is only the *present* annual increase? Until they can do this, the number must be continually increasing. Indeed, I do not believe our southern brethren, in general, intend to do any thing more than to provide a sort of *safety valve*, by this Society, to serve as an outlet for their free blacks and supernumeraries. In our country, acts of the legislature are to be taken as to the expression of the public feeling, on all great subjects.—Towards the blacks, the language of each successive legislature has been, "Our father made your yoke heavy, but we will add the… to; our fathers chastised you with whi… we will chastise you with scorpions." … thing must be done, to avert the …

retarded; and that the same prejudice will continue to have a similar operation, so long as it shall continue to exist. Not that there are wanting men of humanity among our West Indian legislators. Their humanity is discernable enough when it is to be applied to the *whites*; but such is the system of slavery, and the degradation attached to slavery, that their humanity seems to be lost or gone, when it is to be applied to the *blacks*. Not again that there are wanting men of sense among the same body. They are shrewd and clever enough in the affairs of life, where they maintain an intercourse with the *whites*; but in their intercourse with the *blacks* their sense appears to be shrivelled and not of its ordinary size. Look at the laws of their own making, as far as the blacks are concerned, and they are a collection of any thing but—wisdom."† If these remarks are not applicable to the slave laws of our own states, let the contrary be shown.

* See Ep. vi. 5, 9. Col. iii. 22. iv. 1.

† "Thoughts on the necessity of improving the condition of the slaves, &c. with a view to their ultimate emancipation." p. 10, 11.

(To be Continued.)

CURE FOR DRUNKENNESS.

In speaking, on a former occasion, of the remedy for Intemperance proposed by Dr. Chambers of this city we expressed ourselves with a considerable degree of caution. As it is a subject of great importance to the community, and one on which they ought to be explicitly and accurately informed, we have within the past week spent more than o… whole day in making a personal investiga… into cases where the remedy has been … plied, and into the nature of the medic… the hope of coming to a full and satisf… conclusion. The result of our enquiries … be seen in the sequel.—*N. Y. Obs.*

The remedy is not the se… posed by Dr. … it is, the c… bers. … con…

runners had established themselves. By the time of the Civil War they lived mainly in the eastern counties of Virginia, Maryland, and North Carolina; the Southern cities of Baltimore, Charleston, Mobile, and New Orleans; the Northern cities of Boston, New York, Cincinnati, and Philadelphia; isolated areas in the Old Northwest such as Cass County, Michigan, Hammond County, Indiana, and Wilberforce, Ohio; and rural areas in which blacks had mixed freely with Indians, such as those in Massachusetts, North Carolina, and Florida.

THE UPSURGE in the number of free blacks after the Revolutionary War came largely because the Revolution's underlying doctrine—the fundamental equality of men—caused many whites and free blacks to react against the institution of slavery. This reaction had a particular effect in the North, where there was feeling in favor of the abolition of slavery. Before the end of the eighteenth century, slavery was prohibited in several Northern states, and programs had been set up for gradual emancipation in others.

In the South, the Revolution gave a different impetus to emancipation. Many slaves were manumitted, or set free, in order to serve in the Revolutionary War.

Another common way for slaves to gain freedom was for their white masters to set them free when they became disabled to work. This relieved th of having to care for their slaves was not profitable to do so. Some n left wills that said their slaves shou be set free after their death. Some slaves with a record of particularly meritorious service were set free either by their owner or by the state.

The number of free blacks also multiplied through the excess of births over deaths. Babies born to free black mothers were free, whether or not their fathers were slaves. Some free children also resulted from the union of white women and black slave men, though the penalties for such unions were heavy. In 1850, more than a third of the total number of free blacks in the U.S. were mulattos.

FREE BLACKS enjoyed fairly high legal status during the Colonial period, and their status improved further due to their important role in the Revolutionary War. After the war these citizens gradually became more and more isolated because of the animosity of whites, especially in the

Andrew Bryan (l.) was a pioneer Baptist minister. Photograph above shows the first black Baptist church in Savannah, Georgia.

South. The presence of a large and growing number of free blacks who were taking an important role in society made white slaveowners uneasy because it reminded them and, more importantly, their slaves, that the foundation of slavery—the assumed inferiority of the black man and his "natural inclination" to servitude—was false. To put the proud free blacks "in their place," Southerners began maligning them and showing open hostility. Gradually the status of the free black was lowered until by the time of the Civil War there was little apparent difference in some places between a free black and a slave. To keep down the number of free blacks, many states passed laws that made former slaves leave the state after they were manumitted.

Every attempt was made to prevent free blacks from uniting, either among themselves or with slaves. By 1835 there were laws against free blacks entertaining slaves or visiting them in their homes. Almost everywhere in the South free blacks were forbidden the right of assembly. They could not hold church services without a licensed white minister being present. Free blacks could not testify against whites, but slaves could testify against free blacks.

The doctrine of the inherent inferiority of all blacks, which was being advanced more strongly as a justification for slavery, had its effect in the passage of humiliating laws limiting the action of free blacks. One of the doctrine's first manifestations, for instance, was the passage of laws against intermarriage between blacks and whites. Other laws limited the economic development of free blacks. In Georgia, by 1830, a free black had to get his white guardian's permission to buy goods on credit; and in many states it was illegal for blacks to buy or sell alcoholic beverages. In 1818 Georgia even forbade free blacks to own real estate, but this law was repealed the following year in most areas of the state. After the Revolutionary War some states passed laws, modeled on a Pennsylvania statute of 1725, which said an unemployed free black who was able to work could be bound out to service by a court. Some states made blacks post bonds as security that they would not become economic burdens on the public.

Most states which wrote their constitutions during the Revolutionary period did not exclude blacks from voting, and in several, such as Maryland, North Carolina, New York, and Pennsylvania, many blacks voted for several years. But all

Richard Allen was the first bishop of the African Methodist Episcopal Church and the first national leader of the black community.

Absalom Jones, a Philadelphia leader, founded the first black episcopal church.

Southern states entering the Union after 1789, except Tennessee, denied blacks the vote. After 1800, Northern and Southern states in which blacks had the vote passed discriminatory legislation. Maryland barred black voters in 1810, Tennessee in 1834, North Carolina in 1835, Pennsylvania in 1838, and Indiana in 1851. In 1823 New York instituted a property qualification for black voters of $250 and a residence requirement of three years.

When the War of 1812 with England broke out, few objections were made to blacks fighting, but little effort was made to enlist them in the service. Most black soldiers served in menial capacities, though a few, including William Burleigh of Philadelphia, who fought in the Battle of North Point, became heroes. One-tenth of the crews on ships in the Upper Lakes were blacks, and many were lauded for valiant service. Blacks were important in the American victory at the Battle of New Orleans.

Despite their important service in two wars, by 1820 the history of black Americans had been so distorted, and the animosity caused by the competition for jobs had become so sharp, that in Philadelphia whites began driving blacks away from the Fourth of July celebrations in Independence Square, claiming that they had played no part in establishing the nation.

In some instances the free black's limited freedom exposed him to extra burdens without affording him a share in the benefits his labors produced. In 1859 blacks in Baltimore were required to pay school taxes but were not allowed to send their children to the public schools the taxes supported.

Some states attempted to eliminate the

Daniel Coker was a powerful AME leader. He later emigrated to Liberia.

free black class. These states passed laws which made it easy for blacks to re-enslave themselves, ostensibly as a means of escaping the burdens of freedom. Tennessee passed such a law in 1857, and Texas, Louisiana, and Maryland followed in successive years. Few blacks took advantage of these laws. In 1859, Arkansas went a step farther and passed a law that required blacks to choose masters "who must give bond not to allow such Negroes to act as free."

Gradually, during the years before the Civil War, it became more difficult for a free black to keep his freedom. A white person might claim he was a slave, and the black often had little defense against the charge. Many were simply kidnapped and enslaved. All Southern states made blacks carry passes; and a black without a certificate of freedom was presumed to be a slave. By 1860, a black could not move about freely in any Southern state. In North Carolina, free blacks were forbidden to travel outside their home county. At ports in the Atlantic Seaboard states and in Alabama, Mississippi, and Louisiana, free black sailors could not leave arriving ships to enter the city.

As early as 1793 Virginia had passed a law forbidding free blacks to enter the state, and by 1835 most Southern states and some Northern ones had laws barring entrance or making entrance difficult. In Georgia the penalty for breaking the law was one hundred dollars, and a black who could not pay might be sold into slavery. A law also prevented free blacks from leaving that state for extended periods and then returning.

Whites' fear that free blacks would foment and aid a slave insurrection was expressed in other laws. Virginia, Maryland, and North Carolina, as well as other states, forbade blacks to carry weapons.

It was not only in the South that free blacks met such hostility. Some Northern states restricted black immigration, and in New York State whites rioted against blacks from time to time. In southern Ohio an angry white populace forcibly prevented the 513 freed slaves of Virginian John Randolph from settling in the area.

THE POVERTY in which discrimination kept most free blacks was a great hindrance to advancement. All states required free blacks to work and to have visible means of support, but they often made it hard for them by imposing economic restrictions on the kind of work blacks could legally do. The scarcity of available occupations for blacks was made more acute by laws such as that passed by Maryland in 1805, which forbade free blacks to sell corn, wheat, or tobacco without first obtaining a license. Georgia in 1829 passed a law against free blacks working as typesetters. In 1831 North Carolina forbade blacks to serve as traders or peddlers without a license, and South Carolina made it illegal to employ a black as a clerk.

Nevertheless, there were a good number of free blacks in both the North and the South who lived comfortable, and sometimes affluent, lives. Many worked in lucrative crafts or professions. Some owed their knowledge and skills to apprenticeships, and to the practice in many places of training slaves as artisans. One survey in Charleston showed that blacks worked in more than fifty occupations, many of which were highly skilled, including the building trades, making clothing and food, operating machines, and piloting ships. In Boston in 1860 the two thousand free black residents engaged in almost one hundred occupations, including paper-hanging, engraving, quarrying, photography, and tailoring, as well as the ministry, teaching, law, and dentistry. There was similar variety in occupations in New York and, to a lesser extent, in Cincinnati. In Philadelphia, blacks could be found in more than 130 skilled occupations. In New Orleans just before the Civil War there were black teachers, jewelers, architects, and lithographers. In almost all communities could be found free black carpenters, barbers, cabinet makers, and brickmasons. Many communities had free black shopkeepers, salesmen, and clerks, even when the laws forbade it. In 1859

James Varick became the first bishop of the African Methodist Episcopal Zion Church.

more than half of all American seamen were black.

In both Northern and Southern cities, blacks tended to be most successful in small business ventures based upon personal service. They won their widest reputation in cooking and food preparation. They enjoyed great success in the catering business in some areas, and some had successful tailoring concerns whose clients were prominent citizens. Black contractors were successful in Cincinnati and in other Ohio cities, and there were several flourishing livery stables in eastern states.

At the top of the economic ladder among free blacks were a few businessmen and landowners who managed to amass fortunes despite the generally unfavorable attitudes of the nation's whites toward significant black advancement. Thomy Lafon, a tycoon of New Orleans, left an estate valued at a half million dollars. A philanthropist, Lafon had done so much for the advancement of New Orleans that the state legislature ordered his bust placed in a public institution. Another businessman, Jehu Jones of Charleston, was proprietor of one of that city's best hotels, built at a cost of more than forty thousand dollars. James Forten of Philadelphia, who started out as an errand boy on the docks, built a sailmaking plant into the largest black industrial establishment and amassed a fortune of more than one hundred thousand dollars. Anthony Westone was head of a famous millwright business in Charleston.

In 1800, blacks in Philadelphia owned almost one hundred houses and lots. In New York by 1837 they owned $1,400,000 in taxable real estate and had $600,000 in savings banks. In Maryland in 1860 free blacks paid taxes on more than $1 million worth of property. In Virginia, blacks owned more than sixty thousand acres of farmland, and their city land was valued at $463,000. A large number of New Orleans blacks were affluent. In 1860 they owned property worth more than fifteen million dollars.

Some free blacks owned slaves. Most such slaveowners had bought their relatives or friends to rescue them from the worst aspects of slavery, but were prevented from giving them their official freedom because of legal restrictions. Others owned enough slaves to benefit from them financially. Cyprian Ricard, for instance, bought an estate in Louisiana, including its ninety-one slaves. Charles Rogues had forty-seven slaves and Marie Metoyer fifty-eight. There were

Bethel African Methodist Episcopal Church was organized in Philadelphia by Richard Allen and his followers.

Peter Williams, pictured in the doorway, was a leader of the group which withdrew from New York's John Street Methodist Episcopal Church to organize the African Methodist Episcopal Zion Church.

several black owners with many slaves around Charleston and New Orleans.

The success of blacks in some occupations and the virtual monopoly they enjoyed in a few angered whites who looked upon the growing black population as an economic threat. In 1842, when many whites were out of work because of a severe depression, the unemployed in Philadelphia broke up a black parade celebrating the abolition of slavery in the West Indies. The whites attacked scores of blacks, and burned the new African Hall and Presbyterian church. The labor situation was worsened by later influxes of immigrants from Europe. In some cities, blacks organized associations of mechanics, coachmen, caulkers, and other workers. These organizations were outlawed in some parts of the Deep South.

Christopher Rush became a bishop of the AME Zion Church.

ONE OF THE MOST enduring and important phenomena for blacks during and after the Revolutionary War was the rise of the black church. In addition to the spiritual benefits it afforded, the black church served as an important training ground for leadership. Blacks who had been effectively cut off from the political process of the nation and from formal education developed techniques of organization and attitudes of leadership that were useful not only in building the churches into viable institutions but also for guiding the development of the community.

In the early years after the Revolutionary War, when the fervor of freedom was

The African Free School was established in
1787 by the New York Manumission Society.

still strong, it had appeared that the established churches, notably the Methodist and the Baptist, would insist upon complete integration of houses and modes of worship. In 1784 the Methodists said that slavery was "contrary to the laws of God" and told members to liberate their slaves within twelve months, a position from which church leaders were later forced by Southern factions to retreat. In 1789 the Baptists said slavery was a "violent depredation of the rights of nature and inconsistent with a republican government." They, too, were forced to abandon their liberal position.

Up to this time, many blacks had attended white churches, though they were usually restricted to segregated sections. Before laws were passed to forbid the practice, black ministers, such as North Carolina ministers Ralph Freeman, Henry Evans, and John Chavis, preached to white congregations. There had been precedents for this in the North. Lemuel Haynes had long served white congregations in several Northern towns, and the Reverend Samuel Ringgold Ward was pastor of a white congregation in Cortlandville, New York. Even so, discriminatory practices in the churches caused black members to split off and build their own congregations.

Black Baptist churches began to spring up during the Revolutionary War. George Liele, a resourceful leader, founded one in Savannah in 1779. Whites as well as blacks came to hear the preaching of Andrew Bryan, who carried on Liele's work. Whites tried to close the church at the end of the war; they whipped church members and put Bryan in prison. His master supported him, however, and the church became the starting point for the organization of black Baptists in Georgia.

Meanwhile, black Baptist churches continued to appear in other areas. In 1809 thirteen black members of a white Baptist church in Philadelphia were dismissed to form a church of their own. Under the leadership of a former slave, a Rev. Burrows, it became an important institution. In that same year, the black Baptists of Boston organized a church with the help of the Reverend Thomas Paul, who, about the same time, was organizing the church that later came to be known as the Abyssinian Baptist Church in New York.

Another of the pivotal figures in the movement for formation of black churches was a former slave, Richard Allen. Allen, who saved enough money to purchase his freedom from his Delaware master in 1777, began preaching in the Methodist churches there. In 1786 he

moved to Philadelphia, where he began holding prayer meetings for blacks. When officials of predominantly white St. George's Methodist Episcopal Church proposed to segregate the many blacks who came to hear Allen preach, he decided on the need for a black church. At one service in St. George's in 1787, white officials pulled Allen, Absalom Jones, and William White from their knees because they were praying in the "white" section of the church. The blacks withdrew from the church and formed the Free African Society. In 1794, Allen organized the Bethel African Methodist Episcopal Church. That same year, Jones organized the St. Thomas Protestant Episcopal Church, becoming its first pastor.

Branches of the A.M.E. Church began springing up in various towns in Pennsylvania, Maryland, and New Jersey. By 1816 the various churches had grown to the point where it was possible to unite them as a national organization. The conference held that year in Philadelphia chose Allen as bishop. By 1820 there were four thousand black Methodists in Philadelphia alone, and in the Baltimore district almost two thousand. Soon the organization reached as far as Pittsburgh to the west and Charleston to the south. But the opposition sparked by the Denmark Vesey insurrection in 1822 checked growth in the Southern states.

Establishment of another denomination, the African Methodist Episcopal Zion Church, came in 1796 as a result of discrimination in the New York Methodist churches. Blacks withdrew from the John Street Methodist Episcopal Church there and set up a new one. Leaders of the movement were Peter Williams, father of the first black priest in the Protestant Episcopal Church, James Varick, George Collins, and Christopher Rush. By 1822 the church had overcome schisms within and opposition from without and was stable enough to elect James Varick as bishop and to set up an expansion program.

Black churches were distrusted in slaveholding parts of the nation, largely because whites feared that black ministers

After leaving the U.S., actor Ira Aldridge (left and above) achieved fame in the great theaters of Europe.

would exercise too much authority over their slave congregations, and might cause trouble on the plantations. Between 1820 and 1860 the South passed laws against or discouraged free black participation in religious life. In Charleston, for example, a campaign against the A.M.E. Church, which had made much progress there, succeeded, in 1822, in stopping its activities. By the time of the Civil War, white pressure had greatly lessened the effectiveness of the black churches in the South.

There was also considerable opposition to the education of free blacks, particularly in the South where laws were passed against education of both slaves and free blacks. Even so, many blacks obtained education in the South, sometimes secretly and sometimes with the knowledge of the authorities. In Baltimore, for instance, the Bethel Charity School for blacks flourished for several years after it was founded in 1816. In Charleston, South Carolina, there were laws against the education of blacks, but an 1850 survey showed that a large number of black adults could read and write. In New Orleans, some free blacks attended white schools; others gained education through the efforts of the free black population.

CLOTEL;

OR,

THE PRESIDENT'S DAUGHTER:

A Narrative of Slave Life

IN

THE UNITED STATES.

BY

WILLIAM WELLS BROWN,

A FUGITIVE SLAVE, AUTHOR OF "THREE YEARS IN EUROPE.

With a Sketch of the Author's Life.

"We hold these truths to be self-evident: that all men are created equal; that they are endowed by their Creator with certain inalienable rights, and that among these are LIFE, LIBERTY, and the PURSUIT OF HAPPINESS." — *Declaration of American Independence.*

William Wells Brown was the first black to write a novel. The plot concerned the illegitimate black daughter of a U.S. president.

In the West, too, acquisition of education was difficult. In 1829 Ohio passed a law which barred blacks from the public schools. Twenty years later the state provided for separate schools, but appropriated only a small amount for the black schools. The same situation obtained in Indiana and Illinois. Michigan and Wisconsin had a better educational record but until the Civil War few blacks in these areas were educated at public expense.

Similar forces were at work in the North. When Prudence Crandall, a white Quaker teacher, opened a school for black females in Canterbury, Connecticut, in 1833, the villagers tried to burn it. The state passed a law against free establishment of schools for blacks, and Prudence Crandall was convicted. She appealed the case successfully, but whites attacked the school, which was closed for the protection of the students. In the village of Canaan, New Hampshire, the opening of integrated Noyes Academy in 1835 brought an unusual response from angry white villagers. After failing in one attack on the school, the villagers returned with men from other towns and, with one hundred yoke of oxen, pulled the school to a swamp a half mile away.

The Revolutionary War was a major factor in the development of educational opportunities for blacks. In 1787 the Manumission Society established the New York African Free School, which became

Edmonia Lewis was a famous sculptress. Norbert Rillieux's process (below) for refining sugar was patented.

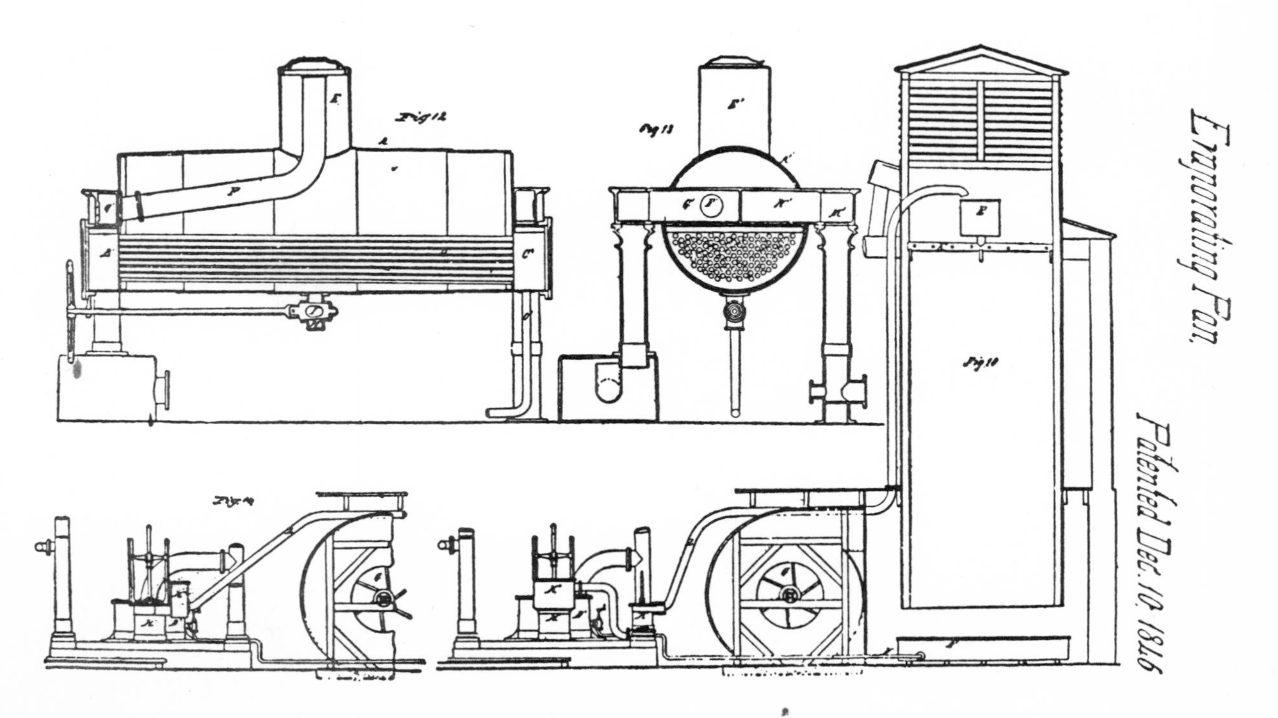

one of the best known schools for blacks of its time. The school's enrollment, which did not exceed sixty students during its first ten years of operation, was up to five hundred by 1820.

During the nineteenth century, educational opportunities gradually widened. In New England, New York, and Pennsylvania, schools for blacks became common. The first such school, in Washington, D.C., was built in 1807 by three former slaves. It wasn't until 1824, however, that a black teacher, John Adams, taught in the District of Columbia. In 1800 the city of Boston refused to establish a school for blacks, but black citizens organized a school which flourished for many years. The city finally opened an elementary school for black children in 1820. In New Orleans, the *Ecole des Orphelins Indigents*, or School for Needy Orphans, founded in 1840, was supported by such wealthy free blacks as Thomy Lafon, Madame Couvent and Aristide Mary. In Virginia and North Carolina some free blacks were taught by whites and other free blacks. By 1850, there were about one thousand free blacks in schools in New Orleans, and fourteeen hundred in Baltimore. Of the two thousand free blacks in Boston, almost fifteen hundred were in school. By the coming of the Civil War there were 32,629 blacks in schools in the U.S.A. and its territories.

During this same period, there were advances in higher education. In 1826 John B. Russwurm became the first black student to graduate from an American institution of higher learning, Bowdoin College in Maine. Before the coming of the Civil War, blacks were attending Harvard Medical School, Oberlin, Rutland College, and other white institutions. Three outstanding black educators, Charles L. Reason, William G. Allen and George B. Vashon, held for a time the professorship of belles lettres at Central College in McGrawville, New York.

An important step toward the establishment of a system of widespread higher education of blacks came in 1851 when a young New York white woman, Myrtilla Miner, went to the District of Columbia and established what was later to become a college bearing her name. In 1842 the Institute for Colored Youth was incorporated in Philadelphia under the leadership of Charles L. Reason. Seven years later Rev. Charles Avery's bequest of $300,000 led to the establishment, in Allegheny City, Pennsylvania, of the Avery college for blacks. Lincoln University in Pennsylvania began as Ashmun Institute

John Russwurm was the first black college graduate and a cofounder of the black press.

MOSS ENG. CO. N.Y.

under Presbyterian sponsorship. It was incorporated in 1854 and admitted students two years later. In 1855 the Cincinnati Conference of the Methodist Episcopal Church decided to raise money for a college which was incorporated the following year as Wilberforce University. Most of the students during its first years were the mulatto children of Southern planters. The school was later reorganized under the sponsorship of the African Methodist Episcopal church.

To provide themselves with institutional means for economic and cultural self-help, free blacks began organizing many cultural, fraternal, and benevolent associations shortly after the Revolutionary War. Lodges and other such organizations, in addition to providing these benefits, afforded members valuable experience in leadership and organization and were a strong force for morality and discipline. The African Society, organized in 1796 by forty-four blacks in Boston, said it would take "no one into the society who shall commit any injustice or outrage against the laws of their country."

But white distrust of any association of blacks that might foment discontent continued to work against blacks. By 1835 blacks were forbidden to hold meetings of benevolent societies in Virginia, Maryland, North Carolina, and several other states. Maryland law said blacks could not have "lyceums, lodges, fire companies, or literary, dramatic, social, moral, or charitable societies." The trend toward the forming of organizations had, however, already grown to great proportions. In 1821, for instance, there was only one benevolent society in Baltimore; fourteen years later there were thirty-five. During the forty years before the Civil War many benevolent societies and fraternal groups were formed in both the North and the South. In 1843 Peter Ogden helped organize The Grand United Order of Odd Fellows, which became one of the major black fraternal groups.

During the eighteenth century literary and artistic works by free blacks began to appear. In time, poets, playwrights, historians, and newspaper editors expressed the aspirations of blacks.

The most noted black literary figure before the Revolutionary War was poetess Phillis Wheatley. Another poet of the same period was Jupiter Hammon, whose *Salvation by Christ with Penitential Cries*, published in 1760, was probably the first published work by an American black.

Samuel Cornish, a Presbyterian minister, was a cofounder of the black press, and an organizer in the Negro Convention movement.

Much of the journalistic writing by blacks was abolitionist in sentiment. The first black newspaper, *Freedom's Journal*, founded in 1827 by Samuel Cornish and John B. Russwurm, included in its opening editorial the promise that "we would not be unmindful of our brethren who are still in the iron fetters of bondage." In 1841 Frederick Douglass used two thousand dollars in contributions from abolitionists in England to begin his newspaper, *The North Star*, named after the guide slaves used to travel to freedom. In 1850 the newspaper's name was changed to *Frederick Douglass' Paper*. Though its original purpose was to attack slavery, it gradually became a generally political organ carrying material on matters that did not necessarily relate primarily to blacks. Other publications of the time included *The Mystery* in Pittsburgh; *The Colored Man's Journal* and the *Anglo-African Magazine* in New York, and the *Mirror of the Times* in San Francisco.

In general, writings against the institution of slavery gave blacks their widest opportunity for self-expression. The most important writers were largely former slaves who had either run away or been freed by their masters. Frederick Douglass, wrote two autobiographies, *Narrative of the Life of Frederick Douglass* in 1845 and, ten years later, *My Bondage and My Freedom*.

Other former slaves also wrote slave narratives. William Wells Brown described his foreign travels in *Three Years in Europe*, published in 1852, and was the first American black man to write a play, *The Escape; or a Leap to Freedom*, which appeared in 1858. He also wrote the first novel by a black. *Clotel, or the President's Daughter*, was published in London in 1853 and in the United States the following year. Another former slave, James W. C. Pennington, who had received the degree of doctor of divinity from the University of Heidelberg, published a *Textbook of the Origin and History of the Colored People* in 1841. He later wrote an autobiography, *The Fugitive Blacksmith*. William C. Nell's *Services of the Colored Americans in the Wars of 1776 and 1812* first appeared in 1852, then was reissued three years later in a revised edition titled *The Colored Patriots of the American Revolution with Sketches of Several Distinguished Colored Persons to which Is Added a Brief Survey of the Condition and Prospects of Colored Americans*. Martin R. Delaney, a leading black physician who made sociological studies of blacks in the United States and Africa, published in 1852 *The Condition, Elevation, Emigration, and Destiny of the Colored People of the United States*. Seven installments of his novel *Blake; or the Huts of America*, were published in the *Anglo-African Magazine* in 1859.

The first internationally famous black

Tom Molineaux, born a slave in Virginia, was America's first champion boxer.

actor, Ira Aldridge, began his career in small roles in Shakespearean plays presented at the African Grove Theater in New York. Aldridge, son of a Presbyterian minister, later studied acting in England and became a star in Shakespearean roles. He was awarded medals by the kings of Prussia and Austria in recognition of his great talent. He died before he could carry out a planned tour of the U.S.

Other artistic figures who achieved fame in the mid-nineteenth century were singer Elizabeth Taylor; Frances E. W. Harper, a poetess and speaker; Edmonia Lewis, a sculptress; and Patrick Reason, a painter and engraver.

In the field of science, a free black of considerable gifts was Norbert Rillieux of New Orleans. Sent by his wealthy father to study in France, he taught applied mechanics in Paris, and by the age of twenty-four had published many scientific papers. In 1846 Rillieux revolutionized the sugar-refining industry in Europe and America by perfecting a vacuum evaporating pan. He established the principles on which modern industrial evaporation is based. Rillieux submitted a complicated proposal for a sewerage system for New Orleans, which was not, however, accepted.

THE IDEA of sending free blacks back to Africa, first mentioned early in the eighteenth century, remained a live issue, partly because some whites believed free blacks threatened the institution of slavery. But not all who favored colonization did so for that reason. Some favored colonization either because they were convinced that blacks could never adjust to Western civilization, or because they believed that returning blacks would take Christianity and civilization to Africa. Some whites in the North thought a decrease in the number of blacks would make it easier for them to find jobs.

A major impetus for the colonization movement was provided in 1815 by black sea captain Paul Cuffe who took thirty-eight blacks to Sierra Leone on one of his own ships and at his own expense. Two years later the American Colonization Society was organized. It made plans to establish a black colony in Africa with the help of federal and state governments.

At first, only free blacks were taken to Africa by the society. But after 1827 masters began freeing slaves to be taken away to the new colony of Liberia. By 1830 the society had settled 1,420 blacks there. Most of those who accepted the invitation to go were free blacks from states in the South who were tired of a seemingly hopeless battle for fair treatment. In the North, practically all blacks were opposed to colonization, particularly of Africa. In 1817,

Black marksmen helped defeat the British at the Battle of New Orleans.

three thousand blacks of Philadelphia, led by Richard Allen and James Forten, met and urged "the humane and benevolent inhabitants of Philadelphia" to reject colonization as an "outrage, having no other object in view than the benefit of the slaveholding interests of the country." Additional meetings were held in other Northern cities in the next ten years.

In 1831 some abolitionists who had supported the idea of colonization turned against it. Reports that were received from Liberia indicated unhappiness among the colonists because of the high cost of living and mismanaged colonial affairs. By the decade before the Civil War the American Colonization Society had ceased to be a viable organization.

The Negro Convention movement was an outgrowth of blacks' desire to establish a basis for united and effective action to alleviate racial troubles. The movement began in 1830 when delegates from New York, Pennsylvania, Maryland, Delaware, and Virginia met in Philadelphia to "devise ways and means for the bettering of our condition." This first meeting considered ideas including raising funds to establish a college for black students and the encouragement of blacks to move to Canada. The following year, a Negro Convention passed resolutions favoring the continued settling of blacks in Canada, and opposing the plans of the American Colonization Society. Other conventions met annually for several years, and less frequently afterward.

In the decade before the Civil War the increasing oppression of blacks prompted the holding of more conventions than ever before. At one of the most important, held in 1853 in Rochester, New York, a National Council of Colored People was formed. By 1854 the mood of the conventions was such that many delegates were willing to openly sanction violence. A clause in one resolution declared that "those who, without crime, are outlawed by any Government can owe no allegiance to its enactments . . . we advise all oppressed to adopt the motto, 'Liberty or Death.' "

Thus, America's free black population, having tried repeatedly to attain their rights and having been repeatedly rebuffed, faced the coming of the Civil War largely united in their determination to gain full citizenship in the nation they had helped to build.

Blacks made up one-fifth of the American crews in some Great Lakes battles in the War of 1812

John Jones was a well-to-do businessman in Chicago.

8

Resistance

SLAVERY WAS NEVER SECURE in America. Its existence depended on the cultural and physical repression of blacks and whites, both of which groups suffered for the benefit of a slaveholding minority. Book burning and other attempts at thought control became common in the American South during the nineteenth century. Slavery fostered self-delusion, hypocrisy, and violence. It perverted religion and the law. The slave system, in addition to being morally corrupt, was economically detrimental to the majority of Southerners, a fact that the slaveholders had to hide from the majority at any cost.

From the beginning, slaveholders were troubled by resistance. This resistance usually took the form of escape by individual slaves. Some of these slaves joined with others to set up settlements in mountains, forests and swamps in the South.

There were also individual whites who, disagreeing with the concept of slavery, either helped ease the burden of slaves or aided them in escaping. Quakers in the South sometimes freed their slaves, gave them money, and helped them to begin successful lives as free men.

The control of slaves was never complete. Though masters could beat and even kill the people they held in bondage, they could not be sure that such measures would not precipitate revenge in the form of sabotage, arson, or murder. Many slaveowners were unable to understand the slave's desire for freedom, and attributed their running away to a "slave sickness." One slave, Henry Bibb, took the trouble to explain in a letter to his master, W. H. Gatewood of Bedford, Kentucky, why he had run away:

> You may perhaps think hard of us for running away from slavery, but as to myself, I have but one apology to make, which is this: I have only to regret that I did not start at an earlier period. . . . To be compelled to stand by and see you whip and slash my wife without mercy when I could afford her no protection, not even by offering myself to suffer the lash in her place, was more than I felt it to be the duty of a slave husband to endure, while the way was open to Canada. My infant child was also frequently flogged by Mrs. Gatewood, for crying, until its skin was bruised literally purple. This kind of treatment was what drove me from home and family to seek a better home for them.

The Revolutionary War, which enunciated and underlined in blood the doctrine of man's inherent equality, gave further impetus to the drive for freedom. The valuable service of slaves in the armed forces also sparked a fresh desire in free blacks and whites to assist slaves in their quest for liberty.

But it was not until the nineteenth century that a strong antislavery movement developed. By that time, ministers, editors, and other opinion makers in the North and the South were speaking out against slavery. But this surge of antislavery rhetoric caused a strong defensive reaction on the part of Southerners who saw a threat to the stability of the institution on which their wealth and style of life were based. While abolitionist sentiment continued to grow in the North, the South stopped at nothing to suppress all manifestations of public discontent.

The abolitionists' activities in the North were opposed by proslavery sentiment that was still strong, but against which arguments and the law could be mar-

Frederick Douglass, a runaway slave, was a leader in the antislavery movement.

shaled. Abolitionists argued that slavery was against the American way of life. Slaves, they pointed out, could not seek employment, had no religious freedom, no marriage or family rights or legal protection, and little opportunity for education. Slavery was economically bad for the country, they argued, because slaves could not be expected to be efficient, and therefore the plantation economy caused great waste of physical and human resources. Slavery, they said, was dangerous to the peace and safety of the nation. They said fear of possible slave uprisings was turning the South into an armed camp, and repression there resulted in bloodshed on both sides.

But in the North, too, proslavery reaction was often harsh. Elijah P. Lovejoy was forced out of St. Louis for questioning the lenient sentence of two persons accused of burning a black alive. He later settled in Alton, Illinois, where he was killed by a mob which destroyed the press on which he printed the abolitionist *Alton Observer*.

The first identifiable white group to actively befriend the black slaves and to work for the ending of slavery was the Quakers, who had aided runaways during the eighteenth century. In 1820 William Swaim was enunciating Quaker opposition to slavery in his *Patriot*, published at Greensboro, North Carolina. Later, Quaker Thomas Garrett of Delaware paid out a fortune in fines for aiding runaway slaves. After one conviction the old man said to the judge: "Thee hasn't left me a dollar, but I wish to say to thee, and to all in the courtroom, that if anyone knows of a fugitive who wants shelter, and a friend, send him to Thomas Garrett and he will befriend him."

The rise of abolitionist sentiment in the

Photograph shows the study in Frederick Douglass's home.

nineteenth century was largely the outgrowth of agitation for abolition that had long been carried on by blacks. Before the Revolutionary War, slaves had brought actions in court against their masters for the freedom which they regarded as their right even before the Declaration of Independence proclaimed the "unalienable rights" of men. During the war and afterward, blacks petitioned state and local governments to outlaw the slave trade and to begin moving toward emancipation.

Before 1800, such free black leaders as Prince Hall, Benjamin Banneker, Absalom Jones and Richard Allen had denounced slavery strongly. Organizations such as the Free African Society issued strong and continuous calls for abolition. These forceful arguments made it clear that slavery was not going to gradually die out, as some theorized.

Benjamin Lundy (top), Wendell Phillips, and William Lloyd Garrison were major antislavery activists.

To work more effectively against the institution of slavery, blacks began organizing antislavery societies. By 1830 blacks had fifty antislavery groups. There was an active group in New Haven, and several in Boston, Philadelphia, and New York. One of the strongest at the time was in New York. It was named after the famous English antislavery leader Thomas Clarkson. Prominent among organizers of such groups was the Reverend Moses Dickson, who established the order of Twelve Knights and Daughters of Tabor in 1844 in Cincinnati. This group did not exclude violence from the means by which it intended to overthrow slavery.

The rise of organized black resistance to slavery frightened the South. Slaveholders were especially alarmed by the activities of black abolitionists like David Walker. Walker, a North Carolina free black, had moved north to Boston where he became a seller of second-hand clothes. In 1829 he published an essay that was to make him the man most feared and hated by Southern slaveholders. The essay was titled *David Walker's Appeal, In Four Articles; Together with a Preamble to the Coloured Citizens of the World But in Particular, and Very expressly, To those of the United States of America.* In it Walker expressed his conclusion that slave revolts were justified for the ending of that hated institution, and he warned white Americans to head off violence by ending slavery.

To blacks Walker directed an exhortation to revolt:

> Are we Men!! I ask you . . . are we MEN? Did our creator make us to be slaves to dust and ashes like ourselves? Are they not dying worms as well as we? . . . How we could be so *submissive* to a gang of men, whom we cannot tell whether they are as good as ourselves or not, I never conceive. . .

The abolitionist newpaper *The Liberator* revealed the horrors of slavery.

THE LIBERATOR.

VOL. I.] WILLIAM LLOYD GARRISON AND ISAAC KNAPP, PUBLISHERS. [NO. 22.

BOSTON, MASSACHUSETTS.] OUR COUNTRY IS THE WORLD—OUR COUNTRYMEN ARE MANKIND. [SATURDAY, MAY 28, 1831.

America is more our country than it is the whites'—we have enriched it with our *blood and tears.* The greatest riches in all America have arisen from our blood and tears: And they will drive us from our property and homes, which we have earned with our blood.

When copies of the *Appeal* were found in Southern cities from Virginia to Louisiana, slaveholders panicked. Importation of copies was forbidden. The state of Georgia offered $10,000 for Walker if he was taken alive, and $1,000 if dead.

A mob attacks William Lloyd Garrison after an antislavery lecture in Boston in 1835.
The drawing at right appeared above a poem, "My Countrymen in Chains!" published by John Greenleaf Whittier.

But the spirit of resistance exemplified by Walker in his *Appeal* continued to grow. The patient moderation that waited for the attitudes of slaveholders to change gradually yielded to a demanding impatience for blacks to take their fate into their own hands. In 1843 the Reverend Henry Highland Garnet of New York, a former slave, issued a call at a Buffalo black convention for slaves to revolt:

Brethen, arise, arise! Strike for your lives and liberties. Now is the day and the hour. Let every slave throughout the land do this, and the days of slavery are numbered. You cannot be more op-

pressed than you have been—you cannot suffer greater cruelties than you have already. Rather die freemen than live to be slaves. Remember that you are four millions.

Garnet's call for outright revolt was turned down by the convention by a single vote. After the Civil War this fiery orator became president of Avery College in Pennsylvania and served as U.S. Minister to Liberia.

IN THE EARLY NINETEENTH CENTURY, economic developments heightened the divisions in the country. Industrial devel-

Theodore Dwight Weld (below) was one of the antislavery leaders who formed abolition societies in the 1840's and 1850's. Blacks and whites attended an antislavery meeting (right) in Baltimore.

opment in the North tended to make people more interdependent and to foster a growing spirit of social reform. In the South, on the other hand, plantation economy fostered a social order in which power was separated from the people.

The general humanitarian movement gave impetus to the antislavery move-

ment. There was a growing concern for the underprivileged that was manifested in crusades for better working conditions in England and in the search for a better life in America. Closely related to such crusades were the movement for women's rights, peace, temperance, and other reform programs. Black abolitionists, who were received enthusiastically in Europe, helped link the humanitarian movement there with the reform and antislavery movements in the U.S.A. William Wells Brown, Frederick Douglass, and Sojourner Truth were among the many black American reformers who extended their battle beyond the issue of slavery.

Robert Purvis, a well-to-do black, headed Philadelphia's first vigilance committee.

Douglass, who supported the still unpopular movement for women's rights, was the only male speaker at the first women's rights convention. Sojourner Truth was a persuasive speaker for the abolitionist cause as well as for temperance, prison reform, better conditions for working people, and the granting of voting rights to women. In May, 1851, the tall, gaunt, deep-voiced woman spoke at a women's rights convention in refutation of men who said that women should not vote because they are mentally inferior to men:

> That man over there say that women needs to be helped into carriages, and lifted over ditches, and to have the best place everywhere. Nobody ever helps me into carriages, or over mud puddles, or gives me any best place! And ain't I a woman? Look at me! Look at my arm! I have ploughed, and planted, and gathered into barns, and no man could head me! And ain't I a woman? I could work as much and eat as much as a man—when I could get it—and bear the lash as well! And ain't I a woman? I have borne thirteen children, and seen them most all sold off to slavery, and when I cried out with my mother's grief, none but Jesus heard me! And ain't I a woman?

White women's rights leaders were active in the antislavery campaign. Susan B. Anthony, for instance, opened her home in Rochester, New York, to slaves fleeing to Canada.

Contemporary with the rise of militant abolitionism was a great religious revival in the West, which had the effect of directing many people toward social reform. Abolitionists could take advantage of this by pointing out that slavery, contrary to the teachings of many proslavery ministers, was against the teachings of Christianity. Christ, said the abolitionists, taught that all men are brothers and that all are created in the image of God.

While Frederick Douglass, the leading black abolitionist, toured Europe in the 1840s to raise money for the antislavery cause, he also spoke out for Irish freedom, world peace, and political rights for all, regardless of sex, wealth, or color. Said he: "I have held all my life, and shall hold to the day of my death, that the fundamental and everlasting objection to slavery, is not that it sinks a Negro to the condition of a brute, but that it sinks a *man* to that condition."

The growth of reform activity and the increasing emancipation of slaves in the North were occurring while slavery was becoming more important in the South because of the cotton market. More and more, Southerners reiterated the four basic tenets by which they justified slavery: that slave labor was essential to the economic development of the South; that blacks were inherently inferior and destined for subordination; that the church had long sanctioned slavery for converting "heathens" to Christianity; and that the white race, rather than degenerating because of slavery, as abolitionists charged, had achieved a unique and high culture. In 1826 Edward Brown published his *Notes on the Origin and Necessity of Slavery*, which said that "slavery has ever

Charles Lenox Remond, was a lecturer for the American Anti-Slavery Society.

been the stepping ladder by which countries have passed from barbarism to civilization. . . It appears . . . to be the only state capable of bringing the love of independence and of ease, inherent in man, to the disciplined shelter necessary to his physical wants. . . ."

The escalation of defensive reaction to antislavery activity had its most basic effect in that free questioning and free speech on the slavery issue disappeared from the South. People who disagreed with the proslavery dogma were forced out of the region. Scholars and artists who either wanted to uphold slavery or who thought that their well-being depended on a pretense of advocacy produced essays, poems, and songs favoring the institution. The colleges became bastions of proslavery and secessionist doctrine. In their zeal to protect the institution of slavery, state and local governments burned books and newspapers, spied on abolitionists, and either abetted violence and murder or closed their eyes to it. A vigilance committee of South Carolina tried to stop people from reading abolitionist literature by offering $1,500 for the arrest of any persons who distributed David Walker's *Appeal* or the *Liberator*, published by William Lloyd Garrison.

Many educators and ministers joined in the defense of slavery. Because many Northern churches voiced disapproval of the institution, denominations split along sectional lines. By 1845 there were separate Northern and Southern subdivisions of the Baptist, Methodist, and Presbyterian denominations.

Henry Highland Garnet called for open revolt against slavery.

Harriet Tubman conducted some three hundred slaves to freedom on the Underground Railroad.

By this time, the federal government had taken a strong proslavery posture. In 1835 a Charleston mob broke into the post office and burned abolitionist newspapers. When no action was taken, Southern postmasters began regularly taking abolitionist literature out of the mails. In 1835 President Andrew Jackson forbade the Post Office to deliver abolitionist mail in the South.

Violence became common. A Georgian who subscribed to the *Liberator* was dragged from his home by a mob who tarred and feathered him, set him on fire, ducked him in the river, then tied him to a post and whipped him. A white man in Petersburg, Virginia, who said that "black men have, in the abstract, a right to their freedom," was lashed and ordered to leave town. Several whites in Georgia and South Carolina were murdered for the "crime" of mixing with blacks.

But mere repression of Southern opinion adverse to slavery was not enough. The leaders of the slaveholding states tried to extend their sway to the North. In Macon, Georgia, $12,000 was offered for the capture of abolitionist Arthur Tappan of New York, and in New Orleans there was a price of $20,000 on his head.

Because the South's campaign to wipe out adverse opinion was so determined, many abolitionists left the South, a good number heading west. Deprived of their voices, their former neighbors in the South gradually came to believe that proslavery feeling was virtually unanimous, and that attacks on it came only from wild-eyed anti-South ranters in the North. This tended to identify "antislavery" with

Sojourner Truth spoke fervently against slavery.

"anti-South," and to make the antipathy of Southerners toward the North even greater.

Sectional animosity had been further intensified by the conflict over the conditions under which Missouri and other potential new states would be admitted into the Union. The Missouri Compromise, passed in 1820 after heated debate, had barred slavery from new states north of the Ohio River.

The appearance of what has come to be called militant abolitionism occurred in the early 1830s. Leading up to the beginning of a new wave of activism were such events as David Walker's publication of his *Appeal*, the publication of Garrison's antislavery publication, *Liberator*, and

Former slave Samuel Ringgold Ward and poetess Frances E. W. Harper were active abolitionists.

the Nat Turner insurrection. These were manifestations of growing and converging waves of resistance to slavery.

Abolitionists increasingly adopted the militant stance that a "higher law" justified circumvention or outright breaking of the laws of the nation in order to achieve justice for enslaved blacks. White abolitionists openly praised the slave revolt led by Turner, in contrast to abolitionists' usual practice of advocating only resistance that was passive or at least not aggressively violent. Jabez Hammond of New York said in 1839 that only force would end slavery, urging that black military schools be set up in Canada and Mexico.

But even in the North there was oppo-

A white mob killed abolitionist newspaper editor Elijah P. Lovejoy in Alton, Illinois, and destroyed his press.

sition to this wave of militancy. Merchants whose business was largely dependent on the existence of slavery, and white workers who saw the freeing of slaves as a threat to their ability to compete successfully for employment, were made fearful and angry by the emergence of an increasingly united movement by persons seemingly determined to eliminate slavery at the cost even of their lives. With their positions threatened, these groups reacted violently. Supposedly "respectable" Boston merchants led a mob that almost killed Garrison. In October, 1835, gangs of rowdy whites broke up abolitionist meetings in New York, Massachusetts, and Vermont.

When it became clear that Southern slaveowners were not going to allow the demise of slavery, and that the rest of the nation had neither the inclination nor the means to bring about its phasing out, many abolitionists abandoned gradualism. Garrison said the only solution was immediate and unconditional abolition. Before assuming his leadership among white abolitionists, Garrison had spent time in jail for an allegedly libelous attack on a ship's captain who carried slaves to New Orleans. He later worked on the abolitionist publication, *Genius of Universal Emancipation*. Incensed by the vacillating and compromising tone that many antislavery spokesmen adopted, he became the foremost spokesman for militant abolitionism. In January, 1831, he began producing the *Liberator*. Said Garrison of his efforts to turn opinion against slavery: "I will be as harsh as truth, and as uncompromising as justice. On this subject I do not wish to think, to speak, or write, with moderation . . . I am in earnest; I will not equivocate; I will not excuse. I will not retreat a single inch. And I will be heard."

No institution or person was sacred to Garrison. He once publicly burned a copy of the American Constitution, which he called "a bloodstained document" because it treated black humans as property. These actions so frightened slaveowners that in October, 1831, the Georgia legislature offered $4,000 for Garrison's arrest.

Particularly influential in the northeast, Garrison was named leader of the New England Anti-Slavery Society when it was formed in 1831 by fifteen persons dedicated to the attainment of immediate emancipation of slaves. Among prominent New Englanders who regarded Garrison as their leader in the fight for abolition were poet John Greenleaf Whittier, Wendell Phillips, Lucretia Mott, Lydia Maria Child, and Maria Weston Chapman.

Garrison was strong in his condemnation of the American Colonization Society, which, with the cooperation of the state and federal governments, was working to move American free blacks to the new colony of Liberia in Africa. The colonization society, said Garrison, "inflicted a great injury upon the free and slave population by strengthening the prejudices of the people, by discouraging the education of those who are free, by securing passage of severe laws, and by lulling the whole country into a deep sleep."

Wendell Phillips and other abolitionists spoke frequently to audiences at Boston Common.

Garrisonism met more opposition than other forms of abolitionism. In the Border States and the West, James Birney and Theodore Weld remained popular leaders who counseled more moderate approaches, including insistence on political action. In 1837 Weld, in his *The Bible Against Slavery*, argued strongly against slavery, on religious grounds.

In the North and West, the growing sentiment for abolition resulted in the formation of many local organizations that worked toward that end by disseminating information against the institution of slavery, raising money for abolitionist work, or giving direct aid to escaping slaves. The membership of these organizations often included the leading citizens of a community. Boston's vigilance committee, for instance, was formed to thwart the efforts of slavecatchers sent north to bring back fugitives. Among its members were writer James Russell Lowell, Rev. Theodore Parker, educator Samuel G. Howe, and lawyer and novelist Richard Henry Dana.

A national abolitionist organization, the American Anti-Slavery Society, was organized in 1833. Arthur Tappan, a wealthy New York merchant, was its first president. Among its leaders were Theodore Weld, James G. Birney, William Goodell, Joshua Leavitt, Elizur Wright, Samuel May, and Beriah Green. Encouraged by the abolition of slavery in the

Whites opposed to the antislavery movement burned the Pennsylvania Hall in Philadelphia.

British Empire, the society worked within the American system to bring about abolition in the U.S.A. New York members published four periodicals: *Human Rights*, *Anti-Slavery Record*, *Emancipator*, and *Slave's Friend*, all of which were distributed widely in the North, and, where possible, in the South. The society had many agents who organized local units to raise money for the abolitionist cause. By 1836 it had seventy lecturers largely recruited from the ministry, theological seminaries, and the universities.

Though the society steadily gained

strength, many militants deplored its moderate practices. The society was unwilling to let women act as leaders of the movement, and its members were wary of criticizing churches that did not speak out clearly against slavery. In 1839 Garrison tried to take over the organization. In the following year his followers were elected to important offices at a convention, and women were given places of responsibility. Garrison's increasing influence, and his demand that members follow his leadership and boycott popular elections, drove many whites and blacks out of the society. New York abolitionists who were opposed to Garrison's bid for power organized, under the leadership of Lewis Tappan, the American and Foreign Anti-Slavery Society. This organization sought to end slavery by appealing to morality, and said that political action was needed to change laws that stood in the way of emancipation.

In 1840, members of this society became the nucleus, with the Tappan wing of the American Anti-Slavery Society, of the antislavery Liberty party. This party nominated James G. Birney for president in two successive elections, but he only polled sixty thousand votes. It seemed that most citizens were unwilling to vote for a candidate who ran on the issue of slavery alone.

Though the abolitionists in 1840 were split between two national bodies, state and local organizations continued to be effective in keeping agents in the field, publishing newspapers, and distributing antislavery literature.

Braving a winter storm, fugitive slaves reach an Underground Railroad station.

In 1848 another attempt was made to win political control of the nation when the Liberty party merged into the Free Soil party, dedicated to preventing any extension of slavery. This did not seriously challenge the Democratic party, which continued in power and continued to garner the favor of slaveholders. It remained for the Republican party to take advantage of the knowledge gained from the defeats of the Liberty party, and to broaden its appeal to voters other than confirmed abolitionists.

Blacks played important parts throughout the period of formation of antislavery groups. Vigilance committees that raised funds to help slaves were often dominated by blacks. David Ruggles became secretary of the New York Vigilance Committee in 1835. Robert Purvis headed the first vigilance committee formed in Philadelphia, and was followed in the leadership position by William Still. The first presiding officer of the Philadelphia Female Anti-Slavery Society was a local dentist, Dr. James McCrummell. In 1847 Frederick Douglass was elected president of the New England Anti-Slavery Society. The committee designated to draw up the Declaration of Intentions of the American Anti-Slavery Society met at the Philadelphia home of Frederick A. Hinton, a local black leader. Its first board of managers included Peter Williams, Robert Purvis, George B. Vashon, Abraham Shadd and James McCrummell. Among blacks who promoted the American and Foreign Anti-Slavery Society were Christopher Rush, Samuel Cornish, Charles B. Ray, and James W. C. Pennington.

The first official participation by blacks in a national political convention came at the Liberty party's meeting in Buffalo in 1843. Five years later Frederick Douglass was present at the founding of the Free Soil party, and he later endorsed its candidates in his newspaper. Most free blacks favored taking advantage of the ballot, and many joined the Free Soil party.

THE ANTISLAVERY MOVEMENT used every means to turn the nation away from slavery. The efforts of abolitionists led to a flood of petitions to Congress, but proslavery forces were strong enough to defeat this thrust. In 1836 the House of Representatives adopted the "gag rule," which provided that petitions against slavery would not be brought up for discussion. The rule was seen by abolitionists and many moderates as an unconstitutional denial of the right to petition for redress of grievances. Former President John Quincy Adams was among congressmen

Levi Coffin's house in Wayne County, Indiana, was a major Underground Railroad station.

who fought against the rule, but it was not rescinded until 1845. Another congressman, Representative Joshua Giddings of Ohio, threw the House of Representatives into turmoil by what amounted to a public acknowledgement that slaves had the right to use violence to escape bondage. When slaves revolted aboard the ship "Creole," Representative Giddings opposed treating them as common criminals and praised them for seeking freedom. The House censured him, and he resigned and returned home. But his constituency reelected him and he returned to Congress.

Underground Railroad passengers flee from Maryland to Delaware. At right, fugitives from Norfolk, Virginia, arrive in Philadelphia.

Though the antislavery movement was largely extinguished in the South by intense repression, it flourished in the North, particularly among the intellectual and artistic classes. Northern writers who wrote, spoke, or acted against slavery included Herman Melville, Nathaniel Hawthorne, Ralph Waldo Emerson, Henry

David Thoreau, John Greenleaf Whittier, Henry Wadsworth Longfellow, William Cullen Bryant, and Louisa May Alcott. Colleges produced many antislavery workers. Western Reserve University produced many students who became active in the movement. Oberlin College became an important center of abolitionist activity after a theological seminary was established there with money from such antislavery philanthropists as Arthur and Lewis Tappan of New York. Theodore Dwight Weld influenced many Northern and Southern students at Lane Theological Seminary in Cincinnati to join the cause of abolition. Students from Lane went out to organize groups to help blacks. They taught black youths and participated in the Underground Railroad.

Meanwhile, the atmosphere of repression continued to build in the South. The growth of aggressive abolitionist activity in the North brought to the surface antipathies in many Northerners who before had remained silent on the issue of slavery. Abolitionists continued to be met with violence. By 1850 the idea that force would be needed to overthrow slavery was

Slavecatchers who surrounded a black man's home in Christiana, Pennsylvania, were met by fatal gunfire.

a doctrine increasingly voiced, even in Congress.

More and more antislavery leaders moved to the West. The spread of antislavery doctrine there brought increasing numbers of converts, and inflamed public passions. James Birney, who moved from Kentucky to Ohio, barely escaped with his life when a mob in Cincinnati destroyed his printing press in 1836. Levi Coffin, a Quaker, left North Carolina and carried on abolitionist activities in Indiana.

PARTICIPATION OF BLACKS in the antislavery movement was a critical factor in its success. Many whites who objected to slavery only on vague principle became actively involved in the struggle after meeting black movement leaders. Blacks were among the most effective abolitionist orators, and white abolitionists often introduced black agents to white audiences to show what blacks could attain if given the opportunity. The foremost black orator on abolition was Frederick Douglass. A runaway slave from Maryland, he was introduced to the organized abolition movement in 1841 when he attended an antislavery convention in Nantucket, Massachusetts. He was later employed by several antislavery societies and soon became one of the movement's best known speakers.

Douglass was a speaker and activist. He refused to leave Northern railroad cars that were designated for whites. Said he: "I was often dragged out of my seat, beaten, and severely bruised, by conductors and brakemen." His home in Rochester, New York, was a station on the Underground Railroad. Douglass's arm was once broken by a mob as he spoke against slavery. Douglass was one of many activists who came to believe that the abolition of slavery would require violent conflict. He expressed this philosophy in a speech in 1857.

> The whole history of the progress of human liberty shows that all concessions yet made to her august claims, have been born of earnest struggle. The conflict has been exciting, agitating, all-absorbing, and, for the time being, putting all other tumults to silence. It must do this or it does nothing. If there is no struggle there is no progress. Those who profess to favor freedom and yet deprecate agitation, are men who want crops without plowing up the ground, they want rain without thunder and lightning. They want the ocean without the awful roar of its many waters.
>
> This struggle may be a moral one, or it may be a physical one, and it may be both moral and physical, but it must be a struggle. Power concedes nothing without a demand. It never did and it never will. Find out just what any people will quietly submit to and you have found out the exact measure of injustice and wrong which will be imposed upon them, and these will continue till they are resisted with either words or blows, or with both. The limits of tyrants are prescribed by the endurance of those whom they oppress. In the light of these ideas, Negroes will be hunted at the North, and held and flogged at the South so long as they submit to those devilish outrages, and make no resistance, either moral or physical. Men may not get all they pay for in this world, but they must certainly pay for all they get. If we ever

get free from the oppressions and wrongs heaped upon us, we must pay for their removal. We must do this by labor, by suffering, by sacrifice, and, if needs be, by our lives and the lives of others.

One of the most famous black women in the antislavery movement was Sojourner Truth. Born Isabella Baumfree about 1797, she belonged to a Dutch master in New York, and spoke English with a Dutch accent all her life. She was sold several times, finally becoming the property of John Dumont, who refused to emancipate her when New York freed all its slaves in 1827. She ran away, leaving her children behind. When her son Peter was sold to an Alabama owner at the age of five, she went to court and succeeded in getting him back. Always jealous of her rights, she fought segregation on New York streetcars by refusing to move to the black section until conductors decided it was better to leave her alone.

It was not until 1843 that she decided to leave her job as a domestic servant and travel around the country, spreading her ideas. She adopted a new name, Sojourner Truth, saying: "The Lord gave me Sojourner because I was to travel up and down the land showing the people their sins and being a sign to them. Afterwards I told the Lord I wanted another name, 'cause everybody else had two names; and the Lord gave me Truth, because I was to declare truth unto people." She traveled through New England and the West, impressing audiences by her speech and deep voice, and the moving message of hatred for slavery which she expressed in a religious-mystical manner.

Margaret Garner killed two of her children rather than let slavers return them to bondage. She later drowned herself.

Free blacks provided much of the manpower and the spiritual enthusiasm in the rise of militant abolitionism. When Garrison began publishing his *Liberator*, most of his early subscribers were blacks. One black abolitionist sent Garrison a check for $50, and contributions from blacks helped him make his first voyage to England.

The militant message of the *Liberator* echoed earlier publications by blacks. Robert A. Young in 1829 published his *Ethiopian Manifesto, Issued in Defence of the Blackman's Rights, in the Scale of Universal Freedom.* In it he, like David Walker, prophesied that a messiah would arise with the strength to free his people.

Ellen Craft dressed as a man and posed as the white owner of her husband William as they escaped on a train from Georgia.

At least as important as the publications that were issued by blacks and whites were the black "agents" who toured the country speaking and working for the cause. Among the better known agents, besides Douglass, were Henry Highland Garnet, William Wells Brown, Frances E. W. Harper, Theodore S. Wright, Lunsford Lane, Charles Lenox Remond and his sister Sarah, and Abraham Shadd. Blacks who carried the abolitionist message to England were Douglass, Brown, the Remonds, Pennington, Garnet, William Craft, Samuel Ringgold Ward, Nathaniel Paul, and Alexander Crummell.

Probably no phenomenon was as persistently troublesome to slaveholders as the slaves' unquenchable desire for freedom. Its constant manifestation was a loss of slaves who braved the threat of beatings and death, and the unknown dangers of swamps and mountains, to leave a known state of bondage for an unknown and often tenuous freedom. The growth of an organized movement to increase such loss by aiding slaves seeking freedom caused a rise in sectional hatred in the nation.

In the earliest days of slavery, many slaves who escaped did not leave the region where they had lived. Some slaves formed communities in the swamps and forests for survival. As early as 1672 Virginia passed laws to deal with slaves who ran away and formed armed bands that "committed depredations" on the colony. Most escapes were individual efforts by slaves who decided to take their chances alone rather than to submit to further slavery. With the growth of communities of runaways, the escape of women and children along with the men became more common. George Washington complained in 1786 of a slave, escaping from Alexandria to Philadelphia, "whom a society of Quakers, formed for such purposes, have attempted to liberate." In 1787, Isaac T. Hopper, a white teenager in Philadelphia, began developing a program for helping slaves escaping from the South. A few years later escaped slaves were receiving help in a number of towns in Pennsylvania and New Jersey. By the end of the eighteenth century Philadelphia had become an important center in aiding slaves to escape, largely because of the antislavery work of the Quakers in the city. In the early nineteenth century these efforts spread into western Pennsylvania, Ohio, Illinois, and Indiana.

The year of "incorporation" of the Underground Railroad is sometimes given as 1804. In that year General Thomas Boude, a Revolutionary War officer, bought Stephen Smith and took him to Columbia, Pennsylvania. They were followed by Smith's mother. The Boudes refused to surrender the woman when her owner showed up. The people of Columbia supported the Boudes, and resolved to champion the cause of runaways.

Increasingly, organized efforts on behalf of runaways reached into the South. By 1819 there were well-organized secret methods in effect to get slaves out of North Carolina. By that time sentiment in favor of helping fugitives was strong in Ohio. Gradually, news sifted through, especially to slaves in the Border States, that they would be free if they could get out of the South. Slaves in Kentucky knew that across the Ohio River were the free states of Illinois, Indiana, and Ohio, where they could find help in starting new lives. By the time of the rise of militant abolitionism, the movement was widespread.

There are several stories about how the name Underground Railroad came into common use. One source says that it happened after slave Tice Edwards escaped from his Kentucky master in 1831 and got across the Ohio River. His master, losing all trace of him, said the slave must have "gone off on an underground road."

From 1831—about the time of the rise of militant abolitionism—to the Civil War, the Underground Railroad operated in violation of federal law. Because it was a definite attempt to undermine the system of slavery, on which much of the economy and social order of the South was founded, it became an increasing cause of hatred and strife between the South and the North and West. It is estimated that between 1810 and 1850 the South lost one hundred thousand slaves with a monetary value of more than $30 million.

Underground Railroad lines began on Southern plantations and ran either to the Ohio or upper Mississippi River in the West, or to points in Pennsylvania and New Jersey in the East. It is not known how many persons worked on these lines, but the names of more than 3,200 agents have been identified.

Ohio, because of its geographical posi-

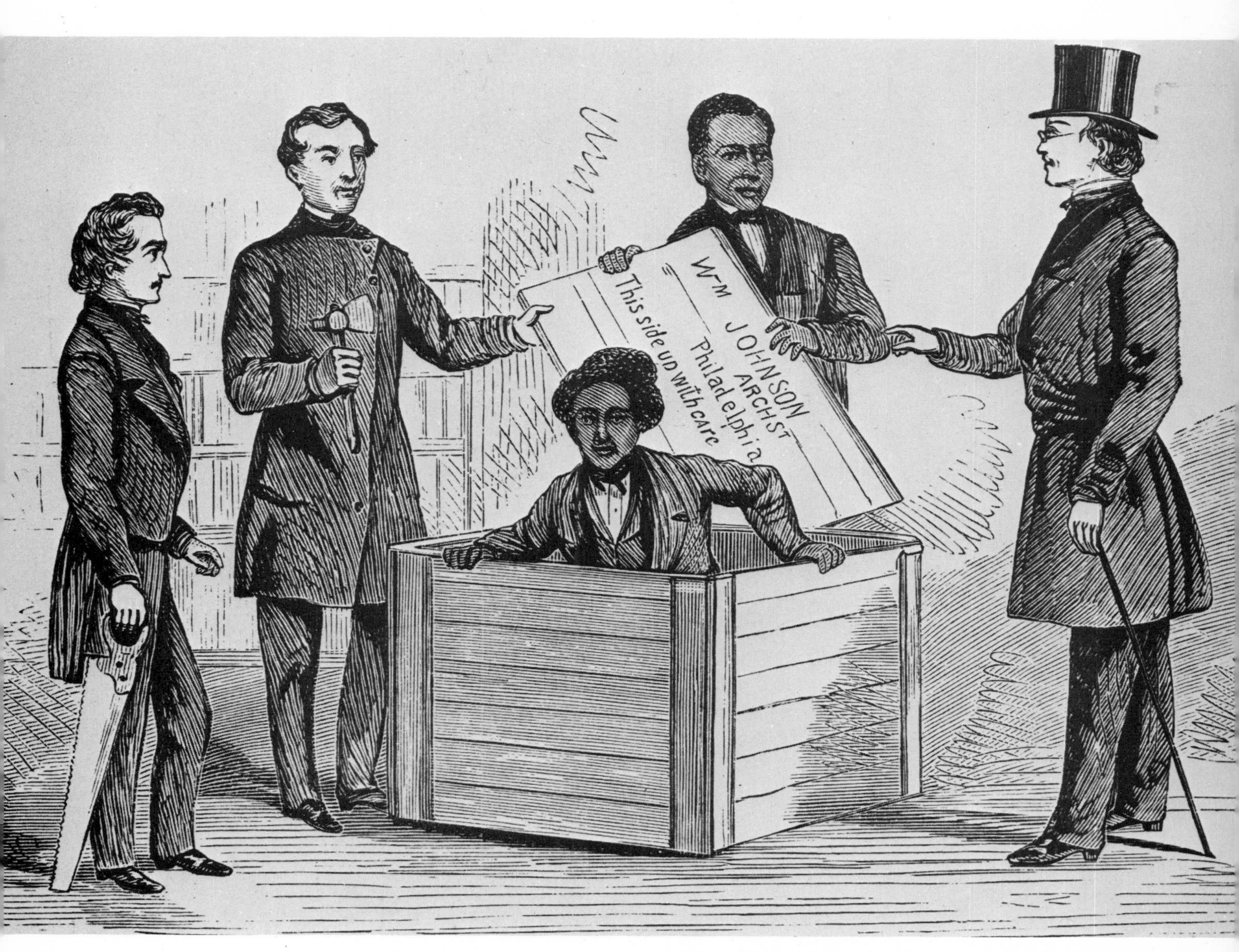

Henry "Box" Brown, a Virginia slave, had himself shipped in a box to Philadelphia and freedom.

Fugitive Slave Bill.

As passed by the Senate and House of Representatives, Sept 12, 1850, and approved September 18, 1850, by President FILLMORE.

AN ACT to amend, and supplementary to the act entitled, "An act respecting fugitives from justice, and persons escaping from the service of their masters," approved, Feb. 12, 1793.

SECTION 1. That persons who have been or may hereafter be, appointed Commissioners in virtue of any act of Congress, by the Circuit Courts of the United States, and who in consequence of such appointments, are authorized to exercise the powers that a *justice of the peace or other magistrate of any of the United States may exercise* in respect to offenders for any crime or offence against the United States, by arresting, imprisoning, or bailing the same under and by virtue of the thirty-third section of the act of the 24th of September, 1789, entitled "An act to establish Judicial Courts of the United States," shall be and are hereby *authorized and required to exercise and discharge all the powers and duties conferred by this act.*

SEC 2. And be it further enacted, That the Superior Court of *each organized territory* of the United States, shall have the same power to appoint commissioners to take acknowledgements of bail and affidavits, and to take depositions of witnesses in civil causes which is now possessed by the Circuit Courts of the United States; all commissioners who shall be appointed for such purposes by the Superior Court of *any organized territory* of the United States, shall possess all the powers and exercise all the duties conferred by law upon the commissioners appointed by the Circuit Court of the United States for similar purposes, and shall moreover exercise and discharge all the powers and duties conferred by this act.

SEC. 3. And be it further enacted, That the circuit courts of the United States and the superior courts of each organized territory of the United States, shall, from time to time, *enlarge the number of commissioners, with a view to afford reasonable facilities to reclaim fugitives from labor*, and to the discharge of the duties imposed by this act.

SEC. 4. And be it further enacted, That the commissioners above named shall have concurrent jurisdiction with the Judges of the Circuit and District Courts of the United States, in their respective circuits and districts within the several States, and the judges of the superior courts of the territories, severally and collectively, in term time and vacation; and shall grant certificates to such claimants, upon *satisfactory proof* being made with *authority to take and remove such fugitives from service or labor*, under the restrictions herein contained, to the State or territory from which such persons may have escaped or fled.

SEC. 5. And be it further enacted, That it shall be the duty of all marshals and deputy marshals to obey and execute all warrants and precepts issued under the provisions of this act, when to them directed; and should any marshal or deputy marshal *refuse* to receive such warrant or other process, when tendered, or use all proper means diligently to execute the same, he shall on conviction thereof, be *fined in the sum of ONE THOUSAND DOLLARS to the use of such claimant* on motion of such claimant, by the circuit or district court of the district of such marshal; and after arrest of such fugitive by such marshal or his deputy, or whilst at any time in his custody under the provisions of this act, should such fugitive escape, *whether* WITH OR WITHOUT THE ASSENT OF SUCH MARSHAL OR HIS DEPUTY, such marshal shall be liable on his official bond to be prosecuted for the benefit of such claimant, for the *full value* of the service or labor of said fugitive in the State, territory or district whence he escaped; and the better to enable the said commissioners when thus appointed, to execute their duties faithfully and efficiently; in conformity with the requirements of the Constitution of the United States and of this act, they are hereby authorized and empowered, *within their counties* respectively to appoint in writing under hands *any one or more suitable persons* from time to time, to execute all such warrants and other process as may be issued by them in the lawful performance of their respective duties, with authority to such commissioners or the person to be appointed by them to execute process as aforesaid, to summon and CALL TO THEIR AID THE BYSTANDERS, or *posse comitatus* of the proper county, when necessary to insure a faithful observance of the clause of the constitution referred to, in conformity with the provisions of this act—AND ALL GOOD CITIZENS ARE HEREBY COMMANDED TO AID AND ASSIST IN THE PROMPT AND EFFICIENT EXECUTION OF THIS WHENEVER THEIR SERVICES MAY BE REQUIRED as aforesaid for that purpose; and said warrants shall run and be executed by said officers anywhere in the State, within which they are executed.

SEC. 6. And be it further enacted, That when a person held to service or labor in any State or territory of the United States, *has heretofore or shall hereafter* escape into another State or territory of the United States, the person or persons to whom such services or labor may be due, or his, her or their agent or attorney, duly authorized, by power of attorney, in writing acknowledged and certified under the seal of some legal officer of court of the State or territory in which the same may be executed, may pursue and reclaim such

A strong Fugitive Slave Law passed by Congress in 1850 was part of a compromise arrangement urged by Henry Clay to quiet slavery controversy.

tion and the fervor of its settlers for abolition, was the chief center of Underground Railroad activities. There were hundreds of stations there and in Illinois and Indiana. The Railroad's routes in Illinois came together in Chicago, and from there slaves went to Canada. Even when fugitives reached Ohio or Pennsylvania there was still danger because planters, slave traders, and sheriffs often chased them northward. In the Philadelphia area there were many stations along routes that led west to Buffalo and east to New England.

The Underground Railroad usually operated at night. Often, escaping slaves assumed disguises. Those with light complexions posed as white persons. In the escape of Mr. and Mrs. William Craft, light-skinned Ellen dressed as a man and posed as the owner of her darker-skinned husband as they rode north on a train. There were instances in which runaways were provided with white babies so that people would believe that they were nurses. Often men posed as women and women as men. In one famous escape, Henry "Box" Brown was shipped from Richmond to the Philadelphia home of William Still by the Adams Express Company. The trip took twenty-six hours. There were other incidents of slaves being put in boxes and shipped by rail or boat.

Underground Railroad "conductors" transported slaves in covered wagons, carriages, and farm wagons with hidden compartments. During the daytime the fugitives were sheltered at "stations"—barns, attics, or other places of hiding. At such stations, which ideally were within ten or twenty miles of the next stop along the line, fugitives could rest, eat, and wait for the next night's trip. Word of the progress of passengers was passed along the "grape vine telegraph" to stations further on. One secret message, mailed by a "conductor" to the next "stationmaster" in 1859, gave needed information to those who knew its true purpose: "By tomorrow evening's mail, you will receive two volumes of 'The Irrepressible Conflict' bound in black. After perusal, please forward..."

A great deal of money was needed to carry on the freeing of the thousands of slaves liberated by means of the Underground Railroad. Fugitives needed food and clothing, and sometimes money for such necessities as boarding a train to escape a pursuer. Some runaways were given enough funds to enable them to appear sufficiently rich so that persons would assume they had been free long enough to accumulate wealth. Vigilance committees, notably in Philadelphia and New York, raised substantial amounts for these purposes. Philanthropists contributed, as did conductors and other Underground Railroad workers. The Quakers were among the leading groups in raising funds to help the Railroad.

One of the most daring and resourceful white conductors was the son of a Virginia slaveholding family. While growing up, John Fairfield came to hate the institution of slavery and decided to live in a free state. Before going North he helped a slave friend to escape to Canada. Whites tried unsuccessfully to arrest him. When blacks heard about his deed, some sought his help in releasing their friends and relatives. Blacks in the North and in Canada would give him money and descriptions of particular slaves, and he would bring them out. In Louisiana, Alabama, Mississippi, Tennessee, and Kentucky, he affected daring rescues. He posed sometimes as a slaveholder, sometimes as a black trader, or a peddler of eggs and poultry. His most spectacular exploit was the taking of twenty-eight slaves to freedom by organizing them into a funeral procession. He was shot during one of his missions, but he continued his work until 1860 when he is thought to have been killed during a slave insurrection in Tennessee.

Blacks were among the most important figures in the operation of the Underground Railroad. One fugitive slave from Kentucky, John Mason, became a conductor, and in one nineteen-month period transported 265 slaves to the Canadian home of black missionary William Mitchell. Mason was captured and sold back into slavery, but he escaped again. He helped a total of about 1,300 slaves escape. Elijah Anderson, the "general superintendent" of the Underground Railroad in northwestern Ohio, worked from 1850 until he died seven years later in Kentucky State Prison. During this period, he transported more than one thousand slaves to freedom. Josiah Henson, born a slave, escaped to Canada with his wife and two children and then returned to the South to help other slaves escape. To avoid arousing suspicion, he once went to Kentucky by a roundabout route that took him through New York, Pennsylvania, and Ohio. He took thirty slaves out of Kentucky to Toledo in a two-week period. A black woman, Jane Lewis, of New Lebanon, Ohio, regularly rowed escaping slaves across the Ohio River.

Persons who entered the South to free slaves showed great courage, but even greater was the courage of those free blacks who lived in the South and acted as

Harriet Beecher Stowe's novel *Uncle Tom's Cabin* convinced hundreds of thousands of readers of the evil of the slave system.

UNCLE TOM'S CABIN;

OR,

LIFE AMONG THE LOWLY.

BY

HARRIET BEECHER STOWE.

VOL. I.

Underground Railroad conductors amid ever present danger of discovery.

In the North, free blacks helped by raising funds, providing shelter and transportation for fugitives, and helping to organize the Underground Railroad's network. Northern blacks prominent in the work were Robert Purvis, William Still, David Ruggles, Frederick Douglass, J. W. Loguen, Martin Delany, and Lewis Hayden.

One of the greatest heroes of the Underground Railroad was Harriet Tubman. She escaped from slavery and brought to freedom her sister, her two children, and her aged mother and father. A frail woman, she suffered from dizzy spells. She could not read or write, but she showed great ingenuity in managing escapes of slaves. After her own escape to the North she said:

> I looked at my hands to see if I was the same person now I was free. There was such a glory over everything! The sun come like gold through the trees and over the fields and I felt like I was in heaven.

Sometimes called "The Moses of her People," Harriet Tubman is said to have gone South nineteen times to bring out more than three hundred slaves. She raised money for her Underground Railroad trips by working as a domestic. She usually began her journeys out of the South on Saturday nights, so that she and the fleeing slaves could get a good head start before Monday. Impatient with cowardice, she carried a gun and threatened to kill any slave who wanted to turn back. She also carried drugs to put to sleep any babies who cried and endangered the group. So incensed did slaveowners become at her work that rewards adding up to $40,000 were offered for her capture.

As early as the latter part of the eighteenth century the escape of slaves prompted special federal legislative action. The first Fugitive Slave Law, enacted in 1793, gave the master of an escaped slave the right to follow and capture him anywhere, and to obtain a certificate from any federal or state magistrate warranting him to return the slave to the state from which he fled. The law did not provide for trial by jury, and conviction required only the master's oral testimony or an affidavit certified by a magistrate of the state from which the slave was said to have fled. The law was always hard to enforce, but it seemed to many to indicate the national government's approval of

In denying Dred Scott's freedom suit in 1856, the U.S. Supreme Court in effect overturned all the antislavery laws.

slavery. It was not until 1842 that the Supreme Court ruled in the case of *Prigg* vs. *Pennsylvania* that state officials did not have to help return fugitives. The decision made even less effective the Southern effort to recover slaves.

By 1850, however, the number of slaves escaping from Kentucky and the lower South led to a stronger Fugitive Slave Law, which required Northern citizens to return runaway slaves to their owners. The law offered a fee to federal officers for captured slaves, and provided for a penalty of six months imprisonment and a $1,000 fine for a person helping a slave escape.

The law did more to exacerbate sectional animosity and excite abolitionist activity than it did to stem the flow of slaves from the plantations. Groups such as the Quakers expressed disapproval of the law and determination to help runaways "in defiance of all the enactments of all the governments on earth."

For the South, passage of the law was a signal for an intensive manhunt in the North. Southern authorities sent people North to bring back fugitives and to spy on abolitionist groups. But such agents met opposition from Northern groups.

John Brown's raid on Harpers Ferry arsenal was the first step in a projected slave uprising.

Blacks and whites took direct action to head off implementation of the law. A rising number of violent incidents caused a congressional committee to report that the effort to recapture runaway slaves in the North "often leads to most unpleasant, if not perilous collisions." When Southerners seized Jerry McHenry, a runaway slave who had been living as a free man in Syracuse, New York, members of the Liberty party, led by Gerrit Smith and William Seward, rescued him as he was being taken back. The community supported the rescue, and no prosecution was undertaken. Among prominent lawyers who defended fugitives seized under the law in Massachusetts were former presidents John Quincy Adams and John Adams.

Black and white abolitionists broke into jails and attacked U. S. marshals to free recaptured fugitives. In 1851 a black vigilance committee in Christiana, Pennsylvania, killed two posse members who had come to claim two runaways. Of this so-called Christiana Riot, Frederick Douglass later wrote:

> The thing which more than all else destroyed the Fugitive Slave Law was the resistance made to it by the fugitives themselves. A decided check was given to the execution of the law at Christiana, Pennsylvania, where three Negro men, being pursued by Mr. Gorusch and his son, slew the father, wounded the son, and drove away the officers and made their escape to my house in Rochester. The work of getting these men safe into Canada was a delicate one. They were not only fugitives from slavery but charged with murder, and officers were in pursuit of them. There was no time for delay. Happily for us, the suspense was not long, for it turned out that on that very night a steamer was leaving for Toronto, Canada.

Two white men and several blacks were tried for treason after the Christiana incident, but were acquitted.

In defiance of the Fugitive Slave Law, abolitionists sometimes helped slaves escape from courtrooms in broad daylight. The first man arrested in Boston under the law was Frederick Jenkins, known as Shadrach. A group of black men, led by Lewis Hayden, who had escaped from slavery, walked Jenkins out of a courtroom as a U.S. marshal was preparing to take him back to his owner. Hayden, who had hidden fugitives in his house before, put two kegs of dynamite in his cellar and said he would blow it up rather than admit slavecatchers. The cost of returning a slave under the Fugitive Slave Law was often many times the monetary value of the slave. In 1854, twenty-two military units, including marines, cavalry, and artillery, were sent to hold back thousands of Bostonians who tried unsuccessfully to free Anthony Burns who was being returned to his master in Virginia. That capture and retrieval cost $40,000. The Richmond (Virginia) *Enquirer* editorialized: "We rejoice, but a few more such victories and the South is undone."

The violent feeling brought on by each case under the Fugitive Slave Law served to heighten the antipathies on both sides of the slavery issue. After the law was passed, a group of Canadian blacks who had escaped from American slavery held a convention in New York. Many of these Canadians joined the Underground Railroad and brought others out of slavery.

Osborn Anderson escaped and wrote a book.

Lewis S. Leary was killed at Harpers Ferry.

THE FUGITIVE SLAVE LAW of 1850 was part of a combination of laws by which Congress tried to resolve the growing antagonisms engendered by uncertainty over the slavery policies that would be followed in newly acquired territories.

There were three main attitudes toward the slavery question in the new territories: some persons wanted total exclusion of slavery, others thought the people of the territories should decide for themselves what the policy would be, and still others felt that slavery should not be legally excluded anywhere.

The Compromise of 1850, of which the strengthened Fugitive Slave Law was a part, provided that: (1) California would enter the Union as a free state; (2) the other territories would be organized without mention of slavery; (3) there would be no slave trade in the District of Columbia. The compromise failed to satisfy either faction in the slavery controversy. After it was passed, Alabama, Georgia,

Mississippi, and South Carolina seriously considered secession. Southerners said they would stay in the Union only if the Fugitive Slave Law, as well as other provisions of the compromise, were strictly observed.

The brief sectional truce brought about by the Compromise of 1850 was finally destroyed by the Kansas-Nebraska Act of 1854. Introduced into the Senate by

Dangerfield Newby was the first of John Brown's men to die.

Stephen A. Douglas, the act in effect repealed the Missouri Compromise. It provided that Kansas and Nebraska should be organized as territories, and that the slavery question be decided by the territorial legislatures. Immediately after Congress passed the act, armed settlers from the North and South went to Kansas. For years abolitionist and proslavery forces fought and bled for Kansas. The strife there was a preliminary to the Civil War.

A further exacerbation of feeling in the North came with the Dred Scott decision in 1857. Scott, a Missouri slave, had been carried to Illinois by his master and then to a fort in the northern part of the Louisiana Purchase, which had been designated as free territory by the Missouri Compromise. When Scott returned to Missouri he sued for his freedom on the grounds that living in free territory had made him free. In the decision on *Scott* vs. *Sanford* the U.S. Supreme Court majority said Scott could not bring suit in the courts because, as a slave, he was not a U.S. citizen. Chief Justice Roger B. Taney, a Maryland slaveholder, said that since the Missouri Compromise was unconstitutional, masters could take their slaves into free states and continue to own them. Abolitionists regarded this statement as open advocacy of slavery by the U.S. Supreme Court. The decision was discouraging to most Northerners, but Frederick Douglass looked beyond the temporary setback:

> Judge Taney can do many things, but he cannot perform impossibilities. He cannot bale out the ocean, annihilate this firm old earth, or pluck the silvery star of liberty from our Northern sky.

The beginning of the end of cooperation between North and South came with the advent of the antislavery Republican party, which arose from discussions among Northern Whigs, Free Soilers, and Democrats. The Republicans nominated Abraham Lincoln for president. The party's platform did not call for an end to slavery, but opposed extension of slavery to new territories. In addition, the party announced a program broad enough to attract votes of persons who did not feel strongly on the slavery issue.

ONE EVENT that probably enlarged the vote for the Republican party was the martyrdom of John Brown. Brown, long a worker for abolition, had aided antislavery forces in Kansas, and had helped operate the Underground Railroad from Missouri. After proslavery nightriders set fire to Lawrence, Kansas, Brown said: "I have only a short time to live, only one death to die, and I will die fighting for this [antislavery] cause."

Brown and about a dozen men, including several blacks, began training in July, 1859, at a rented house on a farm across the Potomac from Harpers Ferry. He stored up arms and drilled a growing contingent of men. His plan was to capture the arsenal at Harpers Ferry, attack slaveholders, arm their slaves, and spread revolt throughout the South. He led the attack on the arsenal on October 16, 1859. Federal and state governments sent troops who overwhelmed his band, killing two of Brown's sons.

After Brown's trial he told a reporter for the *New York Herald:*

> I pity the poor in bondage that have none to help them; that is why I am here; not to gratify any personal animosity, revenge or vindictive spirit. It is my sympathy with the oppressed and wronged, that are as good as you and as precious in the sight of God. . . . You may dispose of me easily, but this question is still to be settled—the Negro question—the end of that is not yet.

Brown accepted his conviction calmly, expressing the idea that the loss of his life would further the cause of abolition:

> Now if it is deemed necessary that I should forfeit my life for the furtherance of the ends of justice, and mingle my blood further with the blood of my children and with the blood of millions in this slave country whose rights are disregarded by wicked, cruel, and unjust enactments, I say, let it be done.

Brown was hanged on December 2, 1859. His raid had left large sections of the South in near panic. Rumors of coming insurrections were widespread, and many whites complained that slaves were insolent because they thought their day of freedom was drawing near. The South was on a semi-war footing, with troops drilling regularly as far south as Georgia. Militia commanders in most states asked for additional men.

Harriet Tubman was prevented by illness from joining the John Brown raid. Frederick Douglass was among a number of free blacks who helped raise money for the venture. Like most, though, he thought the mission was foredoomed and refused to participate. When Douglass said at a meeting that he was withdrawing from the undertaking, Shields Green, an illiterate slave who was at the conference, said "I b'lieve I'll go wid de ole man.' " Other blacks who accompanied

Counterattacked by U.S. marines, Brown was captured in an engine house at Harpers Ferry.

Brown were Lewis Sheridan Leary, Dangerfield Newby, John Anthony Copeland, and Osborn Perry Anderson. Leary and Newby were killed; Copeland and Green were captured and hanged, and Anderson escaped. After the failure, Copeland wrote from prison to his brother:

> It was a sense of the wrongs which we have suffered that prompted the noble but unfortunate Captain John Brown and his associates to attempt to give freedom to a small number, at least, of those who are now held by cruel and unjust laws, and by no less cruel and unjust men. To this freedom they were entitled by every known principle of justice and humanity. Dear brother, could I die for a more noble cause?

A convention called in South Carolina six weeks after the election victory of Abraham Lincoln voted unanimously to cut all ties with the Union, to adopt a new flag, and to take over federal buildings in the state. In a few weeks, South Carolina had been joined by Mississippi, Florida, Alabama, Georgia, Louisiana, and Texas. A provisional government called the Confederate States of America was set up at Montgomery, Alabama, in February, 1861, and Jefferson Davis of Mississippi was elected president. Two months later, Confederate forces bombarded Fort Sumter, beginning the Civil War.

Wounded John Brown and his surviving followers are led into a local court shortly after the raid.

". . . the Negro question—the end of that is not yet." John Brown at his trial in Charlestown, Virginia.

9

Civil War

54TH MASS.

No war has affected the political nature and history of America more than the Civil War. During a period of grave internal strife over the issue of slavery, when it seemed that the nation would dissolve into weak and defenseless units, the four-year Civil War (April 12, 1861, to April 9, 1865) unified the country and created conditions leading to the emancipation of the slaves.

It is ironical, however, that whereas black America seemed to be one of the beneficiaries of the war, the leaders of the conflict tried—in the beginning—to ignore the black man. President Abraham Lincoln, when explaining the objective of the Union's declaration of war, made it clear that the last intention of his administration was to crusade for black freedom. "It is a war fought to save the Union," Lincoln said, "and not to interfere with the institution of slavery."

Nevertheless, once the Confederacy fired its war cannons on the Union soldiers at Fort Sumter—an American fortress located in the harbor of Charleston, South Carolina—blacks and abolitionists knew that, despite official phrases, the South had actually struck the first blow for black freedom.

Although more than one cause contributed to starting the Civil War, it is almost impossible to separate the war from the basic issue of slavery. In fact, the political, moral, and economic controversies between the North and the South all revolved around the institution of slavery as a political protectorate, a moral evil, and an economic asset.

In a speech given at a pro-Union rally, abolitionist John S. Rock explained the issue clearly, "Now it seems to me that a blind man can see that the present war is an effort to nationalize, perpetuate and extend slavery in this country. In short, slavery is the cause of the war: I might say, is the war itself. Had it not been for slavery, we would have had no war! Through two hundred and forty years of indescribable tortures, slavery has wrung out of the blood, bones and muscles of the Negro hundreds of millions of dollars, and helped much to make this nation rich. At the same time it has developed a volcano which has burst forth. . . ."

Slavery, among many other things, had become for the South a political identity, better still, a political platform. Every new slave state could be labeled Southern and Democratic, regardless of its location. On the other hand, the North knew that if it were to secure its economic and political superiority over the South, it had either to limit the spread of slavery or abolish it altogether. Once Northerners gained control of the White House, they could check the progress of slavery. The election of Lincoln was the harbinger of an antislavery Congress.

Slavery was a source not only of political controversy but of moral argument. It was the popular belief in the North that slavery was evil. Although most Northerners did not feel that blacks were equal, and, in most cases, did not treat blacks as human beings, they opposed slavery on moral grounds. And it was this moral edge that eventually spurred the North to victory when it became apparent that fighting in the name of the "Union" wasn't a lofty enough ideal to inspire men in battle.

It was through slavery as a moral issue that the abolitionists, though small in number, were able to influence the North's political and military assault on the institution.

Not only was slavery a political and moral factor in the Civil War, it also pro-

Lincoln won the Republican party's presidential nomination at a convention held in May, 1860, at Chicago.

vided an economic motive. Slavery was the nucleus of the South's economy. Cheap labor lowered the South's overhead and made its profits far greater, proportionately, than those of the North with its free labor system. Cotton was in great demand, and the South was enjoying profitable trade with the North and with England and other European powers.

The war was thus a conflict of economies, a war between the Northern industrialists who wanted to buy in an open market and sell in a protected market, and the Southern cotton planters who wanted to both buy and sell in an open market while broadening the economic base of slave power.

Thomas P. Kettell, author of *Southern Wealth and Northern Profits*, was one of many writers contending that it was the unfavorable economic balance between the North and the South that drove the South to secede. Southerners claimed that the North was growing rich from the South and that secession and political independence alone would emancipate the section from economic bondage.

THE SURPRISE of the Civil War is not that the South lost. Rather, it is that the South was able to fight so bitterly and for so long against the tremendous odds favoring the North. The South could not even support itself well in peace, and it was even more astonishing that it was able to fight four long years against the very power from whom it imported most of its goods. The North had expected the conflict to be a lightning war with a quick victory. But the South proved a much stronger war machine than the North had bargained for because it was energized by slave power.

A look at manpower statistics shows how much the South was aided by slave power. At the start of the war, in 1861, the population of the loyal states comprising the Union was 22,000,000, including 430,000 slaves in the Border States of Kentucky, Maryland, Missouri, and Delaware. But the population of the Confederate states was only 9,000,000, and that figure included 3,520,000 slaves and 260,000 free Negroes. The Union military mustered in 1,600,000 soldiers, about 7 per-

Four black crewmen—Robert Smalls (rear), William Morrison (l.), A. Gradine (r.) and John Smalls—delivered the Confederate gunboat *Planter* into Union hands.

The Confederate gunboat *Planter*, which was pirated for the Union by its black crewmen, is moored in harbor.

cent of its white population of 21,570,000. However, the South was able to spare 800,000 men, about 15 percent of its white population of 5,220,000. This was a population proportion more than twice that of the North. Without slavery, the South could not have contributed as many soldiers. But the 3,520,000 slaves behind the Confederate lines worked as laborers, food producers, plantation and factory foremen, and this freed the maximum number of white men to carry arms. Moreover, thousands of slaves were impressed for the Confederate Army as teamsters, cooks, body servants and medics. They loaded and unloaded Southern war material and built many of the breastworks, fortifications, and battery emplacements used by Confederate troops.

In the early part of the war, Northern generals failed to appreciate the value of slaves. In fact, their refusal to accept runaway slaves was of considerable help to the South. One reason for this refusal was their reluctance to appear to be fighting to free slaves. President Lincoln had made it clear that the war was being fought not to free the slaves, but to preserve the Union. He knew that Missouri, Kentucky, Delaware, and Maryland had four hundred thousand slaves, and that these states were fighting for the Union. He believed that once Union soldiers started aiding runaway slaves, it would encourage escapes, possibly even insurrections, in slave states still loyal to the Union.

But it wasn't long before the North realized the potential power of the slaves. The usual custom was that Confederates would come into the Union camps under a flag of truce and collect the runaways, whom the Union generals gladly surrendered. Thousands of slaves were returned to the South before Northern generals realized that by keeping the runaways they could both diminish the South's fighting power and increase their own by putting the slaves to work for the Union.

Union General Benjamin F. Butler, commander of the Department of Virginia, set a precedent on May 24, 1861, when he refused to return three runaway slaves to their master, a Confederate colo-

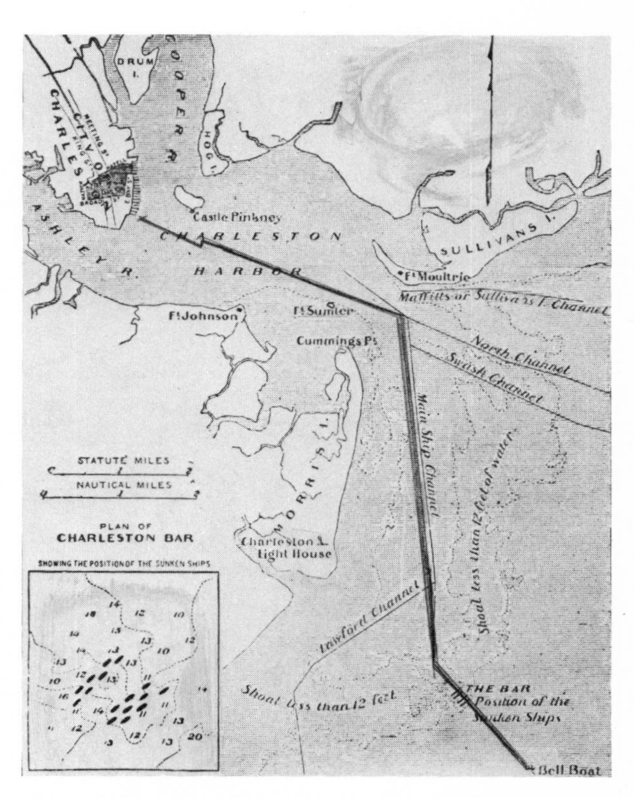

The above map charts the route the black crewmen used to pirate the *Planter.*

By the President of the United States of America.

A Proclamation.

Whereas, on the twenty-second day of September, in the year of our Lord one thousand eight hundred and sixty-two, a proclamation was issued by the President of the United States, containing, among other things, the following, to wit:

"That on the first day of January, in the "year of our Lord one thousand eight hundred "and sixty-three, all persons held as slaves within "any State or designated part of a State, the people "whereof shall then be in rebellion against the "United States, shall be then, thenceforward and "forever free; and the Executive Government of the "United States, including the military and naval "authority thereof, will recognize and maintain "the freedom of such persons, and will do no act "or acts to repress such persons, or any of them, "in any efforts they may make for their actual "freedom.

"That the Executive will, on the first day

nel. Butler reasoned that since the slaves were in service to a military officer of a "foreign" government, they were articles of war to be confiscated once they came under Union control. Butler labeled runaway slaves "contraband," a term that spread like wildfire. Slaves, hearing of the precedent, flooded into Butler's camp, hoping to be saved by that label of liberation. It was, in a way, the first official and successful decision to liberate slaves, albeit indirectly.

Butler's move became policy for other Union generals, and Congress, realizing the military logic behind such an action, eventually echoed Butler's action as official policy in the first Confiscation Act. This act applied only to slaves of masters at war with the Union. The law was passed on August 6, 1861.

Although some slaves and free Negroes had worked for the Confederacy, they involved themselves mostly for reasons other than aiding the Southern cause. Some helped the Confederacy because they hoped to encourage a more liberal attitude and better treatment from their masters. Others helped because they had been brainwashed. Still others helped because they wanted to infiltrate Confederate channels of communication to get information that would be of use to the invading Union soldiers. Some helped because they had been convinced by their masters that Union soldiers raped and tortured all slaves and shipped any survivors to Cuba and South America. At the same time, hundreds of thousands of slaves ran away from their masters and struck other blows for freedom behind Confederate lines.

Official policy apart, blacks knew that a Northern victory meant the eventual end of slavery and an improvement in living conditions for those blacks living in free states. So they were not content to sit on the sidelines and watch white men fight over their destiny.

Photo on opposite page shows an excerpt of the original Emancipation Proclamation document.

Offers of help from black men flooded the White House immediately after the firing on Fort Sumter. From the "Hannibal Guards" in Pittsburgh, the "Attucks Guards" in Albany, Ohio, and countless other hastily organized black regiments in cities throughout the free states came offers to serve the Union in any capacity. Blacks rented dance halls and drilled in preparation for duty at their own expense. Some even volunteered to pay their own way to the Union front lines to smite the rebel force.

In Detroit, Michigan, a military band of black musicians, organized under Captain O. C. Wood, offered to enlist.

In Battle Creek, Michigan, a black physician named Dr. G. P. Miller wrote a letter to the War Department saying that if given permission he could quickly organize a crack task force of black sharpshooters who would take any position assigned them "to pick off the rebels one by one." Miller also said that if his first proposition was refused he had from five to ten thousand blacks standing by to fight as guerrillas "if armed and equipped by the national government."

A Washington Negro was another who wrote a letter to the War Department saying that some three hundred "reliable colored free citizens" stood ready to defend the city. He was Jacob Dodson and claimed among his credentials the fact that he had crossed the Rocky Mountains three times with John Charles Fremont and others. Dodson told the Department that if it wanted the extra hands, "I can be found about the Senate chambers, as I have been employed about the premises for some years." The official response from the War Department was that ". . . the Secretary of War has no intention of using colored soldiers."

In September, 1861, the *Anglo-African* newspaper expressed the black sentiment in an editorial:

> Hence, talk as we may, we are concerned in this fight and our fate hangs upon its issues. The South must be subjugated, or we shall be enslaved. In aiding the Federal government in whatever way we can, we are aiding to secure our own liberty: for this war can only end in the subjugation of the North or the South. We do not affirm that the North is fighting in behalf of the black man's rights, as such—if this was the issue, we doubt whether they would fight at all. But circumstances have been so arranged by the decrees of Provi-

Abraham Lincoln, this nation's sixteenth president, was pressured politically and militarily to issue the Emancipation Proclamation.

Black longshoremen, mostly former slaves, take a break from their work on the James River.

dence, that in struggling for their own nationality, they are forced to defend our rights. . . . Let us be awake, therefore brethren; a generous emulation in a common patriotism, and a special call to defend our rights alike bid us to be on the alert to seize arms and drill as soon as the government shall be willing to accept our services. . . .

Although there were many public offers of black military assistance, the individual requests from popular abolitionists were very influential. Among the most popular abolitionists crusading for black troops were Frederick Douglass, John Rock, William Lloyd Garrison and Charles Sumner. It was these abolitionists who were on hand in strategic situations throughout the history of the war, prodding the government and public sentiment here and there to take steps leading to black liberation. They crusaded for black troops, not only to give them pride in their efforts to break the shackles of their own bondage, but to provide as much manpower as possible to assure a Union victory.

Black labor was an indispensable part of the war machines of North and South.

Douglass, Rock, and Greeley even aided directly in recruiting black troops, once blacks were called officially. Douglass and Rock worked from platforms at various mass meetings held in major Northern cities, and Greeley crusaded through his *New York Tribune* newspaper, writing fiery editorials and public letters to key political figures.

Douglass, a former slave, self-educated and a peerless orator, writer, and editor, was the leading black man of the Civil War period. An occasional visitor at the White House, Douglass had gained prominence as the Socratic gadfly of the administration on issues relating to blacks. When the war came, he personally went out into the field to recruit blacks to serve in the Union Army.

In a famous editorial, "Men of Color, to Arms," he expressed his feelings about the war:

> When first the rebel cannon shattered the walls of Sumter and drove away its starving garrison, I predicted that the war then and there inaugurated would not be fought out entirely by white men. . . . A war undertaken and brazenly carried on for the

perpetual enslavement of colored men, calls logically and loudly for colored men to help suppress it. Only a moderate share of sagacity was needed to see that the arm of the slave was the best defense against the slaveholder. Hence, with every reverse to the national arms, with every exulting shout of victory raised by the slaveholding rebels, I have implored the imperiled nation to unchain against her foes her powerful black hand. . . . Liberty won by white men would lose half its luster. 'Who would be free themselves must strike the blow.' . . . this is the sentiment of every brave colored man amongst us.

At first, Douglass's efforts bore little fruit. Blacks in the North knew that the Black Codes and other discriminatory customs kept them from being first-class American citizens. Many believed they had no stake in the war. Eventually, however, Douglass encouraged many blacks to enlist in the Union Army.

John S. Rock, another black abolitionist. was a doctor, a lawyer, an orator, and a

Blacks worked as blacksmiths, teamsters, cooks, medics, and spies.

Mathew Brady's photograph shows former slaves facing their new freedom.

dentist. He was the first black man permitted to practice law before the Supreme Court. Throughout his life he dedicated his skill and energy to the cause of black freedom. Rock supported blacks fighting in the Civil War, but he demanded first-class citizenship.

> We desire to take part in this contest [the Civil War], and when our government shall see the necessity of using the loyal blacks of the free states, I hope it will have the courage to recognize their manhood. It certainly would be mean enough to force us to fight for your liberty. . . . but even meaner to leave us when we go home to our respective states to be told that we cannot ride in cars, that our children cannot go to public schools, that we cannot vote, and if we don't like that state of things, there is an appropriation to colonize us. We ask for our rights.

Horace Greeley was an advocate of emancipation. Perhaps his most famous exhortation was his August 19, 1862, editorial, in the *New York Tribune*. Addressed to President Lincoln, the "Prayer of Twenty Million" called for the abolition of slavery. Greeley wrote:

> On the face of this wide earth, Mr. President, there is not one disinterested, determined, intelligent champion of the Union cause who does not feel that all attempts to put down the Rebellion . . . are preposterous and futile; that the Rebellion, if crushed out tomorrow, would be renewed within a year if slavery were left in full vigor; that army officers who remain to this day devoted to slavery can at best be but halfway loyal to the Union: and that every hour of deference to slavery is an hour of added and deepened peril to the Union. . . . What an immense majority of the loyal millions of your countrymen require of you is a frank declared, unqualified, ungrudging execution of the laws of the land, more especially the Confiscation Act. The act gives freedom to the slaves of rebels coming within our lives, or whom those lines at any time may enclose. . . .

Despite the offers made by blacks to shed their blood for the Union at the start of the war, the government and white public sentiment were against conscripting blacks. "This is a white man's war," blacks were told. Many blacks were attacked and beaten by white mobs while holding military drills. Even the local police departments warned blacks to cease

A black contraband, employed as a cook in a Union camp, prepares two large cauldrons of bean soup for the troops.

drilling because the only result was "irritation to the local white citizenry."

But the most crushing refusal came from President Lincoln. In his response to Greeley's "Prayer of Twenty Million," he reiterated his intentions.

"My paramount object in this struggle," President Lincoln said, "is to save the Union, and is not either to save or destroy slavery. . . . What I do about slavery and the colored race, I do because I believe it helps to save the Union." But the campaign for recruiting black regiments continued despite the president's response. Union soldiers were dying and the soldiers and their families were beginning to entertain the idea of letting blacks fight and die in their stead.

Lincoln believed that the fifty thousand bayonets from the Border States serving in the Union Army might switch sides if he freed all slaves or enlisted them in the army. The Border States also had over three million citizens whose political support would be very important, once the Union was restored to full representation. Lincoln also felt that the general attitude of most Union soldiers from the free states was anti-Negro.

Eventually, however, the North was forced to recruit black soldiers. Northern public sentiment wanted a victory as quickly as possible, and black soldiers were the keys to it.

The regiments formed by the free Negroes of New Orleans in early 1861 and called the Louisiana Native Guards are believed to be the first black regiments organized in the war. The regiments joined the state militia and marched with other Louisiana troops on November 23, 1861, during a parade in New Orleans. One black soldier later told a Union general who questioned the blacks' fighting ability: "Our fathers were brought here as slaves because they were captured in war, and in hand-to-hand fights too. Pardon me, General, but the only cowardly blood we have got in our veins is the white blood."

Many question why these black regiments volunteered their services to the

Confederacy. A study of the circumstances surrounding these free Negroes affords two explanations. Several of the free Negroes in the regiments had a personal stake in slaveocracy. They were well-to-do, French-speaking Negroes who themselves owned black slaves. Another reason is that, along with their families and slaves, they lived under the constant danger of being impressed into the Confederate Army as slaves and common laborers. Taking the initiative to join the militia themselves, though their service

Former slaves unload war supplies and wash clothes for Union soldiers.

amounted to nothing more than drilling and assuming the role of ready reserves, they could better defend themselves against the prospects of impressment. As for these regiments actually fighting, they were never given orders to fire on anyone.

As soon as the Union soldiers assumed command of New Orleans, the regiments of free Negroes volunteered their services to the Union.

Many historians believe that the First South Carolina Volunteers deserve the distinction of being the first black soldiers actually recruited, trained, and mustered by the Union Army. Although the South Carolina Volunteers served six months without pay (some even died without drawing pay or leaving benefits for their survivors), they could claim their enlistment date back to May, 1862. The man who organized this regiment, General David Hunter, had succeeded General Thomas W. Sherman as commander of the Department of the South and was liberally interpreting orders given to Sherman in October, 1861. Sherman was authorized to use blacks in any capacity he needed, preferably as laborers and spies. Sherman abided by those stipulations, but Hunter, who lacked sufficient manpower to defend South Carolina, authorized the systematic recruiting, enlisting, and training of Negro regiments.

Union troops also employed blacks to chop wood and herd cattle.

Within a week, Hunter had organized 150 blacks into the First South Carolina Volunteer Regiment. Hunter's actions were assailed in Congress, but not strongly enough to end the recruiting of black troops. Hunter had hoped that President Lincoln would come to his rescue and set a policy authorizing across-the-board recruiting and arming of black troops, but the president remained silent. Benjamin Quarles explained the outcome in his book, *The Negro in the Civil War:*

> Hunter was neither ordered to disband his troops, nor given any further means to equip and organize them. When, on August 4, he appealed for commissions for the officers and pay for the men, he might as well have spoken to the wind. Hunter had decided that enough was enough. His Negro soldiers had served without pay for three months, and there was no immediate prospect that the regiment would be officially mustered in. Hence, on August 10, he gave up the experiment, and the troops were all disbanded except for one company. . . . This company, however, was destined to be the first group of Negro soldiers to be given an offensive assignment by the Union.

Black volunteers assemble to enlist as Union soldiers in the command of General U. S. Grant.

Under the leadership of Sergeant C. T. Trowbridge, the company was assigned to St. Simon's Island off the coast of Georgia. Its mission was to flush out a band of rebel guerillas. However, when the black volunteers arrived on the island, they discovered that fugitive slaves had already taken the initiative in pursuing the rebels. During a skirmish with the rebels, the all-black contingent lost its leader, John Brown, who, according to many historians, was probably the first black man to die in an armed encounter with the rebels during the war. This incident indicates that there were probably many other unpublicized encounters between black vigilantes and Confederates.

The South Carolina Volunteers took over the pursuit from the local blacks and hounded the guerillas through the swamps for a couple of weeks, engaging in brief skirmishes. The rebel leader, Miles Hazzard, later confessed: "If you wish to know hell before your time, go to St. Simon's and be hunted ten days by niggers." Despite their services, this surviving company of the Carolina Volunteers suffered the same fate as their cohorts. The government refused to honor their service and to give them the money and credit they had earned. The company was disbanded after another three months.

Eventually, however, when the government decided to support black soldiers, the members of Hunter's disbanded regiments comprised the nucleus of the official First South Carolina Volunteers. The unit was reorganized under Brigadier General Edwin Saxton and was commanded by Colonel Thomas Wentworth Higginson. Higginson, a native of Massachusetts, was a liberal and a brilliant Harvard alumnus. He wrote a book, *Army Life in a Black Regiment,* which detailed his observations of blacks as soldiers and his experiences as their commander. Although the U.S. government mustered the

Recruits board train taking them to enlist in the federal army.

troops in on November 10, 1862, the members refused to forget their previous six months service. They knew they *had* served, and that they thus were the first group of former slaves to be recruited, enlisted, and trained as Union Army soldiers.

Two other early black regiments came out of Kansas. They were the First and Second Kansas Colored Volunteers, groups organized by General (also Senator) James H. Lane in August of 1862, but not mustered into the Union Army officially until January 13, 1863. The regiments were comprised of fugitive slaves from Missouri and free Negroes from the North. Like the South Carolina Volunteers, the Kansas regiments fought for about six months against rebel guerrillas in Kansas and Missouri, without pay or recognition from the War Department.

The bloodiest battle took place in late October, 1862, on the Osage River, in Bates County, Missouri. Lane organized a black task force and sent it on a search and destroy mission against rebel guerrillas on an island in the Osage. The blacks ran into a unit of six hundred guerrillas and fought hand-to-hand in an enviable display of raw courage. One of the blacks was killed and several were wounded. The soldiers had had only about a month's training, but they fought gallantly and even won the plaudits of their enemies. One rebel survivor said that ". . . the black devils fought like tigers . . . not one of them surrendered though we tried to take prisoners." The rebels soon retreated to join their chieftain, William Clark Quantrill.

Whereas the South Carolina and Louisiana colored volunteers were founded in Southern territories captured by the Union troops, the Kansas regiment was the first black unit formed in the North. Another state which recruited blacks was Massachusetts. Governor John A. Andrew, who was authorized by the War Department to raise a couple of black regiments, selected George L. Stearns as the enlistment supervisor. Since Massachusetts had a very small black population, the state raised thousands of dollars and solicited famous black leaders of that day to help recruit blacks from other states. Among those serving as recruiting agents were Frederick Douglass, William Wells Brown, Charles L. Remond, John Mercer Langston, Henry Highland Garnet, and Martin L. Delaney. The unit recruited was named the Fifty-fourth Massachusetts Regiment, and its members came from free states, slave states, and Canada.

THE EMANCIPATION PROCLAMATION was a decisive factor in the Civil War. A child of military necessity and political pressure, the Proclamation changed the tone of the war and gave the North the added power it needed to crush the Southern war effort.

Recruiting posters like this one urged blacks to join the federal army once the government broke the color bar.

Whites attack blacks in New York's draft riots in 1863.

It was clear at the beginning of the conflict that a proclamation of some sort would be necessary, but the man who had the power to issue it, President Lincoln, was reluctant even to use the word "Negro," let alone entertain the possibilities of freeing him. In 1861, Lincoln supported Union commanders who returned runaway slaves to their rebel masters. And when two Union officers, General John C. Fremont in Missouri and General David Hunter in South Carolina, issued emancipation proclamations in their commands, Lincoln repudiated the edicts and criticized both men for taking such initiatives. Later, when the first Union commanders began to recruit black soldiers, Lincoln refused to lend his support in having the black soldiers officially acknowledged and paid by the government.

During this early period, Lincoln maneuvered behind the scenes to placate conservative whites. He urged slaveholders to free slaves on a gradual basis and he championed various plans for the deportation and colonization of freed slaves. But the refusal of slaveholders to accept a compromise and the refusal of most blacks to support the colonization plans made Lincoln realize that there was no alternative to emancipation.

Angry whites burn a black orphanage in New York City during their riots over the draft laws.

The president's ambivalence on this issue stemmed from political and military factors. He was worried about the fifty thousand bayonets and three million votes from the slave states fighting in the Union. He was worried about the legality of an executive order ending slavery. He was worried about the slaves themselves and whether they would take the "proper attitude" to their new freedom. He was worried about the "Copperheads" (Confederate sympathizers) and the possibility of riots in Northern cities. He was worried about public opinion abroad, in England in particular. And he apparently had racial reservations.

In the end, military factors were decisive. It was clear by 1862 that it was going to be a long and bloody struggle and that the North was going to need all the help it could get.

With military circumstances peaking against him, President Lincoln was pressed to issue the Emancipation Proclamation. He knew that there would be some opposition, but he believed the net results would be favorable. His main concern, at first, was the military significance of the Proclamation. He knew it would greatly undermine the South's military strength by turning loose about four million slaves. The Proclamation would also strengthen the Union Army, which would gain additional manpower and put it to work—not just behind cooking stoves, but behind shooting irons.

Lincoln also believed that the Proclamation would win diplomatic support from England, and that this achievement would help the North's military effort by eliminating the possibility that the British would break the North's blockade on Southern ports. Both the North and the South had been competing for British support. The South had been shipping cotton to England, and it was hoped that England's economic needs might encourage her to support the Confederacy. But Lincoln had learned that the British working class sympathized with the slaves and wanted to see them freed. British textile workers even risked being laid off work in order to eliminate the British market for Southern cotton.

Members of the 107th U.S. Colored Troops stand outside the Guard House of their command.

Twelve black heavy artillery units, including the Second U.S. Colored Artillery (light) below, were part of the Union Army.

The history of the emancipation can be divided into five installments. First, there was the Confiscation Act of August 6, 1861. It declared that all slaves used by their masters to aid in the insurrection against the Union were to become the prize and capture of the Union Army.

The second emancipation installment was a package of antislavery legislation passed by Congress in the spring of 1862. The legislation (1) prohibited slavery in U.S. territories; (2) abolished slavery in Washington, D. C.; (3) forbade Union soldiers, through an article of war, to return runaway slaves to their masters, and (4) provided for the eventual suppression of the slave trade.

The third was the Second Confiscation Act of July 17, 1862. It declared all slaves of rebel masters "forever free."

The fourth and major installment was the preliminary Emancipation Proclamation which Lincoln issued on September 22, 1862. It declared free, as of January 1, 1863, all slaves in most areas of rebellious states.

The fifth installment was the Thirteenth Amendment to the Constitution, passed by Congress on December 18, 1865, months after the war had ended and President Lincoln had been assassinated. This amendment legalized and fortified the Emancipation Proclamation. It prohibited slavery or involuntary servitude, except as a punishment for crime, in all parts of the United States.

As a symbol, the Emancipation Proclamation was an important element in this five-step plan. It made a war for union into a war for freedom. Although the freedom in question was actually the freedom of slaves in rebellious states, the white Union public identified psychologically with the war goals. Northerners crusaded for freedom in its abstract form, as an ideal, a moral detergent purifying the nation and broadening the base of world-wide humanity. Union soldiers even marched to the tune of "John Brown's Body," praising the slaves' martyred freedom fighter.

Throughout the North, there were jubilant celebrations. The fact that the Proclamation was to become effective on January 1 gave added meaning to New Year's Day. It was not only the nation's "New Year resolution," it was a "New Era resolution." Blacks held their traditional watch night services, and the churches were crowded with people awaiting the official release of the Proclamation.

At the Israel Bethel African Methodist Episcopal Church, in Washington, D.C., blacks held a watch night service. Old men and women who were former slaves cried, shouted, and testified about the horrors of slavery, the ecstasy of their newfound free-

An unidentified Union soldier poses for a portrait.

dom and what that New Year's Day meant to them and their loved ones still behind the rebel lines. The pastor, Rev. Henry M. Turner, grabbed the first newspaper printing the story and ran a mile to the church. He arrived too tired to read the published Proclamation, so a deacon read it while Rev. Turner caught his breath. The Reverend Turner said later:

> While he was reading, every kind of demonstration and gesticulation was going on. Men squealed and cackled, women fainted, dogs barked, white and colored people shook hands, roosters crowed, songs were sung, and by this time the canons in the Navy yard began to fire. . . . Great crowds of white and colored men marched in front of the White House, praising President Lincoln and promising him that if he showed himself, they would hug him to death. . . . It was indeed a time of times, nothing like it will ever be seen again in this life.

The Proclamation, written with a formal, legalistic flavor, was hailed as a great victory for American democracy. It was about two pages long, but the meat of the document was in one paragraph:

> That on the first day of January, in the year of our Lord one thousand eight hundred and sixty-three, all persons held as slaves within any state or designated part of a state, the persons whereof shall then be in rebellion against the United States, shall be then, thenceforward, and forever free; and the Executive Government of the United States, including the military and naval authority thereof, will recognize and maintain the freedom of such persons, and will do no act or acts to suppress such person, or any of them, in any efforts they may make for their actual freedom. . . . And I further declare and make known, that such persons of suitable condition, will be received into the armed services of the United States to garrison forts, positions, stations, and other places, and to man vessels of all sorts in said service.

Although the Proclamation only freed the slaves in the rebellious states (it did not apply to slaves in Union states and Union-held areas in the South), it made it apparent to everyone that slavery in the United States was on its last legs.

As soon as the war started, slaves had begun to desert the slaveocracy. These slaves freed themselves by running to nearby Union Army camps. Planters with huge slave interests moved their slaves deeper into the Southern interior (some even considered Cuba and South America) to prevent them from running off to the Union Army.

At first the desertions were a mere trickle, because slavemasters strengthened patrols to limit escapes, and Union generals were returning slaves to their masters to be beaten and sometimes killed. As Congress and its generals became more receptive, the flow of desertions thickened. The Confiscation acts sent runaways into Union camps by the hundreds, but the Emancipation Proclamation opened the floodgates of freedom-seeking slaves. Entire plantations swelled the Union ranks.

It is estimated that the wholesale exodus of slaves into Union camps exceeded five hundred thousand. Nevertheless, many of the roughly three million slaves who remained in the South believed they were free. Now that the president of the conquering armies had put his stamp on their walking papers, slaves believed that it was binding and that their servitude was illegal. Many whites feared the Proclamation would be a mandate to the slaves to slit their masters' throats, but the fear was groundless. The slaves rebelled, but few used physical violence. Rather, they refused to work for the rebels, and many cursed their masters or demanded pay. In certain sections the slavemasters did not punish their slaves and began to "respect" them. The slaves were gradually learning about their legal status through "underground telegraph," and they were becoming increasingly intoxicated with the idea of freedom.

This Civil War veteran is photographed before a picture of a gunboat.

As black people sloughed off the bonds of slavery, the Confederate war effort deteriorated. Jefferson Davis himself admitted that "much of our success was due to the much-abused institution of slavery." Now, slavery was dying, and so was the Confederacy.

At the same time, there were new complications in the North. The waves of blacks entering Union camps began to strain the resources of the army. The slaves needed food, clothes, and medical care. Union commanders told slaves to stay put and work the soil of their runaway masters, or to go North where blacks and liberal whites were setting up freedmen's bureaus and other centers to aid the distressed refugees. But the slaves ignored this advice and continued to follow the troops, pitching makeshift tents or sleeping in caves.

Northern relief societies helped ease some of the problems. They followed in the wake of the Union soldiers, clipping off the retinue of slaves, enrolling them in schools and providing medical care and aid. Among the relief organizations were the American Missionary Association, the Western Freedmen's Aid Commission, the

A rare tintype of a black corporal in the Union Army.

Freedmen's Aid Society of Cincinnati, the Assembly of the United Presbyterian Church, the Western Sanitary Commission and the Northwestern Freedmen's Aid Society of Chicago. Many churches, social organizations and individual philanthropists sent money, food, and clothes.

Another post-Proclamation problem was the violent reaction of white laborers who believed the war was becoming a crusade for black freedom. The "Copperheads," Northern supporters of the South, also intensified their propaganda campaign against the war and against slaves by telling the white Northerners that the Proclamation would bring the slaves from the Southern plantations into their living-rooms, dining rooms, and bedrooms. The Copperheads said that the black man was the sole cause of the war, and thus the cause of white men being killed or tortured in rebel prisons.

Northern workers became extremely angry and began to riot against blacks in New York, Boston, Philadelphia, and other major cities. In all cases, the central issues of the riots were unemployment and the war. The precipitating cause in New York was a draft law which made it possible for the well-to-do to evade con-

A black Union Army sergeant poses for a studio portrait.

Union soldier stands guard for his command.

Black soldiers also served the Union as spies (above) and as infantrymen (below).

scription by paying three hundred dollars. At the same time, striking white workers feared the competition of blacks, some of whom crossed picket lines. The grand outcome was that many whites swarmed into the streets, beating and sometimes killing blacks. Even business establishments owned by blacks or employing blacks (white restaurants with black waiters and dishwashers, and white churches with black janitors) were attacked. One of the worst acts was the burning of a black orphanage in New York City. The center, run by Quakers, housed some 250 children. The riots lasted for over a week resulting in many deaths and millions of dollars of damage.

Because blacks knew that the war would destroy slavery, they rallied to the Union cause. As we have seen, there was opposition in the North to the use of black troops. This opposition stemmed largely from bias and a fear of black equality.

Even President Lincoln confessed his lack of trust in blacks as soldiers when he said, "If we were to arm [the Negroes], I fear that in a few weeks the arms would be in the hands of the Rebels." The survival of such an idea was strange, since blacks had already fought gallantly in the War of 1812, and had helped their country to gain its independence. It appears that the prejudices were founded on the idea that the black man's military contributions would reinforce his rights as a human being and citizen on an equal level with whites. As in the Revolutionary War, once whites were threatened, they found racial prejudice was a luxury they could not afford.

Blacks were crewmen aboard several Union war ships, including the ironclad *Monitor*.

Just as Northern white society saw its opportunity in the black man, the black man saw his opportunity in the Civil War. Even in the North, the land of Lincoln, the alleged citadel of liberty, the so-called oasis of freedom, black people were still relegated to economic, social, political, and educational stations inferior to those of whites.

Despite discrimination, most blacks, as in the Revolutionary War and the War of 1812, were optimistic that military service would solve their problems, or at least raise their status as human beings in America.

Said Frederick Douglass:

> Once let the black man get upon his person the brass letters, U.S.; let him get an eagle on his button, and a musket on his shoulder and bullets in his pocket, and there is no power on earth which can deny that he has earned the right to citizenship in the United States.

Corporal Thomas Long, a black soldier in Colonel Higginson's regiment, gave a moving speech to his fellow soldiers:

> If we hadn't been soldiers . . . our freedom might have slipped through the two houses of Congress and President Lincoln and might have passed by for years and nothing been done for us. But now things can never go back, because we have showed our energy and our courage and our natural manhood.

It was this optimistic spirit that inspired blacks to endure the barriers of racial prejudice. And when the call for black troops was made, they came running from all over the country, laborers from the factories, preachers from the pulpits, doctors from lucrative private practices, slaves from the plantations—all willing to die for the flag.

According to official records, some 173,000 black soldiers fought in the Civil War. Of that number, 93,000 came from the seceded states, 40,000 from the Border States, and roughly 52,000 from free states. Some historians estimate that an additional 20,000 mulattoes served in the Union Army as white men. Black soldiers took part in 449 military engagements, of which thirty-nine were major battles. Some 37,000 blacks lost their lives in the Civil War, roughly 21 percent of the total number of black soldiers.

According to black historian John Hope Franklin, the mortality rate for blacks was nearly 40 percent greater than for white troops.

The disproportionately high mortality rate for black Union soldiers was partly a result of racial prejudice and discrimination. Benjamin Quarles said the Negro "faced a number of discriminations: his period of enlistment was longer than that of others, he had little chance of rising to the rank of commissioned officer, his pay was lower than that of whites, he did not receive the same hospital care, he was furnished with inferior firearms . . ." The situation was particularly distressing in the medical field. White doctors were reluctant to serve in Negro regiments. The eight black doctors who received commissions were often sent to white units, where they were insulted and assaulted. Dr. Alexander T. Augustana, for example, left a large, mostly white practice in Canada and was commissioned a major.

On April 14, 1863, while on a train headed for Baltimore, he was attacked by whites, including the railroad guard. The whites tore off his medal insignia and ran him off the train. Later, he returned with an armed federal escort, only to receive another punch in the face while boarding the train. Dr. Augustana and other black doctors said whites clearly preferred death to care at the hands of blacks.

As for arms and supplies, Brigadier General Daniel Ullman wrote a letter in December, 1863, complaining that his Negro soldiers had just been sent into battle with arms which were almost entirely unserviceable. After inspecting several Negro companies stationed in Mississippi, Lorenzo Thomas, adjutant general, made this report: "This regiment, like most of this class of soldiers, have the old flintlock muskets, altered to percussion, which have been in use for a long time. The muskets of this regiment were condemned once, and have been condemned by an inspector a second time."

Black crewmen aboard Union ships were messed and quartered with whites, but their pay was said to be inferior. Some 30,000 blacks served in the Union Navy.

Black soldiers attack the Confederate stronghold at Port Hudson, Louisiana.

Another source of frustration for black soldiers was the discriminatory pay rate. Most black soldiers were recruited with the promise that they would be paid the same amount as white soldiers. In fact, most did more work and were paid half as much as fellow white soldiers. Many blacks served as common laborers (undertaking excess fatigue duty) and as soldiers, too, but they were paid as laborers. This practice caused a storm of protests within and without the Union military. One black soldier, Sergeant William Walker of the Third South Carolina Volunteers, staged a demonstration for equal pay, leading his company into the white captain's tent, where the soldiers stacked up their rifles, signaling their resignation from the army because it had broken its contract with blacks. Sergeant Walker was court-martialed for mutiny and shot.

The two black regiments from Massachusetts, the Fifty-fourth and the Fifty-fifth, also protested by refusing to accept pay for over a year (even when their state legislature had voted to make up the difference) until Congress gave all black soldiers equal pay.

One black soldier explained the problem in detail in a letter he wrote to his sister:

> My dear sister, it is with pleasure that I write these few lines, to let you know how we are getting along. When we enlisted, we were to get $13 per month, clothing and rations, and treatment the same as white soldiers; and now they want to cheat us out of what is justly due us, by paying us off with $10 per month, and taking three dollars out of that for clothing. . . . Why are we not worth as much as white soldiers? We do the same work they do, and do what they cannot. We fight as well as they do. Have they forgotten James Island? Just let them think of the charge at Fort Wagner, where the colored soldiers were cruelly murdered by the notorious rebels. Why is it that they do not want to give us our pay when they have already witnessed our deeds of courage and bravery? They say we are not United States Soldiers. They want

The brave assault launched by black troops against the rebels at Milliken's Bend was acclaimed by Union supporters.

to come around and say we are laborers. If we are laborers, how is it then we do soldiers' duty, such as stand guard, and do picket duty and form a line of battle when the long roll is beat? No, because we are men of color, they are trying to impose upon us. If we had staid at home with our families and mothers, wives and sisters, and dear ones at home, we could have received from $1.00 to $1.50 per day.

After much protest, Congress equalized the pay of black and white soldiers in June, 1864. But by then many black soldiers were in desperate financial straits. Some black soldiers, moreover, were killed in action before they received equal pay.

As for commissions, only about one hundred Negroes were ever commissioned officers in the Civil War, and most of them were not even commissioned by the government. The great majority of black officers were in the Louisiana regiments which enrolled in the army with the stipulation that they could keep their black commissioned officers. Most of the Louisiana officers were replaced with white officers, the standard commanders of the Negro regiments.

Black soldiers were also denied the sta-

tus of prisoners of war. Black captives were usually either tortured and killed or sold into slavery. One white rebel from Mississippi wrote to his mother, "I hope I never see a Negro soldier, or I cannot be a Christian soldier."

About three months after the Proclamation had authorized the enlistment of blacks, Jefferson Davis issued his own proclamation stating that all black soldiers captured would be treated as insurrectionists and traitors and killed. But two months later President Lincoln answered Davis with an "eye-for-an-eye" edict. Lincoln promised Davis that for every Union soldier (black or white) killed in violation of the laws of the war, his troop would execute a rebel soldier, and for every Union soldier sold into slavery, a rebel prisoner would be confined to hard labor.

Although his order restrained Davis, it did not stop Confederate troops from torturing and murdering captured black soldiers. Nothing indicates this more clearly than the Fort Pillow Massacre.

On April 12, 1864, Fort Pillow, a Union

outpost on the Mississippi River, forty miles north of Memphis, was attacked by a rebel unit led by General Nathan Bedford Forrest. About 570 persons, including 262 blacks, were stationed there. It is generally agreed that the garrison surrendered under a flag of truce. But when the rebel soldiers entered the fort and disarmed the captives, they killed, wounded, and buried alive over three hundred Union troops, of whom 230 were black.

Brutal though the Fort Pillow Massacre was, it rallied blacks everywhere to fight with redoubled determination, both to avoid falling victim to the same fate and to repay the Confederacy for its butchery.

Said one black soldier:

> We now call upon our noble brethren in the army to swear anew never to cease fighting, until they shall have made a rebel to bite the dust for every hair of these three hundred of our black brothers massacred in Fort Pillow; and, whenever you may be called upon to measure arms or bayonets, with the rebel horde, give no quarter; take no prisoners; make it dangerous to take the life of a black soldier by these barbarians; then, they will respect your manhood, and you will be treated as you deserve at the hands of these who have made you outlaws. . . . Warriors! Remember that you fight for liberty! Remember the wives and the children you have left behind! Remember, you in New York, the July riots! You from the South, who are soldiers of the Republic, remember your old gray-headed mothers, who are yet behind the lines of rebeldom; remember your daughters, dishonored by those red-handed murderers of your race! Remember, that for two hundred and fifty years, your people have been sold and bartered like so many beasts, and then bow down before God, and swear anew to uphold your country's cause, and the cause of universal liberty.

It was this spirit that inspired black soldiers to fight valiantly on the battlefields. And it was on the battlefields that the black soldiers made believers out of those, including President Lincoln, who doubted their soldiering abilities.

Black soldiers also fought bravely in the Battle of Olustee (Fla.) in 1864. Four Black units took part.

Some 240 black troops were massacred after they surrendered to rebel troops at Fort Pillow, Tennessee. Thereafter, Fort Pillow became a battle cry of revenge for black troops.

The first major battle for black troops was the Union assault on the Confederate defense at Port Hudson, Louisiana. Port Hudson, located thirty miles north of Baton Rouge on the banks of the Mississippi River, was the last Confederate obstacle to the capture of Vicksburg by General Grant. Taking part in the Union's assault on Port Hudson were five black regiments from Louisiana. The fort was protected by a deadly shield of twenty siege guns and thirty pieces of field artillery that could rain death and fire on any troops storming the fort's walls or on any Union ships heading upstream to Vicksburg. Encumbering any troop assaults was a maze of fallen trees, a flooded ditch filled with branches bared and sharpened, and a series of rifle pits and outworks.

The thousand blacks in the Union force were led by black and white officers. Charging up the sloping banks, the black soldiers were mowed down by the Confederate guns. One regiment lost six flag bearers. Benjamin Quarles described in *The Negro in the Civil War* the heroic efforts of a black officer, Captain André Cailloux, to rally his men to victory.

"Steady men, steady," said Captain Cailloux of Company E, First Native Guards, his dark skin actually a bit ashen from the sulphurous smoke. A prominent Catholic layman of wealth and attainment who liked to boast that he was "the blackest man in America," Cailloux had received his civil and military education in Paris. The idol of his men, he moved along the line speaking words of encouragement, now in French (many of his men were French-speaking Creoles) and now in English. His company, the color company, was an especial target for Rebel sharpshooters. Cailloux's left arm was shattered, but he refused to leave the field. Just as he reached the flooded ditch, he shouted, "Follow me!" his last words. A second later a shell hit him and he fell with his body facing forwards to the foe.

Four times, the black soldiers stormed the rebel defense, and each time they were repulsed. Many blacks, injured in the assault, immediately returned to battle with little or no medical treatment. Although these soldiers failed to secure Port Hudson, they earned respect and praise everywhere for their heroic courage. The *New York Times* on June 13, 1863, said "No body of troops—Western, Eastern or rebel—has fought better in the war."

General N. P. Banks, commander of the Department of the Gulf, wrote: "The position occupied by these troops was one of importance and called for the utmost steadiness and bravery. . . . It gives me pleasure to report that they answered every expectation. No troops could be more determined and daring. . . . The history of these days proves conclusively that the government will find in this class of troops effective supporters and defenders." Casualties from the assault included 37 blacks killed, 155 wounded, and 116 missing.

Possibly inspired by their success at Port Hudson, Confederate soldiers decided to attack a Union fortress at Milliken's Bend, twenty miles north of Vicksburg, Mississippi. If the rebels could capture Milliken's Bend, it would help them to defend Vicksburg. The rebels knew that General Grant had drawn men from the fort there in order to strengthen his offensive against Vicksburg.

Milliken's Bend was protected by the Mississippi River and Union gunboats on the east, and by a levee and a thick Osage orange hedge about fifteen feet tall on the west. But open fields and wooded areas to the north and south of the fortress afforded the rebels routes for attack. Defending the fort was a detachment of 1,410 men, of whom all but 160 were black. The black soldiers had put on Union uniforms only sixteen days earlier and had just received guns a day before the Sunday morning, June 7, 1863, encounter with the rebel units from Texas.

The rebels had hoped to capture the fortress before sunrise in order to rob the Union soldiers of effective support from their gunboats. They attacked at about 2:30 A.M. and were pushed back by strong Union gunfire. They rallied, charged again and came face to face with the black defenders. The black soldiers were hindered by malfunctions of the guns. Nevertheless, the black troops engaged the rebels in some of the bloodiest hand-to-hand combat of the war, and held them in battle until sunrise, when the Union gunboats opened fire. The rebels, suffering severe casualties, retreated into the woods, leaving behind hundreds of their dead. Thirty-nine percent of the black defenders were casualties of that battle, and one black regiment, the Ninth Louisiana, with 285 men, reported 66 killed and 62 wounded. This casualty rate of 45 percent is said to have been the highest suffered by any single unit in any battle of the war.

Black troops were also outstanding in the charge at Fort Wagner, the Battle of the Crater, Fair Oaks, Deep Bottom, New Market Heights, Fort Gilmer, the Battles of Nashville and Olustee. At least sixteen soldiers received Congressional Medals of Honor.

Not only was the black man a part of the Union Army, but he was also a very significant part of the Union Navy. Always short of manpower, the navy is said

Black brigades were part of a Union offensive that won the Battle of Nashville in 1864.

The rebels often unleashed dogs against attacking black soldiers.

never to have barred blacks from enlisting and serving in its ranks. The Civil War made it even more urgent for the navy to recruit blacks to help it meet its quota. So in September of 1861, the navy adopted a policy of signing up former slaves. Eventually 29,000 black men, or 25 percent of the Union Navy, were recruited. Blacks were quartered and messed with whites, and, as in the army, they distinguished themselves in warfare. Blacks served as coal heavers, seamen, stewards, cooks, boatswains, firemen, and gunners. Four black men won the navy's Medal of Honor.

They were: Joachim Pease: a black crewman aboard the Union gunboat *Kearsarge*, for his outstanding performance as "loader of the No. 1 gun," enabling his ship to sink the *Alabama*, a Confederate warship.

Robert Blake: a former slave, honored for his service as a powder boy aboard the U.S.S. *Marblehead* during the ship's victorious battle with rebels in the Stono River, off Legareville, South Carolina, December 25, 1863.

John Lawson: black landsman serving aboard the gunboat *Hartford*, for his meritorious service in the Battle of Mobile Bay on August 5, 1864.

Aaron Anderson: a landsman aboard the *Wyandank*, for "carrying out his duties courageously in the face of devastating fire . . ." during a boat expedition on March 17, 1865, to clear the Mattox Creek.

Blacks served on at least forty-nine Union vessels. They suffered eight hundred casualties, approximately one-quarter of the navy's total of 3,220. An additional two thousand black seamen died of disease.

Aside from their duties in military uniform, blacks also served the Union cause as civilians. Although the five hundred thousand slaves who gained their freedom by entering Union camps brought extra responsibilities for the Union soldiers, they also brought strong bodies and intelligent minds that were of great value in the war effort. More than two hundred thousand freed slaves worked within the Union camps as cooks, mechanics, bar-

A black regiment charges rebel troops. Close to 200,000 blacks served in the Union Army, and sixteen were awarded the Medal of Honor.

bers, teamsters, medical orderlies and common laborers. The laborers built fortifications and various groundworks.

Black civilians, within and without the military, also served as spies and scouts. One Union general said that his eyes lit up with joy every time slaves came into his camp "because they never fail to bring us valuable information about the enemy."

In a *New York Times* article, written as early as the summer of 1862, it was reported that, "Some of the most valuable information that General McClellan has received in regard to the position, movement, and plans of the enemy, the topography of the country and the inclination of certain inhabitants has been obtained through contrabands. Even spies and traitors have been detected and brought to the attention of the authorities [by fugitive slaves.] . . ."

General McClellan organized an elaborate intelligence division, headed by Allan Pinkerton, founder of the National Detective Agency. Pinkerton, who held the rank of major, was charged with the responsibility of questioning blacks who entered the Union lines, and planning and directing espionage. Among the blacks interrogated by Major Pinkerton was one William A. Jackson, the personal coachman of the Confederate president, Jefferson Davis. William Jackson's mind was quick and retentive and he was able to impart bits of information he picked up while listening to his former master talk in his sleep, or daydream out loud about some impending military tactics or some recent Confederate blunder.

Pinkerton enlisted several blacks as spies and scouts and sent them on assignments as much as three hundred miles behind enemy lines. They could move about more freely than white Northerners, posing as slaves, and could in many cases get information that would have been otherwise impossible to obtain.

One scout, former slave Jim Williams, joined a regiment from Illinois and led it to his master's plantation in Louisiana where the Union soldiers routed a Confederate unit and took about thirty-one prisoners.

Another runaway slave, William Kinnegy, joined a Union outfit in North Carolina. While on a scouting assignment, he not only managed to obtain valuable information, but also liberated his wife and four children.

Perhaps the leading black spy was John Scobell, who was born in Mississippi. A former slave of a Scotsman, Scobell was well educated and resourceful. He could sing Scottish ballads with impeccable pronunciation, and imitate a field hand. He often disguised himself as a laborer, a cook, or a peddler. Among his major assignments were Dumfries, Fredericksburg, Leesburg, Manassas, and Centerville.

Black women were also active as spies.

Black troops were among the Union soldiers who marched into Richmond, Virginia, the rebel capital, on April 3, 1865. The war ended soon after.

The most celebrated of female spies was Harriet Tubman, who had already distinguished herself as an engineer on the Underground Railroad and in the war led commando raids into enemy territory.

Some blacks also captured military supplies. Such men as Robert Smalls and William Tillman distinguished themselves by taking over or rescuing Southern warships and delivering them into Union hands.

William Wells Brown wrote an account of Tillman's exploit:

In the month of June, 1861, the schooner "S. J. Waring," from New York, bound to South America, was captured on the passage by the rebel privateer "Jeff. Davis," a prize-crew put on board, consisting of a captain, mate, and four seamen: and the vessel set sail for the port of Charleston, S. C. Three of the original crew were retained on board, a German as steersman, a Yankee who was put in irons, and a black man named William Tillman, the steward and cook of the schooner. The latter was put to work at his usual business, and told that he was henceforth the property of the Confederate States, and would be sold on his arrival at Charleston, as a slave. Night comes on: darkness covers the sea; the vessel is gliding swiftly towards the South; the rebels, one after another, retire to their berths; the hour of midnight approaches; all is silent in the cabin; the captain is asleep; the mate, who has charge of the watch, takes his brandy toddy, and reclines upon the quarter-deck. The Negro thinks of home and all its endearments: he sees in the dim future chains and slavery.

Armed with a hatchet, he proceeds to the captain's room . . . strikes the fatal blow. . . . He next goes to the adjoining room: another blow is struck, and the black man is master of the cabin. Cautiously he ascends to the deck, strikes the mate; the officer is wounded but not killed. He draws his revolver, and calls for help. The crew are aroused . . . to aid their commander. The Negro repeats the blows with the heavy club: the rebel falls dead at Tillman's feet. The African seizes the revolver, drives the crew below deck, orders the release of the Yankees, puts the enemy in irons, and proclaims himself master of the vessel.

Blacks also played an important role by assisting Union soldiers (mostly escaped prisoners). Slave cabins were frequently called on by escaped Union soldiers, and their inhabitants were always helpful to the Union soldiers, giving them food, dressing their wounds, hiding them out by day, and leading them to freedom at night. The slaves had in fact built an underground railroad for Union soldiers.

John H. Lawson was one of four black soldiers to receive the navy's Medal of Honor during the Civil War.

Toward the end of the war there was a lively debate in the South over the use of black soldiers. The issue brought strong objections from many Southerners. Memories of Nat Turner, and the other black liberators made most Southerners toss and turn in their beds at night. To arm blacks, many reasoned, would invite more slave revolts.

Another reason for the reluctance of Southerners to arm blacks was that blacks were also needed as laborers on the plantations and within the Southern military camps. When rebel General Patrick Cleburn urged the South to arm slaves, General Howell Cobb made this response:

> The proposition to make soldiers of our slaves is the most pernicious idea that has been suggested since the war began. . . . You cannot make soldiers of slaves, nor slaves of soldiers. . . . The day you make soldiers of them is the beginning of the end of the revolution. If slaves make good soldiers, our whole theory of slavery is wrong.

General Cleburn was a realist, however. He knew that the South was losing the war, and that slavery, at first the South's greatest source of strength, was finally turning its power toward the Union. The institution had backfired, and slaves were running away from their masters and aiding the Union Army. In the famous Battle of Milliken's Bend, one black soldier even captured his former master. Cleburn, in a personal letter to Jefferson Davis, put the situation to him rather bluntly, stating that the South had to choose between keeping slavery or losing the war.

In the fall of 1864, Southern losses in Alabama, Georgia, Virginia, and other areas prompted Davis and his government to consider Cleburn's proposal. Finally, the South's most distinguished general, Robert E. Lee, sent out a plea for black soldiers, echoing Cleburn's proposal that those who serve be freed. His plea proved decisive, and on March 13, 1865, Davis signed a "Negro Soldier Law," which authorized the enlistment and arming of black soldiers to fight for the South. A few thousand blacks were armed and dressed

Sergeant W. H. Carney was the standard-bearer for a black regiment, the Fifty-fourth Massachusetts, that distinguished itself in the Battle of Fort Wagner.

in the rebel gray uniform. A couple of companies of black soldiers even marched in a parade in the Southern capital of Richmond, but by that time it was too late for soldiers of any color to save the South. Less than a month after the "Negro Soldier Bill" was signed, Richmond fell and the Confederacy disintegrated.

The war ended on April 9, 1865, and the claim of victory was shared by several parties. First, of course, the Union's decision over the South was a victory for black people, the slaves in particular, who were the decisive element in its beginning and its outcome. They sabotaged the South's war machinery. They led and fed Sherman and his 65,000 troops all along that triumphant march to the sea. They helped the Union's high command by breaking up some of the South's most elaborate spy rings. The South's defeat meant the abolition of the 250-year-old institution of slavery, and improvements in the black man's lot. Even before the end of the war, state and federal laws were being passed, abolishing the "black laws" of discrimination. The efforts of John Brown, Nat Turner, the Underground Railroad, and the abolitionists had been crowned with victory.

The rebel surrender was also a victory for Northern industry, perhaps the greatest beneficiary. The Southern market had been secured. The immense destruction of property during the war created a need for production and thus a consumer market. Moreover, diplomatic and trade relations with England, Spain and other European countries were improved. The fact that the North had secured its political domination helped to insure freedom and expansion in Northern industry.

The abolitionists also shared in the victory. Their moral crusade for black freedom had succeeded. Never had such a small "pressure group" manifested a stronger influence (proportionate to its numbers) on a nation. Their crusade and its outcome helped to shape the moral creed of contemporary human relations.

Lincoln could claim a personal victory. He was the commander-in-chief, and his decisions helped determine the course of the Northern armies. It was he who maintained that the South had never really seceded from the Union, and it was the power of the Union Army and its military victory that carried the day. Because his decisions resulted in victory, Lincoln was also absolved, in some quarters, of the blame that his earlier "mishandlings" of the emancipation issue brought him.

Some people remained critical of Lincoln, however. They considered him and the entire Union Army as mere pawns in the hands of Providence. They remembered the negative attitudes Lincoln expressed toward issues of urgent interest to

Black volunteers are greeted by their loved ones in Little Rock, Arkansas, after they are mustered out of service.

The House of Representatives, meeting on January 31, 1865, hails the passage of the constitutional amendment abolishing slavery forever.

blacks. They remembered also that he had only acted under uncompromising pressures. They remembered the race riots and the discrimination black people had suffered in the armed services.

But despite all these injustices, the majority of blacks felt that their newfound freedoms almost made up for their previous sufferings. Two hundred and fifty years of servitude had built up such an insatiable hunger for freedom that many blacks were even willing to die for freedom's simple pleasures.

Lerone Bennett Jr., in *Before the May-*

President Abraham Lincoln's funeral train passes through Washington, D.C.

flower, has described what freedom meant to many blacks:

Negro soldiers and civilians had something to cheer about. With the defeat of Lee and the surrender of Joseph Johnston, the freedom of words, of the Emancipation Proclamation and the Thirteenth Amendment, became a freedom involving concrete realities. To the ex-slave, freedom was a serious thing. Freedom was getting married before a preacher and signing a paper and knowing that it was for always and not until the next cotton crop. Freedom was bibles, freedom was churches, freedom was gin. Freedom was two names. A man sat for awhile and decided on a name and if he didn't like it, he could change it tomorrow.

Freedom was getting up when you wanted to and lying down when the spirit hit you. Freedom was doing nothing too. How was a man to know he was free if he couldn't sit still and watch the sun and pull on his pipe when he didn't want to do anything else? Freedom was all this and more, but mostly it was books and legs: an opportunity to learn and the right to pick up and go.

Although blacks exulted in their new freedom, they still faced difficult challenges. They were still not free from racial injustices. They were still unable to vote in much of the country, or work in certain jobs, or use certain public facilities, enjoy equal education and many other privileges. The fight for freedom was not over; it had received new impetus. The voices of the freedom fighters Frederick Douglass, Charles Sumner, John Rock, and others, would still be needed to prevent Congress and the American public from forgetting black America altogether.

Barely had blacks begun to enjoy freedom when they were stunned by the death of President Abraham Lincoln. At Ford's Theater in Washington, D.C., at 10 P.M., April 14, he was shot by John Wilkes Booth, a rebel sympathizer. Lincoln died at 7:30 A.M. the following day.

Thousands of blacks were among the more than one million Americans who either attended the president's wake or viewed his funeral train as it carried his body from Washington to Springfield, Illinois. Elizabeth Keckly, Mrs. Lincoln's personal confidante, was one of the blacks who saw the president's body and wrote a moving account of her experience:

> Morning came at last and a sad morning it was. The flags that floated so gayly yesterday now were draped in black, and hung in silent folds at half-mast. The President was dead, and a nation was mourning for him. Every house was draped in black, and every face wore a solemn look. People spoke in subdued tones, and glided whisperingly, wonderingly, silently about the streets.

The death of Lincoln was a loss, but blacks and liberal whites rallied to continue the fight for freedom. Thus in victory and tragedy, personal and collective, blacks and liberal whites rededicated themselves to the fight for freedom, a fight that persists to this very day and involves the same circumstances, though the names and dates have changed.

A former slave savors his new freedom amidst the smoldering ruins of slavery's empire.